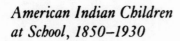

American Indian Children
at School, 1850–1930

American Indian Children at School, 1850–1930

Michael C. Coleman

UNIVERSITY PRESS OF MISSISSIPPI
Jackson

The paper in this book meets the guidelines for permanence and durability
of the Committee on Production Guidelines for Book Longevity of the Council
on Library Resources.

Library of Congress Cataloging-in-Publication Data

Coleman, Michael C.
    American Indian children at school, 1850-1930 / Michael C. Coleman.
        p.   cm.
    Includes bibliographical references and index.
    ISBN 1-60473-009-9
    ISBN 13: 978-1-60473-009-8
    1. Indians of North America—Education—History.   2. Indians of
North America—Biography.   3. Indians of North America—Cultural
assimilation.   4. Ethnology—Biographical methods.   I. Title.
E97.5.C64   1993
371.97'97—dc20   92-37760
                                                               CIP

British Library Cataloging-in-Publication data available

To those American scholars who, since the late 1960s, encouraged me in my study of American history and culture.

And in memory of my sister, Felicity Coleman.

Contents

Preface

WHEN I FIRST READ Francis La Flesche's *The Middle Five* (1900), the account of an Omaha Indian's experiences at a Presbyterian boarding school in the 1860s, I was twice surprised. My first surprise was to discover that La Flesche remembered enjoying much of his schooling, although he himself depicted the sometimes harsh discipline imposed by the teachers. The second surprise sprang from recognition. La Flesche's memories closely coincided with the reports which these same teachers had written decades earlier while he was still a pupil at the school.

Presbyterian and other Protestant missionaries, along with officials and teachers at United States Government Indian schools in the late nineteenth and early twentieth centuries, believed that tribal peoples allowed their children to run wild. Only Christian control, combined with a "civilized" curriculum, would mold the little "heathens" into future citizens of the United States. At Indian schools, the religious and secular educators rigidly divided each day into periods for eating, class work, and physical labor; even play could be indulged in only for a precise number of minutes between other planned activities. Positive and negative incentives varied from school to school and from teacher to teacher. But pupils could be subjected to corporal and other kinds of punishment and occasionally to outright brutality.

Francis La Flesche did not romanticize the Presbyterian mission school. His first day was close to traumatic; later he was often bored by monotonous instruction and religious sermons, and the assault by an outraged teacher on a dull student deeply embittered him. Yet the school introduced him to intense boyhood friendships, and offered him a chance to acquire the skills and knowledge of the powerful American nation. Thus he gained personal satisfaction while simultaneously pleasing his adaptation-minded father. A gifted student who later worked for the Bureau of American Ethnology of the Smithsonian Institution, La Flesche overcame his difficulties at the school. He thrilled to the intellectual challenge as he advanced in the knowledge of English, American history, and mathematics.

Though impressed by the man, I was disappointed in La Flesche the pupil. He should have resisted the missionary contempt for Omaha culture characteristic of these decades of assimilationist education, when

ix

the schools sought to destroy every vestige of "savage" Indian life. Yet La Flesche had his own blend of personal, familial, and ethnic motivations for responding in diverse ways to an educational system which, though alien, was useful to him and his people. His childhood responses to the school were thus strikingly ambivalent—characterized by strongly conflicting feelings and behavior—and complex enough to stimulate further research.

As I began to read other Indian reminiscences, and to write articles based on these sources, I came to realize that La Flesche was by no means alone in depicting his childhood responses to the school as highly mixed. At least one hundred other Indian men and women, who attended missionary and government schools from 1850 through 1930, remembered that as children they too responded in diverse and ambivalent ways. Such school reminiscences ranged from a few chapters or a single chapter within a larger autobiography, to pages, to fragments. These published memoirs of school days constitute the major primary source for the present work.

My interest in pupil responses to the missionary and government school also grew from other influences. My first book, *Presbyterian Missionary Attitudes Toward American Indians* (1985), focused almost exclusively on the missionary side of a many-cultured confrontation. Fairness thus demanded that I examine the campaign of cultural "uplift" from Indians' points of view.

Developments within the discipline of history also pricked my professional conscience. Since the 1960s American historians have increasingly come under the influence of what, three decades later, is still called "the new social history." One of the most impressive achievements of this approach has been to "give voice to the voiceless." It has made historians and perhaps a broader public aware of the experiences, resilience, and achievements of groups till then almost ignored by scholars: women, working people, and, of course, nonwhite peoples such as American Indians.

Responding both to this approach and to the increasing activism of minority groups in America, the field of Indian history has expanded wonderfully in recent decades. Practitioners of "the new Indian history" have gone beyond analyses of government and missionary policies and practices, to examinations of the complex interactions that ensue when cultures meet. David Wallace Adams, Wilbert H. Ahern, James Axtell, Robert F. Berkhofer, Sally Hyer, K. Tsianina Lomawaima, Sally McBeth, William G. McLoughlin, Margaret Connell Szasz, Robert A. Trennert, among others—and I include myself among those others—

have alerted us to the sometimes surprisingly ambivalent responses of Indian children at a variety of schools in the last three centuries. These scholars have also shown us that tribal peoples were more than merely passive victims of the all-powerful white civilization. Indian men, women, and even children were active historical agents, who worked, with varying degrees of success, to adapt white institutions such as the school to their own needs.

Yet although historians are aware of the importance of the school in the campaign to force assimilation upon Indian peoples, we still know relatively little about how Indian schoolchildren themselves saw things. By using their autobiographies, this book thus seeks to contribute to the new Indian history.

The second surprise produced by La Flesche's *Middle Five* was recognition that his memories closely coincided with what missionaries wrote during the 1860s in their reports to the New York headquarters of the Presbyterian Board of Foreign Missions. La Flesche's recollected *attitudes* toward the mission school were quite different from those of his teachers. Yet on point after point they agreed: on the regimentation, the curriculum, the varied responses of pupils, even on particular events. Thus each tends to validate the other: the contemporary correspondence of a number of teachers, and an account written decades later by an ex-pupil. Further, there is equally strong consistency between La Flesche's account of his school days and accounts written by the other Indian autobiographers, and between these and contemporary white sources written by other missionaries and government educators. For the historian, such consistency tends to reinforce the historical credibility of *all*.

Thus the two related, major goals of this study are, firstly, to demonstrate the ambivalent responses of the narrators *as children* to missionary and government schools, as these responses are recalled in published autobiography; and, secondly, to demonstrate the surprising historical credibility of these recollections. In other words, *I am mining the autobiographies for data relating to events and responses that took place decades before the autobiographies were written.*

I write "surprising," because recent studies of autobiographical and historical memory emphasize the distortions and indeed forgetfulness inherent in attempting to remember the past. Further, scholars such as H. David Brumble, Arnold Krupat, David Murray, Gretchen M. Bataille, and Kathleen Mullen Sands indicate the special problems confronting the historian who uses Indian autobiographies as historical sources—especially the complicating role of white collaborators in the production of these narratives. Yet the consistency between autobiographical accounts, and between them and white sources demonstrates the historical accuracy of the Indian narrators' memories of their school years. I thus see this study as a contribution both to the history of American Indian education, and to the scholarly debate on the characteristics of human memory.

I will also examine the extent to which the pupil narrators became cultural brokers—mediators—between the white world and their own. Many historians today are convinced of the importance of such brokers, but the role played by tribal children *while still at school* has not been given due prominence. Considering the tens of thousands of Indian boys and girls who attended American schools and the burdensome hopes often placed upon them, both by their own peoples and by their teachers, their role in this confrontation of cultures needs more intensive analysis.

I do not claim that this group of one hundred autobiographers is representative of all Indian school pupils during these eight decades. But these narrators, male and female, come from a variety of tribal groups, and have left accounts that are rich, varied, and accurate enough for us to begin such an analysis.

The accounts are not uniformly clear on every aspect of schooling, however. Moreover, responses often shifted and overlapped: a pupil might initially accept one element in the curriculum, while resisting another, for example, and then change views on either or both. Thus the nature of the material and of the responses militates against a quantitative analysis of these narrators' experiences.

The chronological span of the book is easily justified. I found no substantial published autobiographical account of school experiences that took place before the 1850s, which was when the assimilationist missionary educational campaign, subsidized by the federal government, began to intensify. By the 1920s an influential group of critics had begun to raise their voices against the culturally intolerant education that had been foisted upon Indians since the beginning of the republic, indeed since colonial times. With the publication in 1928 of *The Problem of Indian Administration* (the so-called Meriam Report), and the appointment of John Collier as commissioner of Indian Affairs in 1933, white America attempted to make amends for past mistakes, to encourage Indian initiatives, and to institutionalize respect for tribal cultures in the schools. Thus 1930 marks a logical cutoff point. The present study focuses upon a distinct and crucial eight decades in the history of Indian schooling.

Nor is it difficult to justify the focus on a distinct kind of school: the so-called Indian school, which missionary societies and the federal government established specifically for the "civilizing" of Indian children. Only in the last two decades of this period, the 1910s and 1920s, did large numbers of Indian children begin to move into state public schools. Few of the narrators in this book enrolled at private schools with white Americans, or at public schools; the vast majority told only of attending Indian schools.

Terminology has been a problem. When referring in general to the aboriginal inhabitants of the present United States, I have used the term "American Indian," rather than "Native American," both of which Indian peoples use as generic terms. But problems persist: should Charles E. Eastman, one of the most celebrated of these autobiographers, be identified as a Dakota or a Santee Sioux? I generally use both designations the first time Eastman appears in the text, and then adhere to the designation he accepted for himself, or which is employed in the autobiography; to avoid repetition I may at times alternate terms (Dakota, Santee Sioux, or Sioux). Further, I have used the personal name that the autobiographer generally accepted, or which appears most prominently on the title page: in this case Eastman, rather than Ohiyesa, the narrator's Dakota name.

Allan Winkler, chairman of the Department of History at Miami University, Oxford, Ohio, arranged my visiting professorship in American studies, 1988–1989, which allowed me both stimulating contact with American students and ample time for research. Without Allan's help I could not have done the intensive research and collecting of materials which a book requires. I also wish to thank the scholar who accepted me as his replacement: that year I always referred to myself as "the poor man's Elliot Gorn." The staffs and faculties of the Department of History and the American Studies Program at Miami were wonderfully welcoming and helpful, especially Mary Kupiec Caton, the acting director of American Studies.

My thanks also goes to the University of Jyväskylä, Finland, for its generous policy of *virkavapaus*—leave of absence. This time the university not only let me go for a year, but paid me part of my salary too. My chairman, Kari Sajavaara, deserves special thanks for encouraging American studies, and for again supporting the application of a historian from Ireland in the Department of English Philology of a Finnish university to pursue American Indian studies in the United States. The libraries and the Inter-Library Loan offices (ILL) of Jyväskylä and Miami universities have graciously accepted my endless barrages of loan requests. For scholars in places remote from their fields of specialization, ILL spells "SURVIVAL."

The Finnish Academy too deserves commendation for financing the trips of Finns and honorary Finns to conferences outside the country. Such trips have been a lifeline to American Indianists in the rest of Europe and in the United States.

The Newberry Library of Chicago awarded me a short-term fellowship, which allowed me examine and collect materials relating to nineteenth-century Indian education. I especially thank Frederick E. Hoxie, director of the D'Arcy McNickle Center for the History of the American Indian, at the Newberry, along with Jay Miller, Violet Brown, John Aubrey, and Ruth Hamilton, also John Sugden and all others, staff and visitors, with whom I worked and talked.

Herman Viola encouraged me to apply for a short-term visitorship at the National Anthropological Archives of the Smithsonian Institution, Washington, D.C. There I read the diaries and correspondence of Francis La Flesche. My trips to the National Archives were too few, but still gratifyingly productive. I located student files from the famous Carlisle Indian School in Pennsylvania, including correspondence written by students and ex-students, along with sources from other Indian schools. Examination scripts are usually the bane of a teacher's life. But reading answers written by young Indian pupils was both an exhilarating and an educational experience.

While studying for my doctorate at the University of Pennsylvania from 1973 to 1976, I almost lived at the library of the Presbyterian Historical Society, Philadelphia. This time I could only make short research trips to my old haunt. But Gerry Gillette, research historian, was as helpful as ever, as were Nora Robinson and the rest of the staff. My thanks also to the ever-encouraging staff of the America Center (United States Information Agency) of Helsinki, for their encouragement both of American studies at the University of Jyväskylä and of my own research. Indeed, the staffs of all the libraries and archives I utilized have been unfailingly helpful and courteous.

A number of people generously agreed to read the manuscript in its entirety: my wife, Sirkka H. Coleman, and Beatrice Coleman, my mother; also David Wallace Adams, Michael Freeman, and Risto Fried. Others read substantial sections: Aiden Coleman, Riitta Myyrrä, Douglas Robinson, and Allan Winkler.

My scholarly debts will be apparent from my notes and bibliography, but I would like to thank Wilbert H. Ahern, Gretchen Bataille, Edward H. Berman, Anne Boylan, H. David Brumble III, Hilary Doyle, Rose-mary Crockett, Robert Crunden, Richard Ellis, Norman Etherington, Nancy Farriss, Elizabeth Glenn, James Glenn, Kevin Gosner, Sally Hyer, James Gump, Päivi Hoikkala, Arnold Krupat, Markku Henricksson and the Klubi at the University of Helsinki, Norris Hundley, Cindy Kasee, Willaim G. McLoughlin, Joan T. Mark, Clyde A. Milner II, Theda Perdue, Charles E. Rosenberg, Margaret Connell Szasz and Ferenc Morton Szasz, John Temple and other members of the NAIC group (North American Indian Council of Greater Cincinnati), and William H. A. Williams. Bo Schöler first mentioned to me that Indians other than Francis La Flesche wrote of their school days. Francis Paul Prucha, S.J., has encouraged me for two decades, and this time lent his expertise at a crucial moment. Seetha Srinivasan has been a supportive and constructively critical editor; I also acknowledge the careful criticisms of the anonymous referees at the University Press of Mississippi. I, of course, am responsible for the final form of this book.

If my children Donagh (18), Tiina (15), and Markus (12) rarely kept MTV and the stereo low enough, they again put up with me while I researched and wrote.

Buiochas daoibh go léir! Thank you all.

Abbreviations

AIC	American Indian Correspondence, Presbyterian Historical Society, Philadelphia
ABCFM	American Board of Commissioners for Foreign Missions
AR	Annual Report
ARCIA	Annual Report of the Commissioner of Indian Affairs
BFM	Board of Foreign Missions of the Presbyterian Church in the United States of America
BIA	Bureau of Indian Affairs (see also OIA)
CCF	Central Classified Files (Record Group 75, National Archives)
CIA	Commissioner of Indian Affairs
NA	National Archives, Washington, D.C.
NAA	National Anthropological Archives, Smithsonian Institution, Washington, D.C.
OIA	Office of Indian Affairs (also BIA)
PCUSA	Presbyterian Church in the United States of America
RG	Record Group (in National Archives: RG 75)

*American Indian Children
at School, 1850–1930*

CHAPTER 1

Introduction: Autobiography and American Indians

What I have told you may not seem to be anything more than a lot of recollections, traditions, opinions and observations. Maybe that's all a person is, a collection of these things.

—Albert Yava, Tewa–Hopi

ALBERT YAVA, WHOSE TEWA people centuries ago migrated to a mesa in Arizona and partly assimilated to Hopi life, was far too modest. Yava told the story of a man balancing at least *three* cultural traditions—Tewa, Hopi, and Euro-American. His account powerfully reinforces H. David Brumble's claim that American Indian autobiographers "can show us an immense range of human ground," and can present the world to us "from a new point of view." [1] They can certainly convey what it was like to have been a young boy suddenly taken from a mesa village, or a young girl carried from a remote Navajo hogan, and plunged into the utterly alien world of the school, with its angular rooms and echoing halls and teachers who spoke an unknown language.

I

Before we enter into the world of the Indian school, it is important to acknowledge that *written* autobiography was unknown to precontact tribal Indian peoples. Indeed many scholars see autobiography as a characteristic expression of modern, Western concepts of the autonomous individual. [2] "[T]he autobiographical project, as we usually understand it," writes Arnold Krupat, "is marked by egocentric individualism, historicism, and writing. These are all present in European and Euroamerican culture after the revolutionary last quarter of the eighteenth century. But none has ever characterized the native cultures of the present-day United States." [3]

3

Some scholars have defined autobiography so exclusively that even important examples of modern Indian self-*writing* would be excluded from the genre, because their narrators are not concerned enough with achieving an individualistic sense of self. Other recent critics, however, take a much broader view. Some have challenged the claim that non-Western peoples lacked a sense of individuality and produced no written autobiography, and many scholars now include almost any kind of self-telling within their definition of "autobiography." For, writes Albert E. Stone, an autobiography "is but an extended reply to one of the simplest and profoundest of questions: who are you, and how did you come to be that way?"[4]

Brumble too cautions against rigidly exclusive understandings of the genre. He suggests a simple but broad definition, one which has also guided the present study: a "first-person narrative that seriously purports to describe the narrator's life or episodes in that life." This definition includes traditional forms of Indian autobiography, narratives told to anthropologists or other white collaborators, self-written narratives, and brief as well as book-length narratives.[5]

If tribal Indians did not write their lives, they developed other methods of self-telling. Hertha D. Wong includes forms such as naming, counting coups, painting tepees and shields, weaving, and dancing, as the "functional equivalents" of autobiography. And Brumble presents six major "preliterate traditions" of spoken Indian autobiography. (1) Coup tales: To establish his worth, a warrior told or acted out accounts of his deeds in battle, especially those involving the touching of an enemy (counting coup). Other warriors might sit in witness upon the veracity of the accounts. (2) Informal autobiographical tales, especially those relating to the hunt or war, but with less stringent demands for accuracy than coup tales. (3) Self-examinations, such as those which Hopi people often carried out to discover whether any personal action had caused an unwanted event. Some of such recollections, Brumble believes, were "strikingly similar to what Christians recognize as a confession." But their purpose was to discover how previous actions, or even dreams, might influence *this* life. (4) Self-vindications: an Indian might tell of his or her life, or of an event, for vindication or to accuse another. (5) Educational narratives: the autobiographies upon which the present study is based contain many cases of traditional Indians recounting life experiences to instruct younger tribal members. (6) Stories about the acquisition of power: Brumble insists that these narratives "more nearly resemble modern autobiography than any of the other types of preliterate autobiography." They are often richly detailed, and, unlike the episodic nature of the other five traditions, this sixth one often links events, to show how claimants came by their relationships with the spirit world.[6]

Perhaps a preliterate Indian was less concerned than an identity-conscious Euro-American autobiographer to ask "who am I?" or "why have I become what I am?" or "might I have been someone different?" The tribal self-teller was generally less concerned with unifying the many stories into a single, coherent life. Each Indian man or woman, writes Brumble, was telling the *stories* of his or her life, whereas the modern autobiographer generally strains for one unifying story.[7]

Admittedly, traditional Indian forms of self-telling were different from modern written autobiography. But when, in the nineteenth century, white Americans began to ask Indians to recount their lives, the concept was not completely foreign to these tribal peoples.

II

The publication of autobiography expanded prodigiously throughout the Western World during the nineteenth and twentieth centuries. Within the United States different ethnic groups, and women, have been caught up in this increasingly compelling need to tell about the self, and all have produced characteristic expressions of the autobiographical genre.[8] Partly influenced by these developments, American Indian men and women also began to write about their lives, sometimes in collaboration with white Americans, sometimes on their own initiative. Specifically American literary developments, such as the frontier hero autobiography and the Indian captivity narrative of colonial times, also had their influence on the development of the Indian subgenre. Arnold Krupat rightly sees modern, written Indian autobiography as "a ground on which two cultures meet," and thus "the textual equivalent of the frontier."[9]

Because so many have been the product of collaborations, modern Indian autobiographies constitute a special kind of subgenre. It is not always possible to disentangle the roles of narrator and collaborator, but it is possible to establish a number of broad categories: "as-told-to" autobiographies; written collaborations; and freely written autobiographies.

As-told-to autobiographies began in an account spoken by an Indian to a white collaborator, often to an anthropologist, who then edited the account into a book accessible to a Euro-American audience. The *Life of Ma-ka-i-me-she-kia-kiak or Black Hawk*, the Sauk and Fox chief, narrated to journalist J. B. Patterson in 1833, was perhaps the first such as-told-to Indian autobiography. The practice continues to this day.[10]

At the suggestion of white Americans, other narrators, such as Don Talayesva (Hopi) and Rosalio Moisés (Yaqui), actually *wrote* an early draft of an autobiography. Their collaborators then extensively edited the manuscript for greater accessibility to a white public. Anthropologist Leo W. Simmons, for example, condensed Talayesva's *8,000 handwritten diary pages* into a powerful 400-page autobiography. Much oral discussion may have taken place between narrator and collaborator before final publication, but such autobiographies, beginning in a written account by an Indian, should be seen as "written collaborations."[11]

The unaided writing of autobiographies by Indians began around the same time as the spoken collaborations. Indeed William Apes, a Pequod, wrote and published an autobiography in 1829—four years ahead of Black Hawk's collaboration with Patterson. And in the late nineteenth and early twentieth centuries other Indians such as G. W. Grayson (Creek), Sarah Winnemucca Hopkins (Paiute), Zitkala-Sa (Gertrude Simmons Bonnin—a Nakota or Yankton Sioux), and Francis la Flesche wrote accounts of their lives. They were, of course, influenced to do so by their exposure to American society. All modern Indian autobiographies are thus "dialogic," to employ Krupat's term for the influence of multiple personal and cultural voices on the finished work. But obviously not all written Indian self-telling was directly initiated by interested whites.[12]

The problematic effect upon Indian autobiography of Euro-American culture in general, and of white editor-collaborators in particular, is a major concern of recent scholars. Gretchen M. Bataille and Kathleen Mullen Sands concede that white collaborators heavily influenced the early autobiographies of tribal women; but these scholars also demonstrate that by the late twentieth century Indian women autobiographers have managed to gain greater empowerment over their own life stories. Arnold Krupat shows the crucial influence that the whole editorial and publishing "mode of production" has had in the making of some of the most famous Indian autobiographies. White editors, in Krupat's view, structured these and other major works. They foisted onto Indian stories major narrative "plots" deeply embedded in the Western psyche: those of comedy, irony, romance, and tragedy (to use the classic categorization of literary critic Northrop Frye). Patterson, for example, structured the story Black Hawk told him into the form of "comedy"—not in the sense of making it amusing, but by allowing the defeat of the Indians and the triumph of "civilization" appear appropriate: all's well that ends well. More recently, however, Krupat accepts that even in such an auto-biography, heavily "monologic"—single-voiced—in its editor-imposed form, hints of "dialogic" voices escape. However diminished, the many voices of traditional Indian life persist in this and other bicultural productions.[13]

Brumble too is acutely aware of the ways in which white editors, audiences, and ideologies impinge upon Indian autobiographies. "In general," he writes, "the more tightly unified the autobiography of a non-literate Indian, the more likely we are to be seeing the Anglo editor at work." Brumble claims that contemporary Indian autobiography has "come full circle or if not full circle, we have returned at least to a point where the beginnings may once again be seen." Rejecting both the services of an Anglo editor and the coherent, chronological structure of much modern autobiography, Indians such as M. Scott Momaday and Leslie Marmon Silko have gone back to telling their *stories*: bringing together fragments and materials relating to tribal myth and history, and to their own and their families' lives. Perhaps Momaday is responding as much to the fragmentation of modern life, as to his desire to remember as a preliterate Kiowa might have. But his autobiographical strategy can alert the reader to ways beyond the Euro-American of telling one's life, and suggests the need to seek traditional patterns along with modern literary influences in the writings of American Indians.[14]

Brumble and other scholars have thus shown us the many-sided and changing nature of American Indian autobiography, preliterate and modern. Responding to deep traditions in their own tribal cultures, and later to Euro-American influences, Indians have told, acted out, painted, and written their lives, sometimes on their own initiative, sometimes less so. And in many of the autobiographies they narrated to non-Indians or wrote themselves in the last century and a half, they included full, rich descriptions of their experiences of the school.

III

The historian attempting to utilize Indian autobiographies faces problems, however. The issue of credibility is obviously complicated by the collaborative and "bicultural" nature of many Indian autobiographies. "[S]elf-written autobiography," writes Brumble, "is the subject's *own* fiction, the subject's conception of the self, and so it must always be authentic in that sense at least." But if whole Western "narrative plots" have been foisted onto Indian accounts, or even if collaborators merely translated or edited the language of the narrators, where is experience of the Indian in all this?[15]

Collaboration complicates but by no means negates the historical value of Indian autobiography. Indians such as Anna Moore Shaw (Pima) and Helen Sekaquaptewa (Hopi) wrote autobiographies in which the role of the editor was minimal. Others wrote their own autobiographies. Even where the editor played a more dominant role, careful counterchecking against other Indian and white sources will allow some judgment on the credibility of the Indian voice. Significantly, the accounts of schooling in independently written autobiographies are not discernibly different from accounts in collaborative autobiographies. It is likely, therefore, that memories of particular episodes, such as schooling, survived relatively intact, although an editor may have imposed his or her own structure on the narrator's account.[16]

Even if the Indian voice rings loud and clear, critics who disagree on much else accept that autobiography is a *construction*—often a distortion—and not merely a recollection of the "facts" of one's past life. "Given the notorious weakness of memory," claims Stone, "the autobiographical act as history is more trustworthy as a record of the author's reactivations than of the actor's original behavior and perceptions."[17] Recent studies of human memory by cognitive psychologists, developmental psychologists, biologists, and others reinforce this skepticism about the ability of narrators to remember the distant past accurately.[18] According to these many scholars, an autobiographer creates his or her image of supposedly "true" past in the light of present needs, conscious or unconscious. A burden of the present book, however, will be to show how impressively Indian autobiographers overcame this supposed weakness of memory, and how accurately they recalled their "original behavior and perceptions."

A further problem relates to audience. Sands, for example, has shown how a Papago Indian gave partly different versions of his life stories to her and to an earlier *male* interviewer. But Sands felt that, even while talking to her, the narrator had at least four audiences in mind: his own people; white people; the interviewer; and himself. Similarly, Brumble notes how Albert Hensley, a Winnebago, not only gave varying life stories on two occasions eight years apart, but Hensley knew enough about his audiences and perhaps about Western forms of autobiography to construct "alternative versions of the self" on each telling. La Flesche,

Luther Standing Bear (Brulé Lakota—Sioux), Charles Eastman (Dakota—Santee Sioux), and other acculturated autobiographers often consciously wrote to convince American audiences of the worthiness of
Indian ways. Helen Sekaquaptewa probably had both white and Indian
audiences in mind (neighboring Navajo as well as Hopi). All this greatly
complicates the issue of which "person" is addressing which audience at
any one time.[19] However, it is likely that even the most self-conscious
Western autobiographer has far more than a single audience in mind; his
or her focus too probably drifts from moment to moment in the writing.
The problem of multiple audiences, then, is not necessarily any greater
in the case of Indian autobiographies.

Even if we accept the historical credibility of a particular autobiography, a further question relates to ethnicity. How Omaha was Francis La
Flesche, whose mother was Omaha, but whose father was part-French
and part-Ponca and made his life with the Omahas? Such questions of
tribal identity still provoke bitter controversy among Indian peoples and
among interested whites. And James A. Clinton has recently argued
against simplistic use of racial "blood" as the basic criterion for ethnic
identity.[20] If La Flesche lived his early life as an Omaha and continued to
identify with that tribe, and if some of its members and later historians
accepted him as an Omaha, then he was an Omaha, no matter how
mixed his "blood" or how "acculturated" he became to white society; the
same broad standard applies to other autobiographers.

In securing a valid sample of ethnically diverse narrators, the major
task has been to locate autobiographies in which the subjects describe or
show a discernible influence of schooling. My principal research aids
were the two bibliographies prepared by Brumble: *An Annotated Bibliography of American Indian and Eskimo Autobiography* (1981); with its
supplement, appended to his *American Indian Autobiography* (1988).
These bibliographies list over 600 published autobiographies, from
fragments to full books. The annotations suggest that relatively few of
the autobiographies relate school experiences: of these I located over
forty books and sixty shorter pieces, which contain longer or brief
passages on schooling. The vast majority of the "school" writings were
published in the twentieth century, but generally deal with missionary
and United States Government school experiences beginning in the
1850s and stretching into the 1930s.[21]

Even the simplest quantification of this sample runs into problems. It
is often difficult to decide whether to include a particular fragment or
account as an autobiography, and, if an autobiography, whether to
include it as a "school" autobiography. An account in which an old

Navajo bitterly lamented his father's refusal to send him to school, *is* included, for example, as it demonstrates the narrator's desire for a modern education.[22] It is also difficult to quantify the sample accurately in terms of as-told-to, written collaborations, or self-written autobiographies. Even in the case of books, it is not always clear just how much or how little an editor influenced the narrator. The impression is that the vast majority of these 100 or so school autobiographies are to some degree collaborations.

Obviously there is no claim that these hundred narrators were statistically representative of the tens of thousands of Indian pupils who attended Indian schools during the decades under study. Indeed, the very act of writing or even cooperating in the writing of their own life stories makes the narrators unusual men and women—those who merely acquiesced in the suggestion of an Anglo anthropologist perhaps less unusual than those who initiated such projects. But these Indians provide a highly varied sample. They were members of around thirty different tribal groups, about two thirds were men, and they attended schools across eight decades of crisis in Indian-white relations. Some narrators were of mixed tribal or tribal-white ancestry.[23]

Further, the narrators often told about the responses and motives of fellow schoolboys and schoolgirls of their own and other tribes. The autobiographies, then, open to us more than the responses of the narrators. Representative or not, they open to us the doors of the school.

Of the *schools*, rather. The autobiographies tell us about life in a wide variety of American Indian schools: Catholic and Protestant missionary day schools and boarding schools; and government on-reservation and off-reservation day and boarding schools. A small number of these narrators attended schools with white children, and the present work will touch on these experiences. But, as emphasized in the Preface, this is a study of Indian pupil responses to schools established specifically to Christianize and "civilize" them. Only a few narrators attended institutions of higher education—Charles Eastman, for example, graduated from Boston University as a medical doctor[24]—therefore this study focuses on the childhood and teenage experiences of the narrators.

IV

To analyse pupil responses to the Indian school, and to demonstrate the credibility of narrator recall, requires both chronological and thematic approaches. The present work is chronological in that it examines responses from first encounters with the school to final return home weeks or perhaps years later. But to suggest the influences of tribal cultures upon responses to the school, Chapter 2 will sketch the kinds of traditional education experienced by the autobiographers. Chapter 3 touches upon Indian schooling in the English colonies, and outlines missionary and government educational policies and practices in the nineteenth and early twentieth centuries. Chapter 4 examines why these Indians began to attend school, and the extent to which they did so willingly; and it presents a model for student motivation, a subject of attention throughout the book. The next five chapters are more thematic in focus, examining different pupil responses: to the institutional sides of the missionary and government school, and to the white staff (Chapter 5); to the curriculum (Chapter 6); pupil responses to each other, and pupil mediation between school, home, and white society (Chapter 7); resistance compatible with continued attendance (Chapter 8); and rejection, including running away, and "quitting" with permission from the school authorities (Chapter 9). The pleasures and difficulties of homecoming are the next concern (Chapter 10); this chapter generally confines itself to the period immediately after the return from school. The final chapter presents conclusions and suggestions for potentially important areas of further study (Chapter 11). Throughout, in both text and notes, the study confronts the historical reliability of these accounts of schooling by comparing them to each other and to contemporary and later white American sources.

Notes

(See "A Note on the Citation of Authors," page 202)

1. Albert Yava, *Big Falling Snow: A Tewa–Hopi Indian's Life and Times and the History and Traditions of His People*, edited by Harold Courlander (New York: Crown, 1978), 139, and 1–2, on history; H. David Brumble, *An Annotated Bibliography of American Indian and Eskimo*

Autobiographies (Lincoln: University of Nebraska Press, 1981), and *American Indian Autobiography* (Berkeley: University of California Press, 1988), 211–58, notation, 182–83.

2. Generalizations on autobiography are drawn from the work of scholars of American Indian autobiography, cited in this chapter, plus the following: Paul John Eakin, ed., *American Autobiography: Retrospect and Prospect* (Madison: University of Wisconsin Press, 1991); James Olney, "The Autobiography of America," *American Literary History* 3 (Spring 1991): 376–96; and Olney, ed., *Autobiography: Essays Theoretical and Critical* (Princeton, N.J.: Princeton University Press, 1980); Timothy Dow Adams, *Telling Lies in Modern American Autobiography* (Chapel Hill: University of North Carolina Press, 1990); Herbert Leibowitz, *Fabricating Lives: Explorations in American Autobiography* (New York: Knopf, 1989); Françoise Lionnet, *Autobiographical Voices: Race, Gender, Self-Portraiture* (Ithaca, N.Y.: Cornell University Press, 1989); James M. Cox, *Recovering Literature's Lost Ground: Essays in American Autobiography* (Baton Rouge: Louisiana State University Press, 1989); Philip Abbott, *States of Perfect Freedom: Autobiography and American Political Thought* (Amherst: University of Massachusetts Press, 1988); Richard N. Coe, *When the Grass was Taller: Autobiography and the Experience of Childhood* (New Haven, Conn.: Yale University Press, 1984); Avrom Fleishman, *Figures of Autobiography: The Language of Self-Writing in Victorian and Modern England* (Berkeley: University of California Press, 1983); L. L. Langness and Geyla Frank, *Lives: An Anthropological Approach to Biography* (Novato, Cal.: Chandler & Sharp, 1981); Karl J. Weintraub, *The Value of the Individual: Self and Circumstance in Autobiography* (Chicago: University of Chicago Press, 1978); and Weintraub, "Autobiography and Historical Consciousness," *Critical Inquiry* 1 (1975): 821–48; Robert F. Sayre, "The Proper Study—Autobiographies in American Studies," *American Quarterly* 29 (1977): 241–62; Elizabeth W. Bruss, *Autobiographical Acts: The Changing Situation of a Literary Genre* (Baltimore: Johns Hopkins University Press, 1976); Daniel B. Shea, Jr., *Spiritual Autobiography in Early America* (Princeton, N.J.: Princeton University Press, 1968); William C. Spengemann and L. R. Lundquist, "Autobiography and the American Myth," in *The American Culture: Approaches to the Study of the United States*, edited by Hennig Cohen (Boston: Houghton Mifflin, 1968), 92–110; Barrett John Mandel, "The Autobiographer's Art," *The Journal of Aesthetics and Art Criticism* 27 (Fall 1968): 215–26.

3. Arnold Krupat, *For Those Who Come After: A Study of Native American Autobiography* (Berkeley: University of California Press, 1985), 29. Also, Krupat, *The Voice in the Margin: Native American Literature and the Canon* (Berkeley: University of California Press, 1989), Chap. 4; Krupat, "Native American Autobiography and the Synecdochic Self," in Eakin, ed., *American Autobiography*, 171–94; Brian Swann and Arnold Krupat, eds., *I Tell You Now: Autobiographical Essays by Native American Writers* (Lincoln: University of Nebraska Press, 1987), ix: "That form of writing generally known to the West as *autobiography* had no equivalent" among traditional Indians. Some modern Indians "still have hostile or ambivalent feelings toward the autobiographical form of writing"; Brumble, *American Indian Autobiography*, 136.

4. See, for example, Weintraub, "Historical Consciousness," 841; Weintraub, *Value of the Individual*. For broader views: Fleishman, *Figures of Autobiography*, 472–73; Rodney L. Taylor, "The Centered Self: Religious Autobiography in the Neo-Confucian Tradition," *History of Religions* 17 (1978): 266–83. Quotation: Albert E. Stone, "Modern American Autobiography: Texts and Transactions," in Eakin, ed., *American Autobiography*, 115. The need to avoid restrictive understandings of the genre is a major theme of the essays in this book.

5. Brumble, *American Indian Autobiography*, 182–83, 17. A few of the school autobiographies are in the third person. Krupat, *For Those Who Come After*, adopts a definition that excludes both preliterate autobiography and many examples written by acculturated Indians without the help of an editor: "original, bicultural, composite compositions," xxvii, 28–35. In *Margin*, Krupat distinguishes between two kinds of "Native American autobiography": individually written (autobiography by Indians) and compositely produced (Indian autobiography), both offering "*dialogic* models of the self," an essentially

collective self which is constituted "by the achievement of a particular placement in relation to the many voices without which it could not exist"—voices of other Indians, of two cultures, of collaborator, interpreter, and narrator, 133–34, all Chap. 4. See also David Murray, *Forked Tongues: Speech, Writing and Representation in North American Indian Texts* (London: Pinter, 1991), esp. Chap. 5.

6. Hertha D. Wong, "Pre-Literate Native American Autobiography: Forms of Personal Narrative," *Melus* 14 (Spring 1987): 17–32. Cf. example in Jason Betzinez, *I Fought with Geronimo*, with Wilbur Sturtevant Nye (1959; rpt., Lincoln: University of Nebraska Press, 1987), 34; Brumble, *American Indian Autobiography*, Chaps. 1 and 2. Quotations, 33, 45. Brumble's list does not include all kinds of traditional Indian stories; see Jarold Ramsey, *Reading the Fire: Essays in the Traditional Indian Literatures of the Far West* (Lincoln: University of Nebraska Press, 1983), 3. See also Christopher Vecsey, *Imagine Ourselves Richly: Mythic Narratives of North American Indians* (New York: Crossroads, 1988); George A. Pettitt, *Primitive Education in North America* (Berkeley: University of California Press, 1946), 159–60.

7. Brumble, *American Indian Autobiography*, 37.

8. Fleishman, *Figures of Autobiography*, 313–14; essays in Eakin, ed., *American Autobiography*, Part II. Also, for example, Beth Maclay Doriani, "Black Womanhood in Nineteenth-Century America: Subversion and Self-Construction in Two Women's Autobiographies," *American Quarterly* 43 (June 1991): 199–222; Lois J. Fowler and David H. Fowler, eds., *Revelations of Self: American Women in Autobiography* (New York: State University of New York Press, 1990); Katherine Jellison, "'Sunshine and Rain in Iowa': Using Women's Autobiography as a Historical Source," *Annals of Iowa* 49 (Winter 1989): 591–99; James Craig Holte, *The Ethnic I: A Sourcebook for Ethnic American Autobiography* (Westport, Conn.: Greenwood Press, 1988); Lionnet, *Autobiographical Voices*; Genaro M. Padilla, "The Recovery of Chicano Nineteenth-Century Autobiography," *American Quarterly* 40 (Sept. 1988): 286–306.

9. Krupat, *For Those Who Came After*, 33, 40–44; Gretchen M. Bataille and Kathleen Mullen Sands, *American Indian Women: Telling Their Lives* (Lincoln: University of Nebraska Press, 1984), 5–8.

10. See Bataille and Sands, *American Indian Women*, all Chap. 1. They write mostly of Indian women's autobiographies, but their generalizations apply to the whole subgenre. They establish somewhat different categories than I do. Cf. Swann and Krupat, eds. *I Tell You Now*, xii–iii; Krupat, *For Those Who Came After*, 33–34; Black Hawk, *Black Hawk: An Autobiography*, edited by Donald Jackson (Urbana: University of Illinois Press, 1964).

11. Leo W. Simmons, "Introduction: The Project and the Procedure," in Don Talayesva, *Sun Chief: The Autobiography of a Hopi Indian*, edited by Leo W. Simmons (New Haven, Conn.: Yale University Press, 1924), 1–9; Jane Holden Kelley, Introduction, in Rosalio Moisés, Jane Holden Kelley, and William Curry Holden, *A Yaqui Life: The Personal Chronicle of a Yaqui Indian* (1971; rpt., Lincoln: University of Nebraska Press, 1977), l–liii.

12. William Apes, *A Son of the Forest: The Experience of William Apes, A Native of the Forest. Comprising a Notice of the Pequod Tribe of Indians. Written by Himself* (New York: Privately printed, 1829); G. W. Grayson, *A Creek Warrior for the Confederacy: The Autobiography of Chief G. W. Grayson*, edited by W. David Baird (Norman: University of Oklahoma Press, 1988); Sarah Winnemucca Hopkins, *Life Among the Piutes: Their Wrongs and Claims* (1883; rpt., Bishop, Cal.: Sierra Media, 1969); Zitkala-Sa, *American Indian Stories* (1921; rpt., Lincoln: University of Nebraska Press, 1986); Francis La Flesche, *The Middle Five: Indian Schoolboys of the Omaha Tribe* (1900; rpt., Madison: University of Wisconsin Press, 1963); Krupat, *Margin*, especially 133–34. Also Krupat, "Native American Autobiography," in Eakin, ed., *American Autobiography*, 189, n22.

13. Bataille and Sands, esp. 24–26, Chap. 7; Krupat, *For Those Who Came After*, 28–35, Chaps. 2–5. See also Eakin, Foreword in *idem*, xx: "Krupat demonstrates that in texts as in all else the Indian was dispossessed by the whites"; Krupat, *Margin*, 151–55. Also Murray, *Forked Tongues*, 67.

14. Brumble, *American Indian Autobiography*, 37, 170, 180, Chap. 8; M. Scott Momaday, *The Way to Rainy Mountain* (1969; rpt., Albuquerque: University of New Mexico Press, 1976); and *The Names: A Memoir* (Tucson: Sun Tracks/University of Arizona Press, 1976). Cf. Krupat, *Margin*, 177-87; Leslie Marmon Silko, *Storyteller* (New York: Arcade Publishing, 1981).

15. Brumble, *American Indian Autobiography*, 11, and Chap. 4

16. Bataille and Sands, Chap. 5, esp. 111; Helen Sekaquaptewa, *Me and Mine: The Life Story of Helen Sekaquaptewa*, edited by Louise Udall (Tucson: University of Arizona Press, 1969); Anna Moore Shaw, *A Pima Past* (Tucson: University of Arizona Press, 1974). Also William Bloodworth, "Varieties of American Indian Autobiography," *Melus* (1978): 69.

17. Stone, "Modern American Autobiography," in Eakin, ed., *American Autobiography*, 97. I base this generalization on studies listed in note 2, above.

18. See Michael C. Coleman, "The Credibility of American Indian Autobiographical Accounts of Schooling." Paper delivered to the Annual Meeting of the Organization of American Historians, Chicago, April 3, 1992. Also, David Thelen, ed., *Memory and American History* (Bloomington: Indiana University Press, 1989). This book originally appeared, in its entirety, in the *Journal of American History 75* (March 1989).

19. Helen Mullen Sands, "Telling 'A Good One': Creating a Papago Autobiography," *Melus* 10 (1983): 55-65; Brumble, *American Indian Autobiography*, Chap. 6; Bataille and Sands interviewed Sekaquaptewa a decade after she wrote *Me and Mine*; see *American Indian Women*, 99-112.

20. James A. Clifton, "Alternate Identities and Cultural Frontiers," in Clifton, ed., *Being and Becoming Indian: Biographical Studies of North American Frontiers* (Chicago: Dorsey Press, 1988), 26-33. This sensitivity about ethnic identity is also my impression from conversing with a small number of Indians and interested non-Indians, 1988-89; on La Flesche's genealogy, Jerry E. Clark and Martha Ellen Webb, "Susette and Susan La Flesche: Reformer and Missionary," in Clifton ed., *idem*, 137-39. See also William T. Hagan, "Full Blood, Mixed Blood, Generic, and Ersatz: The Problem of Indian Identity," *Arizona and the West* 27 (1985): 309-26; Krupat, *Margin*, 207-208, including note 5.

21. Brumble, *An Annotated Bibliography*; Brumble *American Indian Autobiography*, 211-57. Also useful: Bataille and Sands, *American Indian Women*, esp. 155-80; Daniel F. Littlefield and J. W. Parins, eds. *A Bibliography of Native American Writers, 1772-1924* (Metuchen, N.J.: The Scarecrow Press, 1981; Supplement, 1985); Roger O. Rock, *The Native American in American Literature* (Westport, Conn.: Greenwood Press, 1985).

22. Ashie Tsosie, in Broderick H. Johnson, ed., *Stories of Traditional Navajo Life and Culture. By Twenty-Two Navajo Men and Women* (Tsaile, Navajo Nation, Ariz.: Navajo Community College Press, 1977), 110-19.

23. For a full listing of tribal backgrounds, see Appendix.

24. Charles A. Eastman (Ohiyesa), *From the Deep Woods to Civilization: Chapters in the Autobiography of an Indian* (1916; rpt., Lincoln: University of Nebraska Press, 1977), 70-75. On the role of Eastman's wife, Elaine, in the production of this and others of Eastman's works, see Elaine Goodale Eastman, *Sister to the Sioux: the Memoirs of Elaine Goodale Eastman, 1885-91*, edited by Kay Graber (Lincoln: University of Nebraska Press, 1978), 173; Brumble, *Annotated Bibliography*, 54-55; Ruth Ann Alexander, "Elaine Goodale Eastman and the Failure of the Feminist Protestant Work Ethic," *Great Plains Quarterly 8* (Spring 1988): 89-101. On Eastman's life, see also Raymond Wilson, *Ohiyesa: Charles Eastman: Santee Sioux* (Urbana: University of Illinois Press, 1983); David Reed Miller, "Charles Alexander Eastman, the 'Winner': From Deep Woods to Civilization. Santee Sioux, 1858-1939," in Margot Liberty, ed., *American Indian Intellectuals* (St. Paul: West, 1978), 60-73.

CHAPTER 2

The Traditional Education of American Indian Autobiographers

You have no education.
>—Capt. Richard Henry Pratt to Spotted Tail (Brulé Lakota), 1879.

O NE OF THE GREAT Western misconceptions is that peoples without formal schooling are uneducated. If, however, we accept a broad definition of education as "the transmission of [a society's] culture and world view to succeeding generations," these American Indian autobiographers had begun their education long before they set foot inside a school. No matter how alien it appeared to them, schooling was a *continuation*, rather than a beginning of their education.[1]

I

"I believe many people will be surprised," wrote Thomas Wildcat Alford, "when told that Indian parents realized just as much responsibility for the training of their young as any other race of people." Like most of the autobiographers, this Shawnee romanticized his early education. But in often detailed descriptions he and they corroborate George A. Pettitt's claim that the education of children was "an intense and lifelong affair" for Indian tribal peoples.[2]

Before schooling was forced upon them by American authorities, Hopis educated their children through what Helen Sekaquaptewa called on-the-job training. The young

> learned to care for the sheep and raise corn in the day-to-day school of experience. Girls learned from their mothers to grind corn, prepare the food, and care for the household. Men and boys met in the kiva in winter time for lessons in history, religion, and traditions—all taught in story and

song. Here also was learned respect for their elders and for tribal and clan codes.

Perhaps Sekaquaptewa did not fully convey the intensity and resulting anxieties of traditional education. She suggested, nevertheless, the warm and all-encompassing enculturation of boys and girls into both the values and skills necessary for mature and responsible adulthood, and for Hopi survival in a harsh desert environment. She also indicated the *holistic* nature of Hopi and other forms of tribal education: the way in which many essential areas of knowledge—spiritual, mythical, ethical, economic—linked together into a whole; and how kin and other responsible adults communicated this knowledge, binding all together within the small community.[3]

The details vary according to tribe, period, and individual experience, and many of the accounts in the book-length reminiscences are far too detailed to be more than touched upon here. But others besides Sekaquaptewa recalled with fondness, and sometimes with surprising degrees of resentment, how the people ensured their growth into functioning members of the community.[4]

Kin bore the primary responsibility for education. But in ways quite different from white society, the whole Indian community often became involved. The Indian boy or girl was, according to Margaret Connell Szasz, "surrounded by expanding concentric circles of people who cared for him or her": father and mother, older siblings, uncles and aunts (especially important in many of the tribal kinship systems), other concerned adults, old people, "specialists," such as proficient warriors and male and female shamans and, perhaps of greatest importance, grandparents.[5]

If parents often had less to do with the upbringing of even young children than is usually the case in contemporary Western society, mothers and fathers sometimes did exercise a major educational influence. Luther Standing Bear, a Brulé Lakota (Sioux), tersely told how, even before he had left the cradleboard, his mother had begun the ceaseless training with its long-term personal and social goals. "Manhood was thus planned in babyhood," he wrote. "My mother was raising a future protector of the tribe. When the days of age and weakness came to the strong and active, there would have to be those to take their places. I was being fitted to take one of those places of responsibility in the tribe." At least until he began school as a boy of ten, Standing Bear appears to have enjoyed a warm relationship with his father. The older man instructed the boy in the opportunities and the dangers of the buffalo hunt, and encouraged him to seek glory and even death, in order to prove himself a man. And Irene Stewart's Navajo father became for her a major educator, especially after the girl's mother died.[6]

Zitkala-Sa learned much from her mother until departure for a distant boarding school sundered the relationship. "Close beside my mother I sat on a rug," wrote the Nakota (Yankton Sioux), "with a scrap of buckskin in one hand and an awl in the other. This was the beginning of my practical observation lessons in the art of beadwork." But more than mere observation was involved: "It took many trials before I learned how to knot my sinew thread on the point of my finger, as I saw her do." Zitkala-Sa credibly conveyed the perfectionism of her demanding teacher, who stimulated the young girl to greater if sometimes resentful effort. "The quietness of her oversight made me feel strongly responsible and dependent upon my own judgment. She treated me as a dignified little individual as long as I was on good behavior; and how humiliated I was when some boldness of mine drew forth a rebuke from her!" Zitkala-Sa also suggested the intensity of the sessions, and the need for release which they built up in her. "Always after these confining lessons I was wild with surplus spirits, and found joyous relief in running loose in the open again." Belle Highwalking felt similar resentment building against her Northern Cheyenne stepmother, who insisted that the young girl stitch beaded mocassins for her brother. "It made me mad," recalled Highwalking, "and I thought her lazy because she told me to bead and sew. I didn't know that she was teaching me."[7]

Other close relatives, including uncles and aunts (especially mother's brother and father's sister), also accepted major responsibility for education. "In the traditional Hopi pattern," wrote Polingaysi Qoyawayma of a matrilineal tribe which traced descent in the female line, "children are advised, instructed, scolded, and sometimes punished by their maternal uncles." Qoyawayma had enjoyed an excellent relationship with her uncle, until her interest in white ways provoked a bitter confrontation.[8]

Charles Eastman, M.D., became one of the most famous of "educated" Indians, an author, lecturer, and spokesman for his people. Rejecting the "popular idea that all the characteristic skill of the Indian is instinctive and hereditary," Eastman insisted that "All the stoicism and patience of the Indian are acquired traits, and continual practice alone makes him master of the art of wood-craft." He acquired these arts from his father's brother. This uncle, mistakenly believing that Eastman's father was dead—executed for his part in the Minnesota Sioux uprising of 1862—accepted responsibility for the education of a sibling's child, a typical pattern in many tribes. Balancing strictness with praise he encouraged the young Eastman to observe, name, and describe the things he had seen each day. "I made many ridiculous errors," wrote Eastman. "He usually informed me of the correct name. Occasionally I made a hit and this he would warmly commend." When Eastman was a little older, his teacher "went much deeper into this science," carefully instructing him on the habits of bears, wolves, and other animals. Eastman also endured the training and hardship appropriate for a future warrior. "With all this," he claimed, "our manners and morals were not neglected." He learned respect for adults, and especially for the aged, along with "generosity to the poor and reverence for the 'Great Mystery.' Religion was the basis of all Indian training."[9]

Grandparents were especially important educators, both as possessors and communicators of much of the tribal lore, and—remarkable though it might seem today—often as constant companions of the young. "I had seen little of my parents," recalled James Kaywaykla of his childhood, spent with his Warm Springs Apache people in flight from Mexicans and Americans, "for my father was a brave warrior, and my mother's place was at his side." As soon as a child could be separated from her, she turned it over to its grandmother. "'It is natural that you should love your grandmother best of the family,'" his mother told the young Kaywaykla. "'She has taken care of you since you were a baby.'" And Eastman related how, with his grandmother as judge, young children tested each other's knowledge, and reinforced basic categories of Dakota perception. On one occasion they argued over which of the four classes of animal the lizard belonged to: the four-legged, the flyers, the swimmers, or the creepers? Eastman argued that the lizard, having four legs, belonged to the first category. But his grandmother overruled him, declaring that as the creature's stomach did not clear the ground, it was a creeper. Similarly Allen James (Pomo) fondly remembered his *great* grandmother's knowledge of such things. Having her around "was like having the entire volume of the Encyclopedia Bretanica [sic] with you all the time. She seems to have all the answers to everything, the complete cure for every desease [sic] and sickness, and the answer to every question, pertaining to the human life in this mortal existence."[10]

Also noting the way in which busy parents delegated care and educational responsibility to grandparents, Mourning Dove (Christine Quintasket), a Salishan who became the first American Indian woman to publish a novel, eloquently indicated how the old as a group could contribute to rearing the young. "Our most important sense of self and continuity," she believed, "came from the very old, who were so kind, gentle, considerate, and wise with us, particularly as children." Vine

Deloria, Sr., a Standing Rock Lakota (Sioux) of part-white ancestry who became an Episcopalian minister, told how he "would stay awake and listen to the most exciting stories, songs, philosophies from those who lived according to the physical and moral laws of Mother Earth. I knew I was hearing all these things which must have gone back to the grandfathers of these [old] men." An equally warm compliment came from the Ponca, Peter Le Clair. "I always liked old men," he wrote of his youth, "and I would sit around and listen to their talks. I always liked to hear them talk about olden times. I used to carry water to them." [11]

Particular skills could require the specialized knowledge and spiritual assistance of experts, who might or might not be closely related. Anna Moore Shaw described how a young Pima girl went to live with a famous basket maker in order to learn this art. Jason Betzinez began his apprenticeship during the Apache campaigns in the 1880s. "Geronimo asked me to go with him as his assistant," he wrote. "I was now old enough to be a warrior, and the way to learn was to go on several raids with an experienced man, taking care of his horses and equipment, standing guard, and cooking his meat for him. That was the Apache custom." No young man would be trusted as a warrior until he had undergone this apprenticeship: "Now I was to get my chance." [12]

Mourning Dove sought to become a "doctor" or shaman. "Ever since I was seven years old," recalled the Salish woman, "my parents, my adopted grandmother . . . and other relatives had coached me to hunt for the spiritual blessings of a medicine woman." In this case the adopted grandmother became the girl's tutor. Despite accepting arduous duties around the home and enduring a ten-day fast alone in a "mountain wilderness," Mourning Dove failed to achieve a vision. The older woman then sang a "secret song," and encouraged the girl to seek a particular kind of animal helper: "If you are not afraid tonight, you will see a vision of this power I earned when I was a little girl like you. It is the power of the eagle, chief of birds." Then she gave Mourning Dove the leg bones of an eagle, decorated with feathers. Even with such sacred knowledge and material the girl again failed to achieve the desired vision. And although parents and tutor consoled her, it was the tutor who explained the failure: Mourning Dove had brought her dog with her on the vision quest, and thus had not been completely alone. [13]

In some tribes most young men, and not only aspirant shamans, engaged in the vision quest. The actual period spent alone on the mountain or in the forest was a lonely one—Edward Goodbird (Hidatsa) recalled that he was so lonely he would have been happy to meet a ghost. But the vision quest itself was intensely social and educational. Through the agency of one or more tutors, the young Indian entered more deeply into the heritage of the people, and acquired a spirit guide who would help him or her live a more successful and socially useful life.[14]

II

The culture of even a single village was so immensely complex and—stereotype of static "primitive" peoples notwithstanding—so much in flux at any time, that no member could ever hope to know the whole of it. Further, not all members *were meant to know* the whole of a people's heritage, or to participate in every one of its activities. "You might say that there were different levels of knowledge," recalled Albert Yava:

> There were people like me who had picked up a little knowledge of traditions here and there, but who didn't know too much about the inner workings of things. Then there were the ones who'd been educated in the kiva societies. . . . [who] were the "real" Hopis, and the rest of us were unfulfilled, like unripened corn.

Only when Yava, whose father was Hopi and mother Tewa, passed through educative initiation into the One Horn Society did he begin to feel himself a real Hopi. Plains Indians such as the village-dwelling Omahas and the nomadic Cheyennes also evolved hierarchies of prestigious "societies," entry into which depended on age or on military, economic, or other kinds of achievement.[15] This understanding of education as a process in which not all were called to every level, was generally characteristic of Indian peoples.

As emerges clearly in many of the long autobiographies, the sexes received partly different education in skills and knowledge: the hunting and warfare complexes for the boys in many tribes; care of the home, preparation of food, crafts such as beadwork for girls. There was much tribal variation—among the Hopis, for example, weaving was an exclusively *male* activity—and not all tribes insisted to the same degree on rigid role segregation. But differentiation of roles and, as children grew, of education was general.[16] Female autobiographers sometimes mentioned how they were sensitized to the dangers of premature association with the opposite sex. "When I was a a young girl," claimed Belle Highwalking (Northern Cheyenne), "we were afraid of boys when they tried to talk to us, and we never went out at night because, if we did, they caught us." And Mourning Dove recounted in detail the traditional modest dress and careful chaperoning of young Salish women, so they would be "considered valuable" in the eyes of the men. Helen Sekaquap-tewa's Hopi mother told her "about the sex side of life," using "plain language so I would understand." Helen also received instruction in the Hopi moral code, with its insistence, at least for girls, upon the preserva-tion of virginity before marriage. And Helen noted that traditional Hopis objected to school dances because they allowed girls and boys to mingle socially—an ironic criticism, in the light of the efforts of school authorities to severely limit the contact between the sexes.[17]

The sexual division within tribal cultures generally persisted through life. Certain "societies," fraternities or sororities, might only accept members of one sex: a Southern Cheyenne woman recollected how she became a member of the Tipi Decorators society, which was restricted to women. "I was very carefully instructed never to disclose the cere-mony in the presence of males," she told her male interviewer, "so I shall be obliged to discontinue the subject." And when as a girl Mary Little Bear Inkanish, also a Cheyenne but of part-white ancestry, asked her mother about a particular medicine bundle, she received the curt reply: "'Be quiet. That belongs to the men. You aren't supposed to know about it.'"[18]

III

Large areas of cultural knowledge, however, were open to all young Indians. Ironically, Pettitt ignored the evidence which he himself had so impressively amassed in his pioneering study, and claimed that education was "not consciously institutionalized" among Indians. And Standing Bear once claimed that there was "'no system'" in Lakota education. They probably meant to imply that Indian education was nonbureaucratic, lacked schools, written curricula, and was generally implemented orally by kin or other known members of the community.

But such language suggests an image of haphazard, almost casual educating. If we accept a definition of "institutions" as "patterns of behavior . . . to which people become attached as a result of their role in the formation of identity, or through investments of energy or social interests," then education was highly institutionalized in traditional Indian societies. The adults were consciously aware of their varying responsibilities—depending upon their relationship to the children—for transmitting and maintaining "The Hopi way" or "The Apache way." And many of the educational relationships were also highly formal, no matter how much warmth and affection may at times have developed between mentor and pupil. Standing Bear himself insightfully recognized the strain such educational patterns could place upon *adults:* "Perhaps the hardest duty in the performance of parenthood was not so much to watch the conduct of their children, as to be ever watchful of their own . . . example." [19]

Some learning obviously came about through observation. "Watch, learn, imitate"—these were the words Standing Bear once used to describe his experience as a boy. He and others have shown how, although Indian children played some games only for enjoyment, they also patterned others after adult activities. The boys hunted and pretended to go to war; the girls took care of miniature tepees and dolls. Joseph K. Griffis, an Osage of part-white ancestry who grew to boyhood among the Kiowas, later in life watched white children playing. "Their games puzzled me," he wrote. "I wondered how, when they were grown up, they would make a living at such things as 'blind man's buff' and 'drop the handkerchief.' The hunting-game and the war-game, and such like, of my savage boyhood days were the very things that we played in earnest when we became men." [20]

Much more was involved than imitation, however; Indian adults deliberately and systematically employed a variety of educational techniques: instruction in everyday duties, or in specialized knowledge; "hands-on" teaching of everything from beadwork and farming to the arts of war and the hunt; equally careful initiation into the mysteries of tribal ceremony and into sacred experiences such as the vision quest or the sun dance; and, especially important, the telling of stories, tribal history, and mythology. "Groups of boys and girls would go to the houses of the old people," wrote Don Talayesva, "and beg for more stories." The Hopi elders obliged, except in summer when they reminded the children of the work to be done in the fields. Stories about "how we got our pipestone, where corn came from, and why lightning flashed in the sky," declared Standing Bear in a memorable passage, "were the libraries of our people." They were also a form of ethical and moral instruction, stressing as they did the desired norms, such as bravery, female modesty, or the need to conserve the gifts of nature. "To us," wrote Francis La Flesche with a mixture of retrospective pride and awe at the demands of his Omaha upbringing, "there seemed to be no end to the things we were obliged to do, and to the things we were to refrain from doing." [21]

IV

Indian adults devised numerous incentives to encourage compliance with such demands. Love of and respect for kin, especially for grandparents, motivated many children, as did the desire for acclaim. Names had powerful educational and even inspirational functions: a child might initially receive the name of an illustrious ancestor, or one relating to an appropriate event; later he or she might take or be given a name relating to behavior or achievement, or to entry into a society. "A Sioux boy was supposed to distinguish himself in some way to prove his bravery or worth," wrote Standing Bear. "He would then be privileged to take a name indicating what his worthy act was." Albert Yava received a new name during his initiation into the Hopi One Horn Society. Charles Eastman told how a child might be given a new name *to stimulate* achievement. After his band won a lacrosse game, the people changed his name from "The Pitiful Last" (his mother had died shortly after his birth), to Ohiyesa, "The Winner." [22]

Direct praise was probably less used among the Hopis, who discouraged individualism, but it was an immensely powerful incentive in many other tribes: "A child would strive with all his might to win such praise," wrote Alford of his Shawnee childhood. Pettitt noted that "the ego, like a balloon, must be inflated before it can be punctured," and claimed that Indians often employed praise first—then rebuked. But, as accounts by Zitkala-Sa, Eastman, Alford, and others suggest, adults continually balanced approval and criticism to influence appropriate conduct. [23] The desire for praise would later powerfully stimulate Indians such as Standing Bear and La Flesche to success at school. Traditional educational patterns were not inevitably antagonistic to the new form of education.

Adults rewarded socially acceptable ambition with increased responsibility, membership in age-graded or prestigious societies, or positions of leadership or spiritual power. As a young girl Kay Bennett (Navajo) at first resented her mother's insistence that she learn to weave rugs so she could help contribute to family finances. "'You are not pounding the thread down tight,'" the older woman complained, and managed to keep her reluctant daughter at the loom long enough to complete a small rug. Bennett developed a belated sense of pride in her work, however, and began to show off the rug to family and neighbors. Her mother's belief in the young girl's latent ambition to perform as an older member of the household had been justified.

Rain-in-the-Face (Lakota) echoed the desire of boys of many tribes when he spoke of one of the greatest of all rewards a male could achieve: fame among his people for exploits on the battlefield. "I was ambitious to make a name for myself," he told Charles Eastman in an interview. "I joined war parties against the Crows, Mandans, Gros Ventres, and Pawnees, and gained some little distinction." Two Leggings (Crow) was so obsessed with status that even his real achievements on the battlefield brought him but a fleeting sense of satisfaction. His older brother told him that the people thought well of him and believed him to have no fear. "When people spoke like this," said Two Leggings, "it made me even more anxious to become a chief and a pipeholder." [24]

Humiliation, disdain, and spiritual or even physical affliction awaited the unsuccessful, and elders strove to impress the dangers of nonconformity upon their young. "As soon as I was old enough to take advice," wrote Don Talayesva, "he [grandfather] taught me that it was a great disgrace to be called *kahopa* (not Hopi, not peaceable)." Those who lived by the teachings of the people could expect kindness from them, and would reach an advanced age. But, warned the old man: "'Children who ignore these teachings won't live long'." Although Shawnee adults preferred to rely on praise, when this did not work, various negative incentives were employed. "One punishment that was always a bitter one to an Indian child," according to Alford (Shawnee), "was to have some of his faults told to a visitor or friend." And Stands in Timber recounted how, in an earlier generation, Cheyenne girls would openly mock a young man who came home from an unsuccessful hunt or war party. "It was hard to go into a fight, and they were often afraid," he wrote, "but it was worse to turn back and face the women." Tribal girls too had to strive to avoid shame, however. "'Never be lazy,'" the Pima mother told her daughter in an admonition applicable to all these tribes. "'No one wants a lazy wife.'" [25]

In small communities there was no escape from the ignominy of failure. Standing Bear claimed that among the Lakota, "a man living in his tribe without respect was a living nonentity." And Francis La Flesche frankly recalled his sense of boyhood contempt for such a person among the Omaha:

> It was only by the performance of valorous deeds that men won honors in the tribe; but this man had no ambitions to win such honors. As a hunter he was also a total failure, consequently his worldly possessions were not such as could give him distinction.

He finally became "a useless member of the tribe." His equally unsuccessful brother was struck by lightning, undoubtedly seen in Omaha society as a form of supernatural retribution for cowardice and lack of ambition. La Flesche and other narrators convey a sense of intense rivalry as young Indians, especially males, strove to outdo each other to gain recognition and avoid humiliation. Not only was there competition among those of the same generation, but "'You must endeavour to equal your father and grandfather,'" Charles Eastman's grandmother told him. "'They were warriors and feastmakers'."[26]

Angel de Cora (Winnebago) claimed that she never heard a cross word during childhood.[27] And because Indian adults encouraged children to subject themselves to physical pain, its constant use as punishment would have been counterproductive. But many narrators recalled, with varying degrees of bitterness, the physical punishments they received.

Edward Goodbird, of the village-dwelling Hidatsa in North Dakota, fondly remembered much of his childhood, but vividly described the treatment meted out to those who disobeyed their elders. It "was not the custom of my tribe for parents to punish their own children," he wrote. But when necessary, "usually the father called in a clan brother to do this"—a common tribal practice of deflecting the child's resentment away from his parents. Goodbird noted how "a very naughty boy" might be rolled in a snow bank, or ducked in water. Indeed on one occasion his uncle administered the latter punishment:

> Flies Low [the uncle] caught me up, my legs over his shoulder, and plunged me, head downwards, into the pail. I broke from him screaming, but he caught me and plunged me in again. The water strangled me, I thought I was going to die.[28]

Goodbird's pain and fright were mild compared to the near-traumatic suffering of Don Talayesva and some Hopi children initiated into the Kachina Society by the kachina spirits in their impressive masks. Taken to a kiva (a semisubterranean ceremonial chamber), children might be instructed, admonished, gently or severely whipped by these spirit beings in what was intended to be a deeply affecting educational and disciplinary ceremony. Talayesva, who claimed to have been the naughtiest boy in the village of Old Oraibi, received special treatment. He took the first four blows of the kachina's whip without crying, and thought that the ordeal was over. "[B]ut then the Ho Katchina struck me four more times and cut me to pieces. I struggled, yelled, and urinated," wrote Talayesva in a stark and unflattering passage. "Blood was running down over my body. . . . I tried to stop sobbing, but continued to cry in my heart—and paid little attention to the other floggings." More shock followed, deepening the resentment against adults: when the kachinas removed their masks, the children discovered that they were ordinary members of the community! Yet the severe treatment apparently had some of the desired effect. Later Talayesva thought of the initiation "as an important turning point in my life, and I felt ready at last to listen to my elders and to live right." There may have been an element of formula acceptance in these words; but, after years at American boarding schools, Talayesva finally returned to Hopi life as a young adult.[29]

Ostracism, even if temporary, was perhaps the most devastating of punishments. In a study otherwise emphasizing the often warm and supportive nature of Hopi upbringing, Dorothy Eggan recorded an informant's account of how, as a girl of about six, she had neglected to take care of her baby sister. For about ten days her family insisted that she eat on her own, and no one talked to her. "I was so ashamed all the time," she recalled. The informant was forty when she related the incident, noted Eggan, "but she cried, even then, as she talked."[30]

The tribal societies of the narrators were often close to hunger or in constant danger from enemies. So these Indians generally recognized the need for strict discipline, for body-hardening and character-building training, and for occasionally painful, frightening, or humiliating punishments. Indeed, although such descriptions lend a hard edge to the autobiographies, they do not detract from the generally idealized depiction of childhood. They seem to prove, after all, that Indian children were resilient little boys and girls. Echoing this sense of pride, Asa Daklugie claimed that as young Apache warriors "we'd been trained more rigidly" than at the self-consciously rigid Carlisle Indian Industrial School in Pennsylvania.[31]

V

All this perhaps suggests that tribal methods of education combined positive and negative incentives in harmonious balance. But these autobiographies also allow us glimpses of dysfunctionality and occasionally of downright skepticism, which indicate that tribal societies too could produce serious tensions and intergenerational conflicts.

As narrator descriptions demonstrate, Indian children often disobeyed instructions. Two Leggings, the obsessively ambitious Crow, continually defied his elders and mentors as he sought glory on the battlefield, with or without the socially approved "medicine." James Kaywaykla (Apache) also disobeyed his elders on a number of occasions. As youths Asa Daklugie and a friend became so dissatisfied with their anomalous age status between the children and the men in Apache society, that they ran away from the camp of Mangas, son of the famous Mangas Coloradas. And Mourning Dove later regretted scornfully refusing the sacred herbal knowledge of her grandmother. Ah-nen-la-de-ni (Daniel La France), a Mowhawk of part-French Canadian ancestry, did not as deliberately reject his grandmother's knowledge, but the effect of his indifference was the same. "I could have learned much if I had paid attention to her," he confessed,

> because as I grew older she took me about in the woods when she went there to gather herbs, and she told me what roots and leaves to collect, and how to dry and prepare them and how to make the extracts and what sicknesses they were good for. But I was soon tired of such matters, and would stray off by myself picking the berries . . . and hunting the birds and little animals with my bow and arrows. So I learned very little from all this lore.

John Stands in Timber also implied the existence of a such generation gaps when he recalled why he failed to appreciate a Cheyenne ceremony: "I was at the age when I didn't pay attention to those things, and there was no chance later." [32]

Narrators sometimes mentioned the difficulty of living up to the constant adult demands that they harden themselves for life. Many Navajos commented on the relentless work ethic forced upon them by their families and by the harsh Arizona environment. With perhaps a touch of humor Kay Bennett remembered her mother exclaiming: " 'I must find more work for them to do or they will become lazy' "—just when the girls were "sitting around the hogan and relaxing in the warm sun." And Anna Moore Shaw told of a Pima mother waking boys with the words: "You never rest until you die." Daklugie remembered how his uncle, Geronimo, "personally directed much of the training of the young boys for the warpath." He instructed them to jump into the cold water of the stream, "even when it meant breaking the ice." He allowed them to approach the fire for a while, with "teeth chattering," but then made them jump into the water again. Significantly, Daklugie did not romanticize the training. "Of course, nobody wanted to obey, but one look at the stout switch in Geronimo's hand prevented any refusal." [33]

Occasionally a narrator admitted to cynical deception of such elders.

John Dick (Navajo) remembered his father's strictness, and the constant demand that he work. Yet when his father told him to develop strong legs by running home with the horses instead of riding one, Dick did not always carry out this instruction:

> I do have a confession to make: Once in a while I cheated. When I was where no one could see me, I would rope a tame horse and ride off to get the other ones. When I got closer to home I would loose the horse that I used and innocently bring them all back on foot the rest of the way. What a life!

He justified his action with the comment, no doubt as accurate for children elsewhere as for young Indians: "I think everyone has a notion to try to get away with something like that at times."[34]

Other narrators made similarly frank admissions of their human frailty. Although they generally enjoyed listening to the stories of their elders, occasionally they recount falling asleep during such educational sessions. Black Eagle (Ponca) told of his severe father, who used to instruct his children at breakfast. "I always got tired of it," Black Eagle reported. "I'd whisper, 'He ought to hurry up. I want to eat.'" Hardly the idyllic image of wise elder and rapt child.[35] Yet it is in such descriptions and in those of resentment or even disobedience that a more fully human picture of Indian life emerges.

Resentment does not necessarily imply a deep skepticism of tribal values, but occasionally such a socially dangerous attitude did surface. When faced with the awesome technological power of white civilization, or even with the strange new world of the school, some Indian children began to question the wisdom of their elders. But this could happen even before full contact with American life. Indians who rebelliously attempted to engage in activities inappropriate for their age, or without having first acquired the socially sanctioned spiritual powers, in part rejected major tribal values in their pursuit of personal goals. Frank Mitchell often expressed disrespect for Navajo spiritual values—until he himself became a Blessingway singer (a curing shaman). Another Navajo's evasion of the mandatory morning icy wash caused his sister to question the people's beliefs:

> They told us if we did our physical exercises at dawn and carried ice to the hogan house we would be gifted with wealth. But, the one who seldom took ice-water baths had more wealth than we had. We suffered with half-frozen bodies for nothing.[36]

Such open questioning of tribal values was not common, but Daklugie remembered the anguish when he received conflicting orders from respected adults. Juh, his father, had instructed him that his first duty was to protect the girl who would be his wife, but Geronimo, his uncle, had told him that the people came first. "It was puzzling," Daklugie remembered. "At nights I lay awake trying to unravel the problem." And James Kaywaykla alerted us to a fact about tribal cultures easily forgotten: "There was a belief that he who killed at night must walk in darkness to the Place of the Dead," he reported. "I cannot say that all Apaches believed this, but many did. Like White Eyes, we had skeptics among us."[37]

VI

Nevertheless, the elders of these autobiographers achieved a high degree of success in educating their children into responsible manhood and womanhood. The educational patterns recalled by the narrators are mutually reinforcing and broadly similar to those presented by Pettitt when he surveyed data from a large number of tribes, and to those in Szasz's more recent study.

Indian education was essentially designed to preserve the heritage of the tribe, but that need not imply a blind rejection of new experiences. Indian parents, and occasionally grandparents or tribal leaders, often *encouraged* young Indians to seek a school education, in order to secure a livelihood in the modern world or to become mediators between their peoples and American society.

Even when older Indians themselves resisted white culture, some attempted to adapt their traditional teachings to new realities. Jim Whitewolf recounted how his Kiowa Apache grandfather, in classic fashion, brought other old men to tell stories to him. Then the grandfather himself lectured the boy. First pointing out that Indian peoples no longer fought each other as in the "old days," he emphasized the necessity for hard work. "He told me that now I didn't need to have a fast horse to do fighting, *but that he wanted me to take care of my horses so I could use them to farm with, like the white people were doing so I could have something*" (emphasis added). Sanapia, a Comanche medicine woman, also recalled how quickly her grandmother saw the utility of a new skill—writing— to help preserve the old wisdom:

> She tell me [sic] always to remember what she tells me and I did. She tell me that I should write it down, but at that time I didn't even know what writing is, but my grandma did.

And Rosalio Moisés, a Yaqui whose family fled from Mexico to Arizona at the beginning of the twentieth century, also remembered how his father quickly realized the potential of the same new skill for the preservation of tradition. In 1908, after Rosalio had learned to read and write, his father bought a notebook, and "dictated the names of ancestors and relatives along with their birth and death dates. He also dictated an account of the Yaquis telling of battles he had been in." Sadly, the book was later lost.[38]

VII

"It is commonly supposed that there is no systematic education of their children among the aborigines of this country," wrote Charles Eastman in 1902. "Nothing could be further from the truth." In countering such stereotypical thinking, Indian autobiographers often romanticized traditional upbringing, but they also demonstrated that education was a deeply serious business for traditional Indians. "All the customs of this primitive people were held to be divinely instituted," wrote Eastman, "and those in connection with the training of children were scrupulously adhered to and transmitted from one generation to another."[39] Nothing less than the very survival of the people depended on the success of this on-going, communitywide enterprise.

Traditional education obviously made great demands upon Indians of all ages. The fact that it took place within what Sioux medicine man Lame Deer called a "warm blanket" of kin and community meant that school could come as a cold, terrible shock. "I will remember the first night I spent," said Mildred Stinson, an Oglala Lakota (Sioux), of arrival at boarding school as a seven-year-old. "I'll never forget it as long as I live. . . . There was nobody to say goodnight to me. . . . And I remember I cried all night. And oh, I was never so lonesome, and although there were probably two hundred children there in the same dormitory with me, I felt like I was all alone."[40] Except, perhaps, in cases of serious disobedience or neglect of duty, few Indian children would ever have experienced such isolation within their own educational environment. In certain ways then, traditional education left young Indians poorly prepared for the rigors of the school; in other ways it was to prove a surprisingly effective preparation.

Tribal education did not turn the young Indian into a passive prisoner of culture; each boy or girl was an individual with his or her blend of ethnic, familial, and personal characteristics. But the tribal educational experience provided a major motivational influence—indeed a cluster of influences—upon the Indian child's responses to the school.

Nowhere in these autobiographies are there more memorable images of the cyclical nature of this traditional education, or of the power of the old stories to move children, than in the account given by Chris, a Mescalero Apache. "My smallest girl is just at the age when she is interesting to watch," he informed his interviewer in the 1930s. "I was telling stories. She listened for a while and then she said, 'I'm tired,' and went out." Soon Chris heard her talking outside: "I listened. She was telling stories. She had got the children together and was telling them the same stories."

Later, in a reversal of customary roles, the same girl could be heard recounting similar stories *to her grandmother*. And still later she stepped before a group of people who were exchanging stories. "She wasn't a bit bashful," recalled her proud father. "She didn't have a smile on her face at all. 'It's my turn to tell a story,' she said. 'There was a very old man and he went to get a bucket of water to wash his clothes.' She just got that far, and everyone began to laugh at her. Just as soon as they laughed she stopped and jumped back like a little chipmunk." The context suggests that the laughter was good-natured, an expression of surprise at one so young presuming to educate. But the girl had already done her part both in passing on the stories to her own age group, and in convincing adults that the stories still lived for the young.

And so the telling and learning went on between the generations—until a break occurred in the cycle. The same Apache father later noted how some boys had been "teasing" him to allow his son go with them to boarding school. On the eve of departure the boy told his father: "I'm going to see my grandmother before I go off to school. It might be the last time I'll see her."[41]

And the last time she, or perhaps any older people, might instruct him in the ways of the Mescaleros. As the next chapter will demonstrate, a major goal for generations of Euro-American missionaries and secular educators was to effect just such a break in the cycle.

Notes

Chapter epigraph is quoted from Richard Henry Pratt, *Battlefield and Classroom: Four Decades with the American Indian, 1867–1904*, edited by Robert M. Utley (Lincoln: University of Nebraska Press, 1964), 222.

1. Jean Barman, Yvonne Hebert, and Don McCaskill, "The Legacy of the Past: An Overview," in Jean Barman et al., eds., *Indian Education in Canada*. Vol. 1. *The Legacy*, (Vancouver, B.C.: University of British Columbia Press, 1986), 1. Indian pupils also absorbed white culture outside the school, but Chapters 2 and 3 in the present volume will compare and contrast Indian education, in the broad sense of the definition above, with American schooling only. See also Margaret Connell Szasz, *Indian Education in the American Colonies, 1607–1783* (Albuquerque: University of New Mexico Press, 1988), 2–3: schooling of Indians was "a single, crucial dimension of the larger process of cultural interaction."

2. Thomas Wildcat Alford, *Civilization and the Story of the Absentee Shawnees*, as Told to Florence Drake (Norman: University of Oklahoma Press, 1936), 18; George A. Pettitt, *Primitive Education in North America* (Berkeley: University of California Press, 1946), 4.

3. Helen Sekaquaptewa, *Me and Mine: The Life Story of Helen Sekaquaptewa*, edited by Louise Udall (Tucson: University of Arizona Press, 1969), 64; Dorothy Eggan, "Instruction and affect in Hopi Cultural Continuity," in George D. Spindler, ed., *Education and Culture: Anthropological Approaches* (New York: Holt, Rinehart & Winston, 1964), on the warmth, intensity, and anxiety of Hopi education, 321–50. The Eggan article was reprinted from the *Southwestern Journal of Anthropology* 12 (1956). Robert W. Rhodes sees a holistic education as one that "encourages understanding of many aspects at the same time and of the interrelationships involved," in "Holistic Teaching/Learning for Native American Students," *Journal of American Indian Education* 27 (Jan. 1988): 26–27.

4. Such recollections in as-told-to autobiographies often reflected the insistence of editors/collaborators that narrators tell of their early lives; traditional Indians generally thought of their life stories in terms of *adult* achievements, Brumble, *American Indian Autobiography*, 49–50. This editorial influence does not necessarily invalidate the accuracy of the subsequent recall.

5. Szasz, *American Colonies*, 11. See 7–24 for an excellent examination of traditional educational practices.

6. Luther Standing Bear, *Land of the Spotted Eagle* (1933; rpt., Lincoln: University of Nebraska Press, 1978), 2. On relations with his father see, for example, Standing Bear, *My People the Sioux*, edited by E. A. Brininstool (1928; rpt., Lincoln: University of Nebraska Press, 1975), 60–67, 141; Irene Stewart, *A Voice in Her Tribe: A Navajo Woman's Own Story*, edited by Doris Ostrander Dawdy, with Mary Shepardson, Anthropological Papers No. 17 (Soccoro, N.M.: Ballena Press, 1980), 43. Also Alice C. Fletcher and Francis La Flesche, *The Omaha Tribe*. 27th Annual Report of the Bureau of American Ethnology to the secretary of the Smithsonian Institution, 1905–1906. (1911; rpt., Lincoln: University of Nebraska Press, 1970), Vol. 2, 327–33.

7. Zitkala-Sa, *American Indian Stories* (1921; rpt., Lincoln: University of Nebraska Press, 1986), 18–21; Belle Highwalking, *Belle Highwalking: The Narrative of a Northern Cheyenne Woman*, edited by Katherine M. Weist (Billings: Montana Council for Indian Education, 1979), 2.

8. Polingaysi Qoyawayma (Elizabeth Q. White), *No Turning Back: A True Account of a Hopi Indian Girl's Struggle to Bridge the Gap Between the World of Her People and the World of the White Man*, as told to Vada F. Carlson (Albuquerque: University of New Mexico Press, 1964), 90–91. Qoyawayma calls this third-person account a biography, but notes that it is based on her reminiscences and tells her life story, Preface. On the educational roles of uncles and aunts, see also Anna Moore Shaw, *A Pima Past* (Tucson: University of Arizona Press, 1974), 35–46; Alford, *Civilization*, 87; Pettitt, *Primitive Education*, Chap. 3.

9. Eastman, *Indian Boyhood* (1902; rpt., New York: Dover, 1971) 11–16, 43–49.

10. James Kaywaykla, *In the Days of Victorio: Recollections of a Warm Springs Apache*, edited by Eve Ball (Tucson: University of Arizona Press, 1970), 8; Eastman, *Indian Boyhood*, 64–69; Allen James, *Chief of the Pomos: Life Story of Allen James*, edited by Ann M. Connor (Santa Rosa, Cal.: privately printed, 1972), 15.

11. Mourning Dove, *Mourning Dove: A Salishan Autobiography*, edited by Jay Miller (Lincoln: University of Nebraska Press, 1990), 78; Vine Deloria, Sr., "The Standing Rock Reservation: A Personal Reminiscence," *South Dakota Review* 9 (Summer 1971): 193–94; Peter LeClair, "Peter LeClair—Northern Ponca: An Autobiographical Sketch with an Introduction and Comments by James H. Howard," *American Indian Tradition* 8 (1961): 18.

12. Shaw, *Pima Past*, 50–52; Betzinez, *I Fought with Geronimo*, 82.

13. Mourning Dove, *Salishan*, Chap. 2; quotations 39, 45.

14. Edward Goodbird, *Goodbird the Indian: His Story*, edited by Gilbert L. Wilson (1914; rpt., St. Paul: Minnesota Historical Society, 1985), 58–59. Also, Kaywaykla, *In the Days of Victorio*, 16; Lame Deer/John Fire and Richard Erdoes, *Lame Deer: Seeker of Visions* (New York: Simon & Schuster, 1972), Chap. 1; Pettitt, *Primitive Education*, Chap. 8; Szasz, *American Colonies*, 15–17.

15. Yava, *Big Falling Snow*, 1–2, 72. See also Peter M. Whiteley, *Deliberate Acts: Changing Hopi Culture Through the Oraibi Split* (Tucson: University of Arizona Press, 1988), 57–61; E. Adamson Hoebel, *The Cheyennes: Indians of the Great Plains* (New York: Holt, Rinehart, & Winston, 1960), Chap. 3; Fletcher and La Flesche, *The Omaha Tribe*, Vol. 2, Chap. 11. Also, Jim Whitewolf, *The Life of a Kiowa Apache Indian*, edited by Charles S. Brant (New York: Dover, 1969), 7–10. Names fictionalized, viii; Luther Standing Bear, *Land of the Spotted Eagle*, 141–47.

16. Nancy Bonvillain, "Gender Relations in Native North America," *American Indian Culture and Research Journal* 13 (1989): 1–28; Sekaquaptewa, *Me and Mine*, 157–61 (on male weaving). On puberty training and girls: *idem.*, 117–18; Kaywaykla, *In the Days of Victorio*, 37–43; Stewart, *A Voice in Her Tribe*, 19–20; Shaw, *Pima Past*, 52–57.

17. Highwalking, *Narrative*, 2. By the 1960s girls were "boy crazy"; Mourning Dove, *Salishan*, 49–50; Sekaquaptewa, *Me and Mine*, 117–19. Cf. Don Talayesva, *Sun Chief*, in which sexual promiscuity is a major theme. See, for example, 78–79, 144–47; also, Stewart, *A Voice in Her Tribe*, 42–43.

18. Anonymous, "The Narrative of a Southern Cheyenne Woman," *Smithsonian Miscellaneous Collections*, edited by Truman Michelson, Vol. 87, no. 5 (1932), 9; Mary Little Bear Inkanish, *Dance Around the Sun: The Life of Mary Little Bear Inkanish: Cheyenne*, edited by Alice Marriot and Carol K. Rachlin (New York: Crowell, 1977), 9; on ancestry, xi–xii. Narrative in third person, but based on Mary's memories, xi–xiii. Also Luther Standing Bear, *Land of the Spotted Eagle*, 147.

19. Pettitt, *Primitive Education*, 22; Standing Bear, *Land of The Spotted Eagle*, 15, 119. Also Szasz, *American Colonies*, 11; Adam Kuper and Jessica Kuper, eds., *The Social Science Encyclopedia* (London: Routledge & Kegan Paul, 1985), 400. See also Robert A. Trennert, "Corporal Punishment and the Politics of Indian Reform," *History of Education Quarterly* 29 (Winter 1989): 596.

20. Standing Bear, *Land of the Spotted Eagle*, 13. Games, *idem*, 34–38; Standing Bear, *My People the Sioux*, Chap. 3; Anonymous, "Southern Cheyenne Woman," 3; Joseph K. Griffis, *Tahan: Out of Savagery, into Civilization. An Autobiography* (New York: Doran, 1915), 205. See also, for example, Alford, *Civilization*, 22–23; Talayesva, *Sun Chief*, 60–63; George Webb, *A Pima Remembers* (Tucson: University of Arizona Press, 1959), 42–44; Fletcher and La Flesche, *The Omaha Tribe*, Vol. 2, esp. 363–70; Pettitt, *Primitive Education*, 44–45: "Primitive play, where it reflected adult pursuits, was to a large extent directed practice rather than merely imitation."

21. Talayesva, *Sun Chief*, 85–86, also 60; Standing Bear, *Land of the Spotted Eagle*, 26–27; La Flesche, *Middle Five*, xvi. Also on story telling: Kaywaykla, *In the Days of Victorio*, 27, and 37–40; Betzinez, *I Fought with Geronimo*, 55; Highwalking, *Belle Highwalking*, 6–10; John Stands in Timber and Margot Liberty, *Cheyenne Memories* (Lincoln: University of

Nebraska Press, 1967), Chap. 1; Mountain Wolf Woman, *Mountain Wolf Woman, Sister of Crashing Thunder: The Autobiography of a Winnebago Indian*, edited by Nancy Oestreich Lurie (Ann Arbor: University of Michigan Press, 1961), 21; Vecsey, *Imagine Ourselves*, esp. xii, 24–29; Pettitt, *Primitive Education*, Chap. 10.

22. Luther Standing Bear, *My Indian Boyhood* (1931; rpt., Lincoln: University of Nebraska Press, 1988), 152–53; Eastman, *Indian Boyhood*, 4, Chap. 5; and *Deep Woods*, 22: he was disturbed when an insensitive teacher asked him his name; Yava, *Big Falling Snow*, 3. Also on naming: Kaywaykla, *In the Days of Victorio*, 28–29; Daklugie et al., *Indeh*, 43; Alford, *Civilization*, 3; Mitchell, *Navajo Blessingway Singer*, 67–68, 295; Jim Whitewolf, *Life*, 39–40, 71; Talayesva, *Sun Chief*, 31–32, 80, 155, 159–60, 306–07; Carl Sweezy, *The Arapaho Way: A Memoir of a Indian Boyhood*, edited by Althea Bass (New York: Clarkson N. Potter, 1966), 61; Pettitt, *Primitive Education*, Chap. 6.

23. Humility, writes Whiteley, "is an important Hopi ideal," though not all live up to it, *Deliberate Acts*, 180–81; Alford, *Civilization*, 21; Standing Bear, *My People the Sioux*, 65, 128, 138, 143, 151, 162–90, for example. Also, Royal B. Hassrick, *The Sioux; Life and Customs of a Warrior Society* (Norman: University of Oklahoma Press, 1964), 33, 68; Pettitt, *Primitive Education*, 50.

24. Kay Bennett, *Kaibah: Recollections of a Navajo Girlhood* (Los Angeles: Westernlore Press, 1964), 124–25 (written by narrator, but in third person); Charles A. Eastman (Ohiyesa), "Rain-in-the-Face: The Story of a Sioux Warrior," *The Outlook* 84 (Oct. 27, 1906): 510; Two Leggings, *Two Leggings: The Making of a Crow Warrior*, edited by Peter Nabokov (Lincoln: University of Nebraska Press, 1967), 33.

25. Talayesva, *Sun Chief*, 51; Alford, *Civilization*, 21; Stands in Timber and Liberty, *Cheyenne Memories*, 63; Shaw, *Pima Past*, 28. Also, Sekaquaptewa, *Me and Mine*, 109–17; Bennett, *Kaibah*, 153–54.

26. Standing Bear, *Land of the Spotted Eagle*, 40; La Flesche, *Middle Five*, 34–36; Eastman, *Indian Boyhood*, 89; also Two Leggings, *Crow Warrior*.

27. Angel DeCora, "Angel DeCora—An Autobiography," *The Red Man* 3 (1910): 279.

28. Goodbird, *Goodbird the Indian*, 17–18. See also Pettitt, *Primitive Education*, Chap. 3.

29. Talayesva, *Sun Chief*, 79–87. Also, for example: Stewart, *A Voice in Her Tribe*, 42; Alford, *Civilization*, 21–22; Mourning Dove, *Salisban*. An unrelated man did the boy's whipping, 78, note 12; Kiowa Apache parents sometimes asked *school* authorities to whip their children, another case of calling in outsiders to administer discipline, Brant, Introduction to Jim Whitewolf, *Life*, 28; Pettitt, *Primitive Education*, esp. 8.

30. Eggan, "Instruction and Affect," 331–32. Also, Griffis, *Tahan*, 27, Standing Bear, *Land of the Spotted Eagle*, 136–37; Kaywaykla, *In the Days of Victorio*, 132.

31. Daklugie et al., *Indeh*, 144. See also Daklugie interpreting for Geronimo, in *Geronimo: His Own Story*, edited by S. M. Barrett (1906; rpt., New York: Ballantine, 1970) 173–74.

32. Two Leggings, *Crow Warrior*, 115, 269–71, for example; Kaywaykla, *In the Days of Victorio*, 131–32; Daklugie et al., *Indeh*, 92–93; Mourning Dove, *Salisban*, 79–81; Ah-nen-la-de-ni (Daniel La France), "An Indian Boy's Story," *The Independent* 55 (July 30, 1903): 1781; Stands in Timber and Liberty, *Cheyenne Memories*, 102. Also, Inkanish, *Dance Around the Sun*, Chap. 4.

33. Bennett, *Kaibah*, 133–34. Work ethic is a central theme of the accounts in Broderick H. Johnson, ed., *Stories of Traditional Navajo Life and Culture, by Twenty-Two Navajo Men and Women* (Tsaile, Navajo Nation, Ariz.: Navajo College Community Press, 1977); Shaw, *Pima Past*, 139; Daklugie et al., *Indeh*, 86.

34. In Johnson, ed. *Stories of Traditional Navajo Life*, 184.

35. Black Eagle, "Xube, a Ponca Autobiography," edited by William Whitman, *The Journal of American Folk-Lore* 52 (April–June 1939): 182. Falling asleep: for example, Daklugie, et al., *Indeh*, 14; Mitchell, *Navajo Blessingway Singer*, 29. Mourning Dove found the story telling monotonous, but stayed awake, *Salisban*, 158. Some stories were meant to put children asleep: Stand in Timber and Liberty, *Cheyenne Memories*, 16.

36. Mitchell, *Navajo Blessingway Singer*, 140, 152–54; Myrtle Begay in Johnson, ed., *Stories of Traditional Navajo Life*, 59.

37. Daklugie et al., *Indeb.*, 146; Kaywaykla, *In the Days of Victorio*, 76. Also, Highwalking, *Belle Highwalking*, 18.

38. Jim Whitewolf, *Life*, 46–47; David E. Jones, *Sanapia: Comanche Medicine Woman* (1972; rpt. Prospect Heights, Ill.: Waveland Press, 1984), xi, 21–22 (Sanapia is a pseudonym); Rosalio Moisés, Jane Holden Kelley, and William Curry Holden, *A Yaqui Life: The Personal Chronicle of a Yaqui Indian* (Lincoln: University of Nebraska Press, 1971), 37. Other examples of adaptive elders, Webb, *A Pima Remembers*, 54–55.

39. Eastman, *Indian Boyhood*, 41.

40. Lame Deer and Erdoes, *Lame Deer, Seeker of Visions*, 34; in Joseph H. Cash and Herbert T. Hoover, eds., *To Be an Indian: An Oral History* (New York: Holt, Rinehart & Winston, 1971), 95.

41. Chris (pseudonym), *Apache Odyssey: A Journey Between Two Worlds*, edited by Morris Opler (New York: Holt, Rinehart & Winston, 1969), 288–91. According to Eve Ball (editor of Daklugie et al., *Indeb*, 263–66) Charlie Smith, Jr., claimed to have been "Chris," but denied the authenticity of the autobiography, claiming that whites may have given some of the information. But see Opler's careful introduction and notes, and the rich account by the narrator. Perhaps Smith attempted to deflect criticism for having revealed much about Mescalero spiritual life. For examples of Indian children exchanging traditional stories *while at school*, see later chapters of this volume.

CHAPTER 3

American Indians and the School

I

IN THE FIRST CHARTER OF Virginia (1606) King James I exhorted the colony to devote itself to the "propagating of Christian Religion to such People, as yet live in Darkness and miserable ignorance of the true Knowledge and worship of God." Thus the colony might "in time bring the Infidels and Savages living in those Parts, to human civility, and to a settled and quiet Government." The words of the English King powerfully expressed that conviction of cultural superiority, which since the seventeenth century has driven Christian and secular "uplifters" of American Indians.[1] Words like these could also constitute what Neal Salisbury calls a "rhetoric of justification." The drive to Christianize and "civilize" Indians was in every century also a drive to pacify them, one which implied their acceptance of European sovereignty and the surrender of vast areas of hunting grounds to colonists.[2] This drive also implied the schooling of Indian children. Complex blendings of idealism, strategy, and, of course, personal motivations have always impelled the educational crusade.

Despite royal exhortation and despite the oft-quoted plea of the Indian depicted on the 1629 seal of the Massachusetts Bay Colony—"Come over and help us"—English colonists did little to fulfill the task. During the seventeenth and eighteenth centuries only a small number of dedicated individuals set about "uplifting" Indians. In near-total ignorance of tribal methods of education, they focused upon the younger generation as the major hope for the future.[3]

The so-called Apostle of the Indians, English-born John Eliot of Roxbury, Massachusetts, developed an approach to be emulated by educators into the present century: the separation of the hopefully Christianized from the unconverted. Some Indians accepted Eliot's innovation that they settle in "praying towns," subject to English laws and mores. English colonists saw such an arrangement as leading to Christianization and civilization. Many Indians saw it as a method of ensuring group survival; although the colonists increasingly dominated relationships, manipulation was rarely one-way. In the middecades of the seventeenth century, fourteen praying towns grew up, and many established their own schools, in which acculturated Indian teachers taught their young the ways of the English.⁴ Other experiments also began: some colonists sent young tribal members to England, or brought them into their homes, in part to exploit their labor, in part to educate them by a process of total immersion. And a number of Indians actually attended Harvard University, the College of New Jersey (later Princeton University), Dartmouth, and the College of William and Mary.⁵

Unlike the more culturally tolerant and adaptive Jesuit missionaries in French North America, almost all missionary efforts in the English colonies, overwhelmingly Protestant, engaged in both deculturation and enculturation of an extraordinarily absolute kind. They generally accepted Indian potential for "uplift," but sought the utter extirpation of the tribal culture and the inculcation of English ideas of religion and "civility," down to the smallest details of appearance and behavior. "The cure for the Indians' disorder," writes James Axtell of this English obsession with social control, "was a strong dose of English order."⁶

The ethnocentric assumptions of English missionaries changed little during the century of the Enlightenment. From the 1730s to the 1760s, according to Szasz, the New England and Middle Colonies "witnessed a flurry of experiments in schooling for Indian youth." Eleazar Wheelock, the founder of Dartmouth College, was perhaps the most important of these experimenters. In 1754 he established Moor's Charity School, at Lebanon, Connecticut. Almost ninety Indian boys and girls attended, some of whom later became cultural brokers by carrying the new learning back to their own and other Indian peoples.⁷

Significantly, Szasz makes no attempt to judge the success or failure of the numerous short- and longer-lived educational enterprises. Even if full statistical information were available, she asks, whose criterion would we use: that of the Indian student, his family, community or tribe; of the missionary-schoolmasters; of the colony; of the missionary organization; or of its financial supporters in the colonies and Europe? Although Axtell admits that by the time of the American Revolution perhaps 500 Indians had "crossed the cultural divide to become Anglicized Christians in all but color and perhaps memory," he nevertheless maintains that the schools "notoriously failed to turn Indian children into English adults."⁸

The colonial educational experiments inspired Protestants of later generations, and established many of the patterns of Indian schooling that would persist in modified forms through the nineteenth and into the twentieth century: the cultural intolerance of the goals, which fused versions of Christianity to Western secular values; the generally nonracist belief in the potential of Indians for "uplift"; the deep faith in the school as the most effective means of achieving these goals; the combining of physical labor with religious and secular instruction supposedly appropriate to the sexes; and the separation of Indian children from the "corrupting" influences of kin and culture. The adaptive, manipulative responses of colonial Indian peoples to the demands of the "civilizers" also characterized Indian responses in later centuries.

II

By the beginning of the nineteenth century, the new United States faced a dilemma: how to combine acceptably humane treatment of the tribes with expansion of the Christian civilization into their lands? For some whites, of course, the dilemma never arose; at most they faced the military problem of how best to dispossess the Indians. But, as in the colonial period, many Americans inside and outside government saw the problem as both real and urgent. If some politically practical solution were not soon found, the explosive expansion of white settlement would destroy the remaining Indian peoples.

The solution appeared to be at hand, in the form of the school. Possessed of what Michael Katz has called the "American faith in public education," early nineteenth-century reformers built new school systems and "helped engineer a lasting popular conversion to public education as both the cornerstone of democracy and as the key agency for the solution of virtually every social problem." To large numbers of Americans the school became, in Barbara Finkelstein's words, a "formidable structure of persuasion," which would inculcate American values, self-control, and Protestant Christianity into an increasingly heterogeneous population.[9]

Since 1789, responsibility for Indian affairs had been exercized by the War Department. In 1824, a special unit within War was set up, called the Bureau of Indian Affairs (BIA) or the Office of Indian Affairs (OIA). In 1849 the BIA was transferred to the new Department of the Interior.[10] But, despite a growing commitment to Indian schooling, for much of the nineteenth century the government chose merely to subsidize the educational work of other groups. Commissioner of Indian Affairs Francis E. Leupp, head of the BIA, accurately reflected in 1905 that the "education of Indian children was practically in the hands of religious associations alone during the first hundred years of our national history." Indeed, one of the most remarkable characteristics of Indian schooling during the decades covered by this study was the close cooperation between the federal government and the churches. Only occasionally did participants question the propriety of the arrangement.[11]

As the century progressed, government financial aid increased. But only in the last decades did federal authorities move from subsidization to actual participation. They began to erect and staff government Indian schools, and attempted to develop an ambitious Indian educational system. By the early twentieth century the federal effort dwarfed the missionary contribution to Indian schooling.

In 1819, the "civilization fund" became law, providing "for the civilization of the Indian tribes adjoining the frontier settlements." Each year the President could expend $10,000 to employ "capable persons of good moral character, to instruct them [Indians] in the mode of agriculture suited to their situation; and for teaching their children in reading, writing, and arithmetic." The President and Secretary of War used the fund to help finance existing missionary enterprises among the Indians. By 1824, there were thirty-two such missionary schools in operation among the tribes, enrolling over 900 children.[12]

Further, many Indian treaties authorized grants to provide schools for the tribes concerned, and much of this money benefited the missionary establishments. Among peoples such as the Cherokees and Choctaws, adaptive leaders of part-white ancestry utilized this treaty money to subsidize American missionary education for their peoples; as in colonial times, Indian initiatives influenced the development of the education campaign. In the pre-Civil War decades, direct government financial aid, important as it was, accounted for perhaps less than 10 percent of the money poured into the effort to "civilize" Indians. The mission societies themselves raised some of the money; Indian treaty money supplied the bulk of it. The missionaries simultaneously capitalized on government moral support and on the increasing military strength of the United States.[13]

Stimulated also by the religious revivals of the Second Great Awakening, Evangelical Protestants threw themselves into the work of "saving the heathen" throughout the world. Quakers, Baptists, Congregationalists, Presbyterians, Episcopalians, Methodists, Lutherans, and others established a throng of missionary organizations. Some of the explosive effort focused upon the Indians of America—"our own heathens," as a Presbyterian tract called them. In this great Protestant crusade, as in the initially smaller Catholic effort, the school had a major, if not *the* major, role to play.[14]

Founded in 1810, the American Board for Commissioners for Foreign Missions (ABCFM) was the first American foreign missionary society. Its "Presbygational" members (Congregationalists and Presbyterians) founded missions in Hawaii, China, Africa, the Middle East, and India, and among such American Indian peoples as the Cherokees, Choctaws, Dakotas, Ojibways, and Tuscaroras.[15] By the late 1820s the ABCFM's eight schools among the Cherokees of the Southeast had become, according to William G. McLoughlin, "an international showpiece," visited by such dignitaries as President James Monroe.[16]

At schools of the ABCFM and of other Protestant missionary societies, the goal remained the extirpation of tribal cultures and the transformation of Indian children into near-copies of white children. The varied curricula totally excluded Indian cultural knowledge, and generally fell into the "half-and-half" pattern: half of the curriculum comprised common school academic subjects, generally the English language, arithmetic, history, geography, and the religion of the denomination. The other half required physical labor appropriate to "proper" gender roles. The boys learned such skills as blacksmithing, woodwork, and—although some came from tribes which practiced agriculture—American methods of farming. The girls learned "civilized" cooking, dressmaking, and other "domestic arts." Thus educated into the ways of the Christian civilization, young Indians would return to their tribes as mediators between cultures. "Soon they will be mingling with their countrymen," declared the ABCFM of Brainerd pupils in 1821, "and imparting their acquired character to others, and they to others still, in a wider and still wider range."[17]

Like fellow missionaries, and like concerned government officials and "friends of the Indian" throughout the century, the ABCFM was convinced that Indians must civilize or die. Yet there was hope for them. "By what law must they perish," asked the ABCFM in 1841, "unless it be that barbarism must retire before civilization? But why should they remain barbarous? Few nations have ever made more rapid strides towards civilization than the Cherokees and the Choctaws previous to the troubles of the last ten years."[18]

Those "troubles," the forced removal of most of the so-called Five Civilized Tribes from the Southeast to the Indian Territory of Oklahoma during the 1830s, temporarily hindered missionary efforts. Again partly through the initiative of acculturated leaders of part-white ancestry, the missionary societies took up the educational work anew in the Indian Territory. Missionary efforts continued elsewhere in the United States and its territories, and by the eve of the Civil War Protestants and

Catholics had established new stations among tribes such as the Omahas of the Midwest and the Nez Perces of the Far Northwest.[19]

After the Civil War, the federal government attempted to surrender the bulk of its responsibility for Indian welfare to the religious bodies. Through its Peace Policy, the administration of Ulysses S. Grant first invited the Friends (Quakers) to suggest church members for appointments as agents and teachers among the tribes. Commissioner of Indian Affairs Ely S. Parker (a Seneca Indian) declared in 1870 that the experiment had "proven such a success" that other Protestant and Catholic churches had been invited to participate. The fused secular and religious goal was "to combine with the material progress of the Indian race, means for their moral and intellectual improvement." By 1872 Presbyterians, for example, had received nine agencies with oversight of 38,069 Indians; Catholics received seven agencies with 17,856 Indians.[20]

Such a crass bundling out of unconsulted Indians did not result in their mass "uplift." It did not even produce more markedly moral administration of Indian affairs. The initially celebrated Peace Policy did not even produce peace; the late 1870s saw some of the most famous of the Indian wars: Custer's Last Stand took place in 1876. By the early 1880s this ambitious experiment in church-state relations was over.[21]

III

The drive to school the children of the tribes would have continued, Peace Policy or not. But, writes Robert H. Keller, "An essential ingredient in Grant's thinking was Indian education." Educational programs became institutionalized within the BIA. Government Indian schooling expanded rapidly after 1876, having received "its first significant government aid under the Peace Policy."[22] As the BIA set about establishing its own schools and forcing the missionary societies to the margin, appropriations increased rapidly: from $20,000 in 1870, to almost $3 million by 1900. The number of government schools also increased: from 150 with over 3,000 enrolled pupils in 1877, to 307 with over 21,000 in 1900. Such superficially impressive statistics tell us little about regularity of attendance, however, not to speak of effective learning.[23]

Also, Keller believes, a "cult of nationalism," began to replace emphasis on the Gospel for government officials.[24] Patriotic indoctrination may have intensified. But missionary and government documents, along with Indian autobiographical accounts, demonstrate that throughout the nineteenth century and into the twentieth both secular *and* missionary educators aimed at the inculcation of American democratic values, intertwined as they supposedly were with Protestant forms of Christianity. Certainly, officials could express the nationalistic goals of the campaign with great stridency. "It is of prime importance," declared Commissioner of Indian Affairs Thomas J. Morgan in 1889,

> that a fervent patriotism should be awakened in their [Indian children's] minds. . . . They should be taught to look upon America as their home and upon the United States Government as their friend and benefactor. They should be made familiar with the lives of great and good men and women in American history, and be taught to feel a pride in all their great achievements. *They should hear little or nothing of the 'wrongs of the Indians,' and of the injustice of the white race* [emphasis added]. If their unhappy history is alluded to it should be to contrast it with the better future that is within their grasp.[25]

In the last quarter of the nineteenth century, then, the BIA found itself overseeing an ever-increasing budget and an expanding educational empire. Yet, as David Wallace Adams notes, the growth in the government Indian school service in these decades was "in many ways a fitful and chaotic story."[26]

Further, although most concerned Americans agreed on goals for the tribes, there was sometimes bitter contention over methods. Educators disagreed, especially about the most appropriate kind of schools for Indians. Should "civilization" be brought to them through on-reservation day schools and boarding schools? These penetrated to the heart of the Indian community, but failed to quarantine children from the "heathenism" of their kin. Or should the Indian be brought to "civilization," through the construction of off-reservation boarding schools, sometimes hundreds or even thousands of miles from the reservation? Both approaches persisted through the period covered by this study. Despite the admitted dangers of exposing unprepared young Indians to the vices of civilization, by the late nineteenth century the large, off-reservation boarding school appeared to be the wave of the future.[27]

Many educators hoped they could supplant Indian parents and turn such distant boarding schools into real Christian homes, in contrast to supposedly inadequate environments from which the children came. According to William P. Dole, commissioner of Indian Affairs in 1863, children who only attended day schools on the reservation retained "the filthy habits and loose morals of their parents." In a manual labor boarding school, however,

the children *are under the entire control of the teacher* [emphasis added];
they are comfortably clothed; fed on wholesome diet . . . in fact, they are
raised and educated like white children and on leaving the school are found
to have acquired a knowledge of and taste for civilized habits.[28]

Control, obviously, was the issue. Yet even boarding schools could
not quarantine the children forever, as C. Robinson, superintendent of
the Haskell Institute at Lawrence, Kansas, lamented in 1888. There was
too much truth to the claim that "Children leaving even the best of
training schools for their homes, *like the swine return to their wallowing
filth, and barbarism*" [emphasis added].[29] Yet the boarding school, especially the off-reservation variety, at least offered the chance of temporary quarantine from such "filth."

The assimilationist vision and energy of Captain (later general)
Richard Henry Pratt triggered the large-scale move to off-reservation
boarding schools, which partly supported themselves through the manual labor of young Indians. This soldier's experience of "civilizing" a
group of Indian war prisoners, and his further experience with young
Indians at Hampton Institute in Virginia (where young blacks also
engaged in the half-and-half regimen), convinced Pratt of the potential of
Indians. In 1879, at a former military facility at Carlisle, Pennsylvania,
he opened his school. Luther Standing Bear, one of the Indian autobiographers, was among the first group of over one hundred boys and
girls who entered Carlisle. By 1900 enrollment had increased almost
tenfold, to 1,218 Indians from seventy-six tribes.[30]

Large numbers of Carlisle pupils took part in the famous "outing"
system, working a few months or more each year for selected white
families or firms, both to earn money for themselves and to gain experience of white life. The fundamental goal was to "individualize" the pupil
by separating him or her from other Indian children—first the separation from kin, then from *all* Indians—and to "lift him up" by total and
solitary immersion in white life. The program, wrote Pratt decades later
in his autobiography, was Carlisle's "right arm." It "enforced participation" in civilized life, and was thus "the supreme Americanizer."[31]

By 1910 a later principal, M. Friedman, admitted that Carlisle was "a
vocational school. It is neither a college or a university." But he outlined
the impressively expanded activities. The pupils spent part of each day
in the classroom, obtaining a common school education, and another
part working at various vocational pursuits such as telegraphy, business
studies, carpentry, tailoring, tinsmithing, printing, baking, sewing, or
agriculture. (In the early twentieth century the school attempted to
modernize its vocational training, dropping harness making as a separate

department, for example.) In one of the few concessions to tribal cultures, pupils could also engage in "native Indian crafts," like jewelry or rug making. They could enjoy the numerous extracurricular activities, such as the debating and literary societies, the band program, or football—the Carlisle team played against Harvard, Yale, and the University of Pennsylvania. Carlisle was a government school, but Friedman assured readers that "while the various students are allowed to select their own denominations in the great Christian church, it has been insisted constantly that every student affiliate with some church." Until its closing in 1918, Carlisle constituted an ambitious, carefully organized, and expensive way of "nationalizing"—Friedman's term for detribalizing—Indians from about ninety different tribes, and of molding them into new citizens.[32]

Further, Carlisle stimulated the establishment of many more government off-reservation boarding schools, with their large multitribal student bodies and ambitious academic and vocational curricula. Many developed their own versions of the "outing" program, which sometimes degenerated into a supply system of cheap menial labor to white patrons. Each school also instituted its tightly organized daily regimen and sometimes harsh military-style discipline, the better to instill in young Indians obedience, self-control, Western concepts of time, and the Protestant work ethic. These schools became, notes Robert A. Trennert, "monuments to regimentation." By the beginning of the new century there were twenty-five off-reservation boarding schools, claiming an average yearly attendance of over 6,000 Indian students, at such widely separated locations as Chilocco (Oklahoma), Phoenix (Arizona), Santa Fe (New Mexico), Flandreau (South Dakota), Fort Lewis (Colorado), and Lawrence (Kansas)—the Haskell Institute.[33]

By 1900 the government also supported eighty-one on-reservation boarding schools, claiming an average yearly attendance in of over 8,000 students, plus 147 day schools for Indians, with an average attendance of over 3,500. These many kinds of schools were, as Commissioner of Indian Affairs William A. Jones proudly declared, "all under complete government control." There were also about thirty schools still subsidized through contracts with the government. In addition, the BIA still assumed a "supervisory care" over a number of mission schools. Their enrollment was less than 2,000.[34]

In the late 1880s Commissioner Morgan attempted to turn this loosely directed collection of schools into a hierarchical, compulsory system, modeled on that of the public schools, with a uniform curriculum, standard textbooks, and similar methods of instruction from school to school. Ideally, students would progress in an orderly fashion from day school (elementary education), to on-reservation boarding school, to Carlisle or Phoenix or another nonreservation boarding school (vocational high school). Morgan did bring a greater degree of coherence to Indian schooling, but it was not possible to ensure uniformity in what was, after all, a haphazard collection of schools, among widely dispersed and culturally different peoples. Even in its own publication, the government admitted that, as late as 1928, few of its schools offered instruction of high school level.[35]

Nor was it possible to "civilize" Indian children who stayed away from school. In 1900 Commissioner Jones conceded that only 26,000 out of an estimated Indian school-age population of 40,000, were even *enrolled* at the above schools. Although absenteeism continued to decline, leading at times to embarrassing overcrowding of available government classroom space, as late as the 1920s large numbers of Indian children did not attend any kind of school.[36]

Thus, throughout the period under review, educators kept insisting on the need for compulsory Indian education, and treaties sometimes included clauses to this effect. Congress passed a number of laws allowing the BIA to compel attendance on particular reservations. And in 1891 a bill for the first time "authorized and directed" the commissioner of Indian Affairs "to make and enforce by proper means such rules and regulations as will secure the attendance of Indian children of suitable age and health at the schools established and maintained for their benefit." In 1893 Congress authorized the Secretary of the Interior to withhold rations and other annuities from parents and guardians who refused to send their children to school—but the next year partly backtracked and forbade the sending of children to off-reservation schools without parental or kin consent. Congress continued to pass laws of compulsion, and authorities on a number of reservations coerced children into school. Enforcement of compulsory laws always remained difficult, however, and the whole issue continued to arouse controversy even among white educators. Nevertheless, the Indian education program constituted, in the words of Frederick E. Hoxie, "a unique level of federal activism on behalf of a non-white minority."[37]

Early in the twentieth century a new trend added both possibilities and complications: Indian children began in ever-increasing numbers to attend state public schools, often with government financial support. In 1900 only 246 did so. By 1930, the cutoff point for the present study, this number had grown to 38,000—over half of the estimated total of 72,000 Indian children at all schools.[38] Few of the narrators of these autobiographies, however, appear to have spent much time in public schools, hence the focus of the present study on Indian schools.

Despite the remarkable expansion of efforts, officials believed that much remained to be done at the turn of the century. Employing the no-nonsense logic of the "friends of the Indian," Commissioner William A. Jones in 1903 exhorted the nation:

> Give the Indian a white man's chance. Educate him in the rudiments of our language. Teach him to work. Send him to his home, and tell him he must practice what he has been taught or starve. It will in a generation or more regenerate the race. *It will exterminate the Indian but develop a man* [emphasis added].

And although the government had taken most responsibility for Indian schooling from the missionary societies, the major goal remained consistent: assimilation into Christian citizenship. The almost complete lack of interest in Indian views on Indian education also continued to characterize the movement. E.M. Yearian, agent for the Lemhi reservation in Idaho, spoke for most of those involved with the tribes when he wrote in 1900: "The sooner we quit consulting the Indian about his welfare, the better for the Indian." [39]

IV

There is controversy among scholars over what happened next. Prucha believes that the goal of most educators remained assimilation of Indians into American society on something like equal terms. [40] Hoxie has argued, however, that around 1900, those in control of Indian educational policy became infected by theories that claimed Indians were mentally limited by their racial "nature." Hoxie sees the New Course of Studies, a systematic curriculum introduced in 1901, as one "of low expectations and practical lessons," deemphasizing academic learning and focused heavily on fields such as agriculture. Its goal, Hoxie believes, was to train Indians in practical but lowly skills that would help them develop economic self-sufficiency necessary for survival when they returned to the reservation. There they would remain caught in a peculiar twilight status: citizens, yet simultaneously dependent wards, under the guardianship of the superior civilization. [41]

An increasingly strong emphasis on the need for practical, vocational education certainly appears in reports of officials around the turn of the century. There was also an increase of appreciative comments on Indian life, which might be taken as either romantic racist sentimentality about interesting but backward peoples, or a genuine growth of sensibility—or, more likely, a confused blending of both attitudes together.[42]

Indeed it is possible to interpret the sometimes ambiguous language of officials in many ways. Commissioner Leupp poured scorn on the idea of an academic curriculum for Indians, most of whom, he believed, would draw a living from the soil. "Now, if anyone can show me what advantage will come to this large body of manual workers from being able to reel off the names of the mountains in Asia, or extract the cube root of 123456789, I shall be deeply grateful," he wrote in 1905. A more realistic approach was needed:

> the ordinary Indian boy is better equipped for his life struggle on a frontier ranch when he can read the simple English of the local newspaper, can write a short letter which is intelligible though ill-spelled, and knows enough of figures to discover that the storekeeper is cheating him.

Boys would also need practical skills about the farm, and girls a rudimentary academic education along with housewifely skills—all a far cry from the goals of visionaries like Pratt, or even of many missionary schools, which provided an impressive academic curriculum. Leupp believed that there was a "line of nature" between races, and thought in terms of the survival of the fittest. Yet he also declared that each Indian should be seen as an individual, who, if he could not be transformed, could be improved. And the commissioner denied that he was imposing a permanent status of inferiority upon Indians: "I would give the young Indian all the chances for intellectual training that the young Caucasian enjoys," he wrote; "no young Indian with the talent to deserve and the ambition to ask for the best there is in American education is likely to be refused." The goal of government policy, in Leupp's view, should still be to lead Indians to assume "the responsibilities of citizenship."[43]

To understand the full complexity of both policy *and practice*, we would need to know the effect of such often ambiguous thinking at hundreds of schools. How completely did teachers incorporate the New Course of Studies into classroom practice? To what extent did they become infected with ideas of race and of "inferior" Indian nature? The autobiographies do not offer conclusive proof on these issues; indeed they lend weight to both sides of the argument. They show, for example, the heavy emphasis on physical labor at many government and missionary schools, but they rarely show that the autobiographers were themselves victims of direct racial prejudice. Even accepting Hoxie's argument that emphases changed in government education policy in the

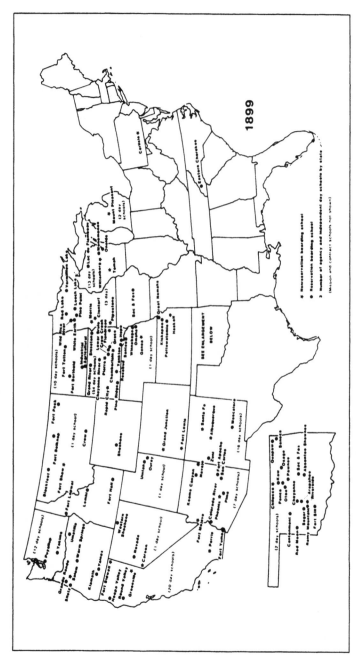

GOVERNMENT INDIAN SCHOOLS, 1899.

The commissioner of Indian Affairs claimed that these government schools enrolled 20,712 Indian pupils. Contract schools receiving government support (including Hampton Institute of Hampton, Virginia) enrolled a further 2,903 Indian pupils. Mission schools by then enrolled 1,261 Indians. State public schools enrolled only 326 Indians at the turn of the century. Actual attendance often fell below these figures.

In addition, after removal to Oklahoma in the 1830s the "Five Civilized Tribes" (Cherokees, Chickasaws, Choctaws, Creeks, and Seminoles) built their own school systems. The United States Government took over these systems in 1906.

Reprinted from *Atlas of American Indian Affairs*, by Francis Paul Prucha, by permission of University of Nebraska Press. Copyright © 1990 by the University of Nebraska Press.

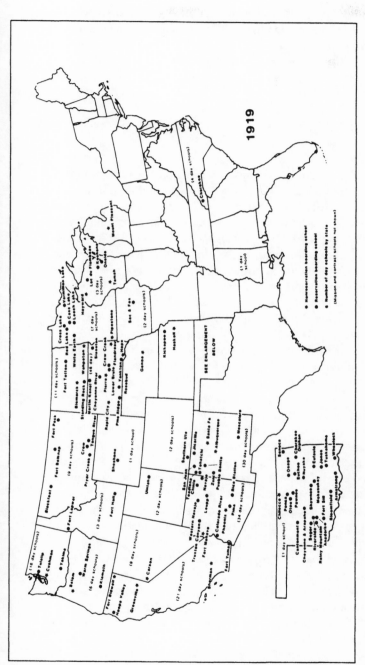

Government Indian Schools, 1919.

The Indian school situation continually changed. In 1918, for example, the government closed the famous Carlisle Indian School. By the end of the second decade of the twentieth century government schools claimed an enrollment of 25,396 Indian pupils. Mission and contract schools enrolled 5,387 Indians. Private schools enrolled 159. But state public school enrollment of Indians had increased to 30,858.

The trend toward greater state public school enrollment of Indians continued through the next decade. By 1930 public schools enrolled 38,000 Indians, compared to 28,000 in government schools, and 6,000 in mission and private schools.

Reprinted from *Atlas of American Indian Affairs*, by Francis Paul Prucha, by permission of University of Nebraska Press. Copyright © 1990 by the University of Nebraska Press.

early twentieth century, it is by no means clear that Indian school-children inevitably faced more racist and limiting educational practices. For, as Trennert points out in relation to the Phoenix Indian School, "changes at the top did not always filter down . . . in the expected way."[44]

V

By the early decades of the present century, then, Indians participated in an expanding and increasingly complicated educational establishment—goverment, missionary, and public school. It was an establishment which, despite its impressive statistical claims, came in for mounting criticism in the 1920s. Rejecting the generally optimistic tenor of government publications, groups of critics such as John Collier and the American Indian Defense Association, the authors of the so-called Meriam Report (1928), and the members of the National Advisory Committee on Education (1931), urged deep and widespread change. "Their findings," writes Prucha, "must have come as a heavy blow to the men and women in the Indian school system."[45]

Produced for the Institute of Government Research by a team of specialists—including the Winnebago Henry Roe Cloud—under the technical directorship of Dr. Lewis Meriam, *The Problem of Indian Administration* devoted over 800 pages to telling the Secretary of the Interior what was wrong. The calm, reasoned, but telling criticisms of the Meriam Report grew from two years of intense research and fieldwork, including ninety-five visits by survey members to Indian "jurisdictions" such as reservations, agencies, schools, and hospitals. Methodically the report presented the failure of the government to seek Indian points of view, to provide adequate health facilities, to ensure their economic subsistence, to train or adequately pay those assigned to assist the tribes; and, of course, government failure to provide adequate schools and relevant curricula. The Meriam Report also encouraged assimilation, but no longer insisted that Indians "civilize or die": the object of the work should be "to fit them either to merge into the social and economic life of the prevailing civilization, or to live in the presence of that civilization at least in accordance with a minimum standard of health and decency."[46]

Although careful not to blame individuals, the Meriam Report scathingly criticized much of Indian schooling. "The most fundamental need," declared W. Carson Ryan, Jr., the professional educator who wrote the eighty-three-page education section, "is a change in point of view." Ryan's own view reflected ideas of community-centered and individual-centered education characteristic of the Progressive movement in education. Whereas in the past Indian children had been removed from the family, he wrote, "the modern point of view in education and social work lays stress on upbringing in the natural setting of home and family life."

Ryan systematically examined areas such as student health, the school physical plants, the caliber and qualifications of staff, the military discipline, the religious indoctrination, the curriculum, the growth of "star" athletic programs, which neglected the mass of students—and found all severely inadequate or ill-conceived. The utilization of pupil labor to support the schools deprived children of proper education, and often amounted to mere exploitation. The "courses of study," so beloved of commissioners and senior administrators, had become insensitively rigid, taking little account of tribal and environmental diversity. In place of the overwhelmingly ethnocentric curriculum, Ryan declared, the Indian needed "to have his own tribal, social and civic life used as the basis for an understanding of his place in modern society." Above all, instead of regimenting Indian children into unthinking soldiers, the schools should try to encourage creativity, so the pupils would emerge capable of living full, independent lives in their chosen communities.[47]

As director of Indian education with the BIA from 1930 to 1935, Ryan attempted to put some of these ideas into action. But with the appointment of John Collier as commissioner of Indian Affairs in the New Deal administration of Franklin D. Roosevelt in 1933, the assault on pre-Meriam educational policies and practices intensified. Collier possessed a near-mystical admiration for tribal cultures and group values—values which, he believed, Western civilization desperately needed if it were to survive. In partnership with anthropologists, the BIA for the first time attempted to build a flexible curriculum that placed positive value on Indian life-styles. Collier too attempted to turn day schools from quarantined bastions of a superior civilization into genuine community centers, responsive to Indian cultural and social needs. Collier was not without his own streak of paternalism, and New Deal Indian programs did not envisage Indians taking control of, or even having a major say in, Indian administration. He too realized that they would have to adapt to modern life. But this need not result in the destruction of all that was Indian, nor should the separation of tribal children from their kin be continued any more than was absolutely necessary. The goal of schooling, Collier believed, should be to produce "adolescents in whom the tie that binds them to their [Indian] homeland *has been strengthened rather than broken* [emphasis added], Indian youths with wide horizons, bilingual, literate, yet proud of their racial heritage, [able] to become completely self-supporting, even though going without some of the mechanical accessories of the present day."[48]

Collier's vision was close to what anthropologist Malcolm McFee would later call a "150% man" or woman, enriched rather than stunted by participation in two cultures.[49] It was a far cry from the absolutist programs of the previous three centuries. And this new approach survived for less than a decade in the BIA. By the end of World War II the cycle had turned again; not quite back to intolerance of all things Indian, but away from such open respect for tribal culture. By the 1950s a fresh call for assimilation arose, now encapsulated in the idea that the government should "terminate" its responsibility for tribal affairs and thus "free" the Indian for participation in American life. Not until the 1960s would there be another attempt to build on both cultures in the education of Indians.[50]

Many of the above developments, as we shall see, lived on vividly in the minds of the Indian autobiographical narrators. Some of the oscillations in twentieth-century policy, especially John Collier's short-lived attempt to change things, clearly affected Noah White, a Winnebago Indian born about 1917. "I went to school without being able to talk English at all," he reminisced in 1970:

> so they had to have an interpreter from my own tribe to interpret for me for the first year or so, until I began to learn the English language. After that, we were forbidden to speak our own language. We were taught to forget our own culture and learn everything we could about the white man's ways. That was in the twenties and up to the middle thirties.
>
> Commissioner Collier had some of that changed, so in some Indian schools we would be able to send for our Indian costumes and hold tribal dances during commencement week. It didn't last long, because the school closed up.

Reflecting the emergence in the late 1960s and 1970s of a new development in Indian-white relations—a movement toward "self-determination" by Indians that goes far beyond the "top-down" New Deal acceptance of tribal culture—Noah continued with his personal history of Indian education. "[I]n most of the schools today, they are trying to revive all the traditions of the various tribes. They are trying to teach basket weaving and bead work. They are trying to teach tribal dances and tribal singing. And in some places they even teach the language. The various tribes are trying to bring back their own languages. There are quite a few of them that have lost their language, however."⁵¹

VI

Unlike most of their white contemporaries, these Indian auto-biographers had experienced as children distinct forms of education: a tribal form; then later, and sometimes interspersed with it, the school. Tribal education and Western schooling were strikingly, often brutally different.

Tribal education took place within a small, often face-to-face community, generally through the agency of kin or "experts" known to the child. The school, even the local reservation day school, strove to separate children from family. Not only were staff not kin; they were almost never personally known to the Indian children before enrollment. Traditional education happened everywhere in the village or in a natural environment. Schooling took place in a specific and generally man-made environment. Traditional instruction was oral, or through example, or "doing" or play. Western educators also used such methods, but before the Indian child could go far at school, he or she had to master a completely new language and then come to grips with "the book." Whereas kin and other tribal educators *enculturated* children into the ways of their own people, white educators forced a double process on the children: *deculturation*, to be followed by the learning of a totally new way of life and thought. Further, the tribal group generally controlled the education of its own children; when these children entered the school, control of many aspects of their education passed to an outside group.

The demands of such an alien system might have overwhelmed tribal children, had there not been surprising compatibilities between the two so apparently different approaches to education. Both systems assumed the importance of continual, incremental learning under the tutelage of adults. Both accepted the importance of spiritual knowledge, discipline and punishment, advance into higher status grades, the winning of particular prizes for tasks well performed, and the separation of the sexes.

Finally, it is a commonplace to contrast the holistic tribal approach to education with the fragmented Western approach. From an educational environment in which all areas of life related tightly to each other, and to the spirit world, the Indian child plunged into an institution which seemed to split knowledge into numerous unrelated "subjects," each assigned its own period in the school day.

Yet below such surface fragmentation, holistic assumptions also operated within the school. Karl Kaestle has noted both the coherence and comprehensiveness of the complex of beliefs espoused by antebellum nineteenth century educators—indeed by many middle- and even working-class Americans. Protestantism, "republicanism," and capitalism were its major, intertwined, and mutually supporting components. These produced a vast number of interdependent religious, social, and political tenets: "republican" government depends upon individual moral character, and on the elevated but dependent role of women; the principles of American Protestantism are the same as those of democratic American "republicanism"; environment, and thus schooling, are decisive to the development of moral character and thus to the republic; Christianity sanctions private property, which is the spur to industry and thus to civilization—and so on. "[I]f you assented to one or more of the propositions, it followed logically that you should be for any one of the others," claims Kaestle. "Conversely, if you assaulted one of the beliefs, you could be portrayed as assaulting the entire belief system, because the beliefs were interdependent." To propose a completely different system of values was to be "genuinely radical and threatening."[52]

The ideas of secular and religious Indian educators, through the antebellum period and even into the early twentieth century, certainly fit this ideological model. Not all subscribed to every tenet Kaestle proposes, and the emphases and combinations of tenets changed from individual to individual and over time; but most educators ascribed to most of them. And it was such a developing but coherent system of thought and assumptions that they presented to Indian children. Like tribal education, then, the school also enveloped the young Indian in a vast network of interdependent knowledge and behavioral requirements—in the holistic cultural environment of the white tribe.

Notes

1. Henry Steele Commager, ed., *Documents of American History* (New York, 1934), 8, quoted in Szasz, *American Colonies*, 46. In this section I rely heavily on Szasz's work. A good interpretive synthesis of Indian mission history is Henry Warner Bowden, *American Indians and Christian Missions: Studies in Culture Conflict* (Chicago: University of Chicago Press, 1981). A short synthesis of Indian schooling: Jon Reyner and Jeannette Eder, *A History of Indian Education* (Billings: Eastern Montana College, 1989).

2. Neal Salisbury, *Manitou and Providence; Indians, Europeans, and the Making of New England, 1500–1643* (New York: Oxford University Press, 1982), 177. Also Salisbury, "Red Puritans: The 'Praying Indians' of Massachusetts Bay and John Eliot," *William and Mary Quarterly* 31, 3d series (Jan. 1974): 27–54; James Axtell, *The Invasion Within: The Contest of Cultures in Colonial North America* (New York: Oxford University Press, 1985), 208, 331–32, and all 131–333; Szasz, *American Colonies*, 219–20.

3. For an illustration of the seal, Szasz, *American Colonies*, 84. Axtell contrasts the English focus on Indian children with the French Jesuit attention to adults, *The Invasion Within*, 179.

4. Szasz, *American Colonies*, esp. 111–23; Axtell, *The Invasion Within*, 282–86; Harold W. Van Lonkhuyzen, "A Reappraisal of the Praying Indians: Acculturation, Conversion, and Identity at Natick, Massachusetts, 1646–1730," *New England Quarterly* 63 (Sept. 1990): 396–428; James P. Ronda, "Generations of Faith: The Christian Indians of Martha's Vineyard," *William and Mary Quarterly*, 3d series, 38 (July 1981): 369–94.

5. Szasz, *American Colonies:* to England, 143–46; in colonial homes, 54, 64–65; at colleges or university, 68–69, 216–17, 257, 263; Bobby Wright, "'For the Children of the Infidels'?: American Indian Education in the Colonial Colleges," *American Indian Culture and Research Journal* 12 (1988): 1–14.

6. Szasz, *American Colonies*, refers to *one* possible case of Catholic schooling for Indians in Maryland, 62–64; Axtell, *The Invasion Within*, Chap. 5; quotation, 138. The willingness of captured Englishmen, women, and children to stay with Indian peoples might have provoked the colonists to deeper thought about the positive characteristics of tribal cultures, Chap. 13.

7. Szasz, *American Colonies*, 191; Chaps. 9, 10; James Dow McCallum, ed., *The Letters of Eleazar Wheelock's Indians* (Hanover, N.H.: Dartmouth College Publications, 1932), esp. 293–98, on enrollment. Cf. Axtell, *The Invasion Within*, 211–13, on Wheelock's possibly racist attitudes.

8. Szasz, *American Colonies*, 261–62; Axtell, *The Invasion Within*, 273–75.

9. Michael B. Katz, *Reconstructing American Education* (Cambridge, Mass.: Harvard University Press, 1987), 23, and Chaps. 1–3; Barbara Finkelstein, *Governing the Young: Teacher Behavior in Popular Primary Schools in Nineteenth-Century United States* (New York: The Falmer Press, 1989), esp. 5–25. Quotation, 24. See also, for example, David Tyack and Elisabeth Hansot, *Learning Together: A History of Coeducation in American Public Schools* (New Haven, Conn.: Yale University Press, 1990); Paula S. Fass, *Outside In: Minorities and the Transformation of American Education* (New York: Oxford University Press, 1989).

10. Theodore Fishbacher, "A Study of the Role of the Federal Government in the Education of the American Indian," unpublished Ph.D. dissertation, Arizona State University, 1967, 68–70; Francis Paul Prucha notes the changing nomenclature of the Department/Bureau/Office of Indian Affairs, *The Great Father: The United States Government and the American Indians*, (Lincoln: University of Nebraska Press, 1984), Vol. 2, Appendix D, 1227–29.

11. *Annual Report of the Commissioner of Indian Affairs* (1905), *House Documents*, Vol. 19, 59th Cong., 1st sess. Serial 4959, 34–35. (Henceforth, ARCIA, followed by citation. The ARCIA reports available to me appeared in different collections of documents or even

separately.) CIA Thomas J. Morgan, for example, criticized the church-state ties, ARCIA (Washington, D.C.: Government Printing Office, 1891), 68–69.

12. The text of the act is given in Report of the Indian School Superintendent, ARCIA (Washington, D.C.: Government Printing Office, 1885), LXXVII–LXXIX; Prucha, *The Great Father*, Vol. 1, 148–52.

13. Prucha, *The Great Father*, Vol. 1, 152–53. On the Cherokees, see, for example, Annual Report (1817), in *First Ten Annual Reports of the American Board of Commissioners for Foreign Missions* (title changes over the years), 1810–1820 (Boston: American Board of Commissioners for Foreign Missions, 1834), 153–58. (Hereafter ABCFM, AR, followed by year and page number); William G. McLoughlin, *Cherokees and Missionaries, 1789–1839* (New Haven, Conn.: Yale University Press, 1984); on Choctaws: Michael C. Coleman, *Presbyterian Missionary Attitudes Toward American Indians, 1837–1893* (Jackson: University Press of Mississippi, 1985), 13–14, 58–62. The Five Civilized Tribes built their own school systems, which the federal government took over in 1906. Report of the superintendent of schools for Indian Territory, with ARCIA, *Reports of the Department of the Interior* (Washington, D.C.: Government Printing Office, 1907), 349–55; Prucha, *The Great Father*, Vol. 2, 909–11. On funding: Fischbacher, "Role of the Federal Government," 65–67.

14. Coleman, *Presbyterian Missionary Attitudes*, 9–17; Robert F. Berkhofer, *Salvation and the Savage: An Analysis of Protestant Missions and American Indian Response, 1787–1862* (1965; rpt., New York: Atheneum, 1972). Berkhofer lists many church societies, 161–80; Prucha, *The Great Father*, Vol. 1, 145, on Catholic mission developments.

15. McLoughlin, *Cherokees and Missionaries*, 102–104; ABCFM, *Memorial Volume of the First Fifty Years of the American Board of Commissioners for Foreign Missions* (Boston: ABCFM, 1861), lists churches established by the ABCFM, 303.

16. ABCFM (1829), 61–65; McLoughlin, *Cherokees and Missionaries*, 132.

17. ABCFM, AR (1821), 49. Letters (copies) by Cherokee girls, 1828–29, detail the curriculum, John Howard Payne Papers, Vol. VIII, Newberry Library, Chicago, 1–62; Berkhofer, *Salvation and the Savage*, Chap. 2; Coleman, *Presbyterian Missionary Attitudes*, 17, 152–55.

18. ABCFM, AR (1841), 51. See also CIA Luke Lea, ARCIA (1852), *Senate Executive Document*, Vol. 1, No. 1, 32d Cong., 2d sess., Serial 658, 293–94; "The only alternative left," wrote C. Robinson, superintendent of Haskell Institute in the school's 1888 annual report, "is civilization or annihilation, absorption or extermination," with ARCIA (Washington, D.C.: Government Printing Office, 1888), 262.

19. Coleman, *Presbyterian Missionary Attitudes*, esp. 13–14, 69, 184–87; Berkhofer, *Salvation and the Savage*, takes the development of missions up to the time of the Civil War; Prucha, *The Great Father*, Vol. 1, 283–92. On Catholic missions, R. Pierce Beaver, "The Churches and the Indians: Consequences of 350 years of Missions," in *American Missions in Bicentennial Perspective* (South Pasadena, Cal.: William Carey Library, 1977), 276–81.

20. ARCIA (1870) *House Executive Document*, No. 1, 41 Congress, 3 Session, serial 1449, 474; ARCIA, (1872), *House Executive Document*, No. 1, part 5, 42 Congress, 2 session, serial, 1560, 460–62; Prucha, *The Great Father*, Vol. 1, Chap. 20; Robert H. Keller, Jr., *American Protestantism and United States Indian Policy, 1869–82* (Lincoln: University of Nebraska Press, 1983); on the implementation of the Peace Policy in specific tribes: Norman J. Bender, *"New Hope for the Indians": The Grant Peace Policy and the Navajos in the 1870s* (Albuquerque: University of New Mexico Press, 1989); Bender, *Missionaries, Outlaws, and Indians: Taylor F. Ealy at Lincoln and Zuni, 1878–1881* (Albuquerque: University of New Mexico Press, 1984), Part II; Clyde A. Milner II, *With Good Intentions: Quaker Work Among the Pawnees, Otos, and Omahas in the 1870s* (Lincoln: University of Nebraska Press, 1982).

21. Prucha, *The Great Father*, Vol. 1, 516–27.

22. Keller, *American Protestantism*, Chap. 11. Quotations, 205–206.

23. ARCIA (1900), *House Document*, No. 5, 56 Congress, 2 session, serial 4101, 44, 23. By 1928 appropriations for Indian education, exclusive of public school tuition, had

increased to $5,923,000, ARCIA, *Annual Report of the Secretary of the Interior* (Washington, D.C.: Government Printing Office, 1928), 13.

24. Keller, *American Protestantism*, 206.

25. I base this generalization about the patriotic practices of both secular and missionary education on the Indian autobiographies, ARCIA, and randomly read agent and missionary reports appended to it, government sources listed in the bibliography (section A, 3), the American Indian Correspondence, Presbyterian Historical Society, Philadelphia (hereafter AIC), also on the secondary sources on government and missionary educational efforts cited in this chapter. Quotation: ARCIA (1889), in Wilcomb E. Washburn, ed., *The American Indian and the United States: A Documentary History* (New York: Random House, 1973), Vol. 1, 432–33. On the patriotism of staff and pupils during World War I, see Robert A. Trennert, Jr., *The Phoenix Indian School: Forced Assimilation in Arizona, 1891–1935* (Norman: University of Oklahoma Press: 1988), 159–63.

26. David Wallace Adams, "From Bullets to Boarding Schools: The Educational Assault on American Indian Identity," in Philip Weeks, ed., *The American Indian Experience, A Profile: 1524 to the Present* (Arlington Heights, Ill.: Forum Press, 1988), 220; see also Adams, "Fundamental Considerations: The Deep Meaning of Native American Schooling, 1880–1900," *Harvard Educational Review* 58 (Feb. 1988), 1–28.

27. The Christian civilization was an ideal. On the admitted "evils" of American life and their potential to corrupt unprepared Indians, see, for example, Coleman, *Presbyterian Missionary Attitudes*, 42–44.

28. ARCIA (1863), *House Executive Document*, No. 1, 38 Congress, 1 session, 1182, 172; also ARCIA (1873), *House Executive Document* No. 1, part 5, 43 Congress, 1 session, serial 1601, 376–77. On the school as home, Coleman, *Presbyterian Missionary Attitudes*, 91–92; ABCFM, AR (1817), 154. On this phenomenon in non-Indian schools, Katz, *Reconstructing American Education*, 12, 43–44.

29. Report of School at Lawrence, Kan., ARCIA (Washington, D.C.: Government Printing Office, 1888), 262.

30. Richard Henry Pratt, *Battlefield and Classroom*, esp. Chap. 21; Luther Standing Bear, *My People the Sioux*, Chap. 14; Report of School at Carlisle, Pa., ARCIA (1900), *House Document* No. 5, 56 Congress, 2 session, serial 4101, 15–16, 502. The affairs of the school can also be followed in the reports appended to ARCIA; in school publications such as *The Red Man*, Vol. 1 (1909)–Vol. V (1913); in the superintendents' Annual Narrative and Statistical Reports from Field Jurisdictions of the Bureau of Indian Affairs,, 1907–938, (M1011), RG 75, NA; Records of Nonreservation Schools, Records of the Carlisle Indian Industrial School, RG 75, NA.

31. United States Indian Service, Training School for Indian Youth, ARCIA (1881), *House Executive Document* No. 1, part 5, vol. II, 47 Congress, 1 session, serial 2018, 245–46; Pratt, *Battlefield and Classroom*, 311, all Chap. 27; ARCIA (1900), *House Document* No. 5, 56 Congress, 2 session, serial 4101, 30–32. Student files gave details of each Indian's "outing" experience, School Records, Records of the Carlisle Indian Industrial School, Records of Nonreservation schools, RG 75, NA.

32. M. Friedman, "Annual Report of the Carlisle School, 1910," *The Red Man* 3 (Oct., 1910), 47–69; on extracurricular activities, see, for example, *The Carlisle Arrow* 12 (Nov. 19, 1915). On closing, Utley, Introduction to Pratt, *Battlefield and Classroom*, xvii.

33. On changes in the "outing" system at other schools, see Robert A. Trennert, Jr., "From Carlisle to Phoenix: The Rise and Fall of the Indian Outing System, 1878–1930," *Pacific Historical Review* 52 (Aug. 1983): 267–91; Trennert, "Victorian Morality and the Supervision of Indian Women Working in Phoenix, 1906–1930," *Journal of Social History* 22 (1988): 113–28. On regimentation: Trennert, "Educating Indian Girls at Nonreservation Boarding Schools, 1878–1920," *Western Historical Quarterly* 13 (July 1982), 281. I examine the subject of discipline in the text, Chapter 5. School list: ARCIA (1900), *House Document* No. 5, 56 Congress, 2 session, serial 4101, 15–16. See also: Sally Hyer, *One House, One*

Voice, One Heart: Native American Education at the Santa Fe Indian School (Santa Fe: Museum of New Mexico Press, 1990).

34. ARCIA (1900), *House Document* No. 5, 56 Congress, 2 session, serial 4101, 16-29.

35. Prucha, *The Great Father*, Vol. 2, 700-707; ARCIA, *Annual Report of the Secretary of the Interior* (Washington, D.C.: Government Printing Office, 1928), 13.

36. ARCIA (1900), *House Document*, No. 5, 56 Congress, 2 session, serial 4101, 22; Fischbacher, "A Study of the Role," 130-31.

37. Fischbacher summarizes and quotes extracts from many of the compulsory schooling laws, "A Study of the Role," 125-31. Quotation, 127; Prucha, *The Great Father*, Vol. 2, 691-92, 705-07, 833-34. Cf. Markku Henricksson, *The Indian on Capitol Hill: Indian Legislation and the United States Congress, 1862-1907* (Helsinki: Finnish Historical Society, 1988), 273. Also 113-15; Frederick E. Hoxie, *A Final Promise: The Campaign to Assimilate the Indians, 1880-1920* (Lincoln: University of Nebraska Press, 1984), 53-70, 69. See also Trennert, *Phoenix Indian School*, 10-11, 35-42, 156-58. On American attitudes toward compulsory schooling for white children, see Chapter 4, note 1, below.

38. ARCIA (1900), *House Document*, No. 5, 56 Congress, 2 session, serial 4101, 22; ARCIA, *Annual Report of the Secretary of the Interior* (Washington, D.C.: Government Printing Office, 1930), 26-27. The CIA does not explain the rise in school-age population from 1900 (see text and note 36 above) to 1930.

39. ARCIA (1903), *House Document*, No. 5, part 1, 58 Congress, 2 session, serial 4645, 3; E. M. Yearian, Report of Agent for Lemhi Agency, Aug. 25, 1900, in ARCIA (1900), *House Document* No. 5, 56 Congress, 2 session, serial 4101, 221.

40. Prucha, *The Great Father*, Vol. 2, 826-35. Referring to Hoxie's doctoral dissertation, Prucha explicitly rejects his view that there was a radical change in government policy in the new century, *The Great Father*, Vol. 2, 814, note 1.

41. Hoxie, *A Final Promise*, Chaps. 6 and 7. Quotations, 196, 210; Trennert accepts Hoxie's argument that racial attitudes changed, yet declares: "Whether such ideas actually influenced government policy is debatable." *Phoenix Indian School*, 59. See also xi, and 68-73. To gain a broader perspective on these issues, see Tyack and Hansot, *Learning Together*, esp. 183-92; Jean Barman et al., "The Legacy of the Past: An Overview," in Barman et al., eds., *Indian Education in Canada*, Vol. 1, 8-9; K. J. King, *Pan-Africanism and Education: A Study of Race, Philanthropy and Education in the Southern States of America and East Africa* (Oxford, Eng.: Clarendon Press, 1971). "Relevant" education was obviously "in the air" for more than Indians in these decades.

42. See, for example, Report of the superintendent of Indian Schools (W. N. Hailmann), in ARCIA (1897), *House Document* No. 5, 55 Congress, 2 session, serial 3641, 329. For a sympathetic view of Hailmann, see Dorothy W. Hewes, "Those First Good Years of Indian Education: 1894 to 1898," *American Indian Culture and Research Journal* 5 (1981): 63-82. Also Francis E. Leupp, in ARCIA (1905), *House Documents* Vol. 19, 59 Congress, 1 Session, serial 4959, 12.

43. ARCIA (1905), *House Document* Vol. 19, 54 Congress, 1 session, serial 4959, 1-13. Quotations 3, 5, 8. "Perhaps in the course of merging this hardly used race into our body politic," wrote Leupp, "many individuals, unable to keep up the pace, may fall by the wayside and be trodden underfoot. Deeply as we deplore this possibility, we must not let it blind us to our duty to the race as a whole," 7; also, William A. Jones, ARCIA (1903), *House Document* No. 5, part 1, 58 Congress, 2 session, serial 4645, 2-7; nineteenth-century Presbyterian mission school curricula sometimes included, along with history, geography, and the three R's, physiology, botany, geometry, chemistry, natural philosophy (the sciences), and natural history (geology and biology); see Coleman, *Presbyterian Missionary Attitudes*, 153-54.

44. Trennert, *Phoenix Indian School*, 85; the tension between policy and implementation is a major theme of Trennert's book; on the 1930s, Margaret Connell Szasz, *Education and the American Indian: The Road to Self-Determination Since 1928*, 2d ed. (Albuquerque: Univer-

sity of New Mexico Press, 1977), 88, 192. See also Larry Cuban, *How Teachers Taught: Constancy and Change in American Classrooms, 1890–1980* (New York: Longmans, 1984).

45. Prucha, *The Great Father*, Vol. 2, Chap. 31, 835–40. Quotation, 837.

46. Institute for Government Research, *The Problem of Indian Administration* (The Meriam Report) (Baltimore: Johns Hopkins Press, 1928). See Chap. 3, on the team's methods. Quotation, 86. See also, Steven J. Crum, "Henry Roe Cloud, a Winnebago Indian Reformer: His Quest for American Indian Higher Education," *Kansas History* 11 (Autumn 1988): 171–84. Trennert believes that, though substantially accurate, the Meriam Report exaggerated the deficiencies and played down the strengths of the government schools, *Phoenix Indian School*, 183.

47. Institute for Government Research, *Indian Administration* (Meriam Report), Chap. 9. Quotations, 346, 371, 372, 373; also Chap. 14, on missionary activities; Szasz, *Education and the American Indian*, Chaps. 2, 3, and 5; Fass, *Outside In*, esp. Part I, on the limits, strengths, and contradictions of Progressive educational ideas.

48. Prucha, *The Great Father*, Vol. 2, 926–31, 940–45, 977–85; Szasz, *Education and the American Indian*, Chaps. 3–8; Collier, in ARCIA, *Annual Report of the Secretary of the Interior* (Washington, D.C.: Government Printing Office, 1935), 129. For an expression of Collier's view of Indian life, 113.

49. Malcolm McFee: "The 150% Man: A Product of Blackfeet Acculturation," *American Anthropologist* 70 (1968): 1096–1107. Also James A. Clifton, "Alternate Identities and Cultural Frontiers," in Clifton, ed., *Being and Becoming Indian*, esp. 29–30. On the manipulative tendencies of the Indian New Deal, see Thomas James, "Rhetoric and Resistance: Social Science and Community Schools for the Navajos in the 1930s," *History of Education Quarterly* 28 (Winter 1988): 599–626.

50. Prucha, *The Great Father*, Vol. 2, 983, 1060–69, 1100–06, 1139–49; Szasz, *Education and the American Indian*, Chaps. 9–15, and Epilogue. On recent developments see also Szasz, "Listening to the Native Voice: American Indian Schooling in the Twentieth Century," *Montana: The Magazine of Western History* 30 (Summer 1989): esp. 52–53, on federal challenges to "self-determination" in the 1980s; Estelle Fuchs and Robert J. Havighurst, *To Live on This Earth: American Indian Education* (Albuquerque: University of New Mexico Press, 1972; 1983 ed., Introduction by Margaret Connell Szasz); the *Journal of American Indian Education* (many volumes), published by the Center for Indian Education, Arizona State University, Tempe, Arizona.

51. In Cash and Hoover, eds., *To Be an Indian*, 104–105. Prucha notes the paradox at the center of Indian quests for self-determination: "All measures leading to increased community control of the Indian schools, however, have been limited by the inescapable fact that the financial support of the schools comes from outside sources," *Great Father*, Vol. 2, 1149; also Szasz, *Education and the American Indian*, 196.

52. Kaestle, Karl, "Ideology and American Educational History," *History of Education Quarterly* 22 (Summer 1982): 123–37. Quotations, 132. Also, Karl F. Kaestle, *Pillars of the Republic: Common Schools and American Society, 1786–1860* (New York: Hill & Wang, 1983); Tyack and Hanson, *Learning Together*, especially 37.

CHAPTER 4

To Go or Not to Go?

Although the school and tribal educational patterns shared more than might be expected, they were radically different approaches to enculturation. Why, therefore, did these narrators first begin to attend school?

Some Indian autobiographers gave fairly detailed reasons for attending a second or a third school; apparently, once the ice had been broken, continuing on to more advanced or distant schools became almost natural for many. But of the hundred or so narrators who left accounts of schooling, only about seventy gave any indication as to why they *first* entered school, and many left the details unclear. So it is impossible to achieve precision on this issue. Nevertheless, this chapter will attempt a rough breakdown of reasons.

The vast majority of these seventy had little choice in whether or not to start schooling. In at least one case out of four, they were coerced—by government officials or persons acting for the government (such as tribal police), or occasionally by missionaries. In about half of the cases, close kin or other tribal members insisted upon schooling for their young; in a number of cases such influences overlapped. A small number, about one seventh of the seventy, enjoyed the privilege of personal choice. But at least a number of those compelled to attend school also wished to do so:

Compelled by "authorities"	17
Sent by tribal members	33
Overlapping influences	9
Personal choice	10
Total number supplying information	69
(of 102 narrators)	

Extrapolating these figures to the group of one hundred, it appears likely that tribal members sent about half of the autobiographers to the alien school. We cannot assume, however, that a proschool family always produced a well-adjusted Indian pupil. Further, some kin only reluctantly accepted the need for schooling, and some were bitterly divided on the issue.

When it came time to continue schooling at a second or third institution, the above proportions no longer held. Large numbers of the narrators (perhaps two thirds) had obviously got the habit, accepting or insisting upon further schooling. Some even resisted kin demands to return to the people, and fled *to* a new school.

I

Not all nineteenth-century white Americans accepted the validity of compulsory education for their children. But more and more came to see the need for compulsion, and the states, rather than the federal government, began to enact the necessary legislation.[1] Congress attempted to impose compulsory education on Indians, but the BIA failed to compel uniform attendance of tribal children in every region. Yet many narrators remembered the sporadic and often shocking attempts of agents, police, and others to compel them or even—quite literally—to drag them off to school. And government officials in the field often corroborated these Indian accounts.

"We were very happy until a new menace occurred," wrote James Kaywaykla, a Warm Springs Apache sent by the government with his people to Florida after the Geronimo campaign in 1886. "Officers and their wives went through the camp and selected over a hundred children to go to school in Pennsylvania." The young Indian traveled part of the way to the Carlisle school by sea: "being out of sight of land frightened us, but not more than the bewildering experience of crossing New York city." The accompanying officer and wife treated the Apache children well. But the authorities made no attempt to seek consent from them or their kin, who were, after all, prisoners of war.[2]

Jason Betzinez, also a young boy with the Apache prisoners, recalled a similar experience. As Betzinez later became especially appreciative of his Christian education at Carlisle, his account of the high-handed method of selection is a powerful one. The young Apaches were lined up like soldiers:

> I well remember that when Captain Pratt came to me he stopped, looked me up and down, and smiled. Then he seized my hand, held it up to show I volunteered. I only scowled; I didn't want to go at all. I was twenty-seven, too old to be a schoolboy. I had never been to any school, didn't know a word of English. This made no difference to Capt. Pratt.[3]

Indians long since at peace with the United States were just as vulnerable. Lame Deer, an Oglala (Sioux) shaman, recalled how one day around 1905 "the monster came—a white man from the Bureau of Indian Affairs." Lame Deer's parents were given a choice of sorts: send their child to school immediately, or have the Indian agency police come for him. "I hid behind Grandpa," claimed Lame Deer. "My father was like a big god to me and Grandpa had been at the Custer fight, but they could not protect me now."[4] A hyperbolic humor characterizes Lame Deer's autobiography, but in this account he accurately portrayed the helplessness of traditional Indian kin in face of the increasingly powerful federal bureaucracy.

Hopis vividly remembered their early brushes with the agents of compulsion: in an act of special insensitivity, considering the antagonism between the two tribes, the government sometimes employed Navajo policemen to apprehend Hopi children. Don Talayesva put the best face on things, and rather than be rounded up, in 1899 he "volunteered" for the local day school below Oraibi on Third Mesa, Arizona. Fred Kabotie was another reluctant beginner. His "Hostile" family—in contrast to those "Friendly" Hopis more willing to adopt selective elements of white culture—did not want him at school. But soon after the famous Hostile–Friendly split at Oraibi in 1906, many of his friends "were caught" by the agency police. "My grandfather must have hidden me carefully," he wrote, but one day the leader of the Friendlies, acting for the white agency authorities, apprehended him. Thus Kabotie, who later became an acclaimed artist, began a career which impressively blended Hopi and American life-styles and values.[5]

Helen Sekaquaptewa, also from a Hostile Hopi family in Oraibi, had especially strong memories of police raids and the ritualistic evasion they inspired. The children and parents "became involved with the school officials, assisted by Navajo policemen, in a serious and rather desperate game of hide-and-seek, where little Hopi boys and girls were the forfeit in the game." There ensued a series of searches and evasions, as a result of which more and more children became pupils of the day school. She gave a graphic account of one close escape, as she hid in an abandoned room full of ashes and other refuse: "We lay on our stomachs in the dark, facing a small opening," she wrote. "We saw the feet of the principal and the policeman as they walked by, and heard their big voices as they looked about wondering where the children were. They didn't find us that day."

The game finally played itself out, however. "I don't remember for sure just how I came to be 'caught'," wrote Sekaquaptewa. "Maybe both my mother and myself got a little tired of getting up early every morning and running off to hide all day." But symbolic resistance persisted to the end:

> it was the rule among the mothers not to let the child go voluntarily. As the policeman reached to take me by the arm, my mother put her arm around me. Tradition required that it appear that I was forced to school.[6]

The element of play and of face-saving gesture could not disguise what was taking place here and on many other reservations. Often against their own will and the will of their families, young Indians entered a system of compulsory education devised by another society, one which sought radical separation of children from kin and "corrupting" social environment.

The believability of such accounts is strengthened by the fact that many of the narrators later came to enjoy much of their schooling. Also, white educators sometimes corroborated the dramatic descriptions. In perhaps the same year as Sekaquaptewa's capture (1903), an unusually critical teacher claimed that children had been "taken forcibly from their homes by an armed body of Government employees and Navajo Indians, under the leadership of C. E. Burton [superintendent of the boarding school at Keams Canyon]." And Burton himself boasted, "At daybreak we went up silently to the village Oraibi and began a search through the houses for the children. As we found them we took them to a kiva near the center of the village and left them under guard by a policeman." This action provoked bitter response from angry Hopis. "I ordered the police and employees to draw their guns, which we did and stood off the mob, having managed to get the children started down the trail to school." Such extreme diligence led to Burton's transfer next year. But a few years later in 1907 Commissioner Leupp conceded that, while Oraibi Hopi parents could choose *which* school their children might attend, all must attend some school. Government authorities at other agencies also advocated and employed compulsion.[7]

But compulsion alone does not explain why so many of the autobiographers first entered the classroom. In their efforts to educate Indian children to the ways of white America, federal authorities and missionary teachers often found willing allies among the Indians themselves.

II

Although traditional education was essentially conservative, we have seen how individual tribal adults realized the need to adapt to, and even exploit, the new education, especially the English language and the skills of reading and writing. Thus half of the autobiographers first attended school because kin or other tribal adults instructed them to do so. In some cases the narrator claimed that he or she had wanted to go anyway, but tribal adults made the decision.

Nowhere is this more powerfully expressed than in the speech given by Joseph La Flesche, father of Francis La Flesche and a principal chief of the Omahas. The older man realized that the world was changing, and this was why he sent Francis and others of his children to school and why he instructed the new Omaha police force to return runaway students. "That you might profit by the teachings of your own people and that of the white race, and that you might avoid the misery which accompanies ignorance," he told the boy,

> I placed you in the House of Teaching of the Whitechests [missionaries], who are said to be wise and to have in their books the utterances of great and learned men. I had treasured the hope that you would wish to know the good deeds done by men of your own race, and by men of the white race, that you would follow their example and take pleasure in doing the things that are noble and helpful to those around you. Am I to be disappointed?[8]

There was little in the speech of the elder La Flesche to indicate that he had internalized the full missionary view of schooling. In these accounts Indian adults developed their own personal or ethnic perspective on the new institution. "While my parents had no school education whatever," wrote G. W. Grayson (Creek) of his part-white kin, "they had a very high appreciation of the advantages following the possession of it, and were unalterably determined that their children should not, like themselves, grow up without some sort of school education." With an education, the father believed, his children would not have to work out in the hot sun, as he had. And some "might attain to positions of honor and trust in the public affairs of the [Creek] nation." White education was to be exploited for more effective performance as an Indian, if a modernizing one. Later when Grayson felt tempted to flee his studies, fear that his father would administer "heroic treatment with the rod" kept him in line.[9]

Charles Eastman, also first sent to school by an acculturating father, described a rending scene when Dakota parents left their daughter at the Santee Normal Training School in Nebraska in the 1870s. The girl "began to run towards them, screaming pitifully." The parents reasoned with her, to no avail. "Then I saw them leading her back [to the superintendent] in spite of her pleading and begging." The whole scene "made my blood boil," wrote this usually strong advocate of schooling. Eastman left little doubt that it was the Indian parents, rather than the school authorities, who caused the girl's suffering.[10]

Asa Daklugie remembered resenting how his uncle, Geronimo, ordered him to become a pupil at Carlisle. But Daklugie credibly explained why one of the last Indians to hold out against white civilization should then advocate schooling. "Without this training in the ways of the White Eyes," wrote Daklugie in a paraphrase of Geronimo's pragmatism, "our people could never compete with them. So it was necessary that those destined for leadership prepare themselves to cope with the enemy. I was to be trained to become the leader." Chris (Mescalero Apache) also recalled how in the early twentieth century an adaptive chief lectured his people on the importance of schooling, as the people would need interpreters. Further, the chief told them: "'We have to learn to hold ploughs, picks, and shovels and build houses and have farms and stock of our own."[11]

According to Jim Whitewolf (Kiowa Apache), many of the children on his Oklahoma reservation did not attend any school. Then in 1891 a chief "went to the agent and told him he wanted all the children of school age in the tribe to go to school, *and that if they didn't their parents should not get* [government-supplied] *rations*" (emphasis added). The parents complied.[12] Indeed, food and other material advantages may often have influenced adults, especially during times of scarcity. Perhaps because as children they were unaware of it, narrators rarely allude to this motivation. White agents, however, sometimes mentioned how Indians accepted schools so their children might be better fed or clothed.[13]

Other narrators noted how Indian initiative could lead to the *continuation* of their schooling. According to G. W. Grayson, the Creek Nation adopted the policy of sending "one or two of the more advanced and promising pupils" to colleges and schools in the surrounding states. In the year 1859 his people chose him, and this future Civil War combatant and Creek politician "readily assented" to study at Arkansas College. In 1870 the Choctaw Nation chose Peter Hudson to attend Old Spencer Academy in Oklahoma.[14]

Many of these beginners and seekers of further schooling went forth with words of wisdom and encouragement ringing in their ears. Thomas Alford recounted the discriminating speech made to him by Shawnee elders before he headed off to Hampton Institute in Virginia. Like Geronimo, some of his people had come to realise that young men should learn reading and writing to understand treaties and other documents: "'it would enable us to use the club of the white man's wisdom against him," said one chief. Probably as the result of his father's respect for a Quaker missionary, Alford began his schooling at the Friends' mission, and later progressed to a local government school. The Quakers then persuaded tribal leaders to send two young men to Hampton, and arranged for scholarships to support them there; Alford's clan selected him.

Just before the journey, two chiefs paid the young travelers a visit. "We all squatted on the ground, in true Indian fashion," recalled Alford, and "very solemnly" the chiefs spoke, reminding the boys of their responsibility as representatives of the Shawnee nation, and of the demands they would later face as chiefs:

> They told us of their desire that we should learn the white man's wisdom. How to read in books, how to understand all that was written and spoken to and about our people and the government. . . . But there was a proviso attached to the promise that we should be chiefs—*a positive demand that we should not accept the white man's religion; we must remain true to the Shawnee faith* [emphasis in original].

In Alford's recall, an element of romantic Indian oratory suffuses the speech. Yet this pragmatic, selective, and manipulative approach of the elders to white education is found in other accounts, too.[15]

Such encouragement of schooling implied some degree of exploitation of the young Indian for the good of the people. Perhaps the most exploitative experience was that of a Zuni, who recalled how his uncle took him to school as an eight-year-old to learn English and act as interpreter when the uncle sold sheep and wool to whites. The boy became progressively more useful, but he also became more interested in school learning. When he sought permission to continue his education at a boarding school, his uncle denied it:

> he thought I already knew enough to get along in any sales. That was all he was worrying about. He thought that if I ever went off to learn some more that I might get spoiled and turn into the white man's way. . . . First he wanted me to learn, but after I wanted to learn too much he sort of refused me. . . . [He] thought that if I learned too much I might learn some kind of trade and that I would quit the sheep business.

From the narrator's account the uncle was far more worried about his own economic stake in the boy than about the boy's foresaking the Zuni way. Considering the difficulties experienced by Indian children at distant boarding schools, the uncle may have been right to forbid his going. But a sense of loss pervades the account by this anonymous Zuni.[16]

Other narrators lend credence to his sense of frustration at the sudden ending of white education by those who had first sent the child to school. Belle Highwalking (Northern Cheyenne) felt she gained little from her first seven years of schooling, and hoped to go to an off-reservation boarding school. Her family withheld permission: "Now I feel bad because I can't speak English well," she wrote near the end of her life. Mountain Wolf Woman (Winnebago) vividly conveyed the devastation she earlier felt when her brothers—one of whom originally insisted she go to school because he liked to hear women speak English—suddenly withdrew her from the Lutheran Mission School at Wittenberg, Wisconsin:

> Then I stopped attending school. They took me out of school. Alas, I was enjoying school so much, and they made me stop. They took me back home. They had let me go to school and now they made me quit. It was then that they told me I was going to be married. I cried but it did not do any good.

Mountain Wolf Woman's mother comforted her, and might have allowed her to continue school. But the older woman reluctantly advised obedience to her brothers.[17]

These and other accounts by women lend some support to the complaints of white observers that Indians were less interested in schooling girls than boys.[18] Zitkala-Sa recalled that both her mother and brother—who himself had spent three years at a school in the East—attempted unsuccessfully to hold the eight-year-old Zitkala-Sa at home. "'Your brother Dawee says that going East, away from your mother, is too hard an experience for his baby sister'," pleaded the mother. The Comanche family of Sanapia lived in southern Oklahoma. Her mother was prepared to allow sons to attend Haskell Institute in distant Kansas, because "boys are tougher than girls." But she would not allow Sanapia go.[19]

Surprisingly, however, there are few such examples. Despite the sexual division of roles within Indian societies, these narrators' families were often willing that girls too acquire some white education. Even if later prevented from continuing, Mountain Wolf Woman and Highwalking did attend school. Other girls, like Anna Moore Shaw (Pima) and Elsie Allen (Pomo), began or continued school with a degree of family acceptance.[20] Perhaps the kin of such narrators believed, as did white educators, that it was pointless to educate males in the ways of the white world, if females possessed only knowledge of traditional life.

Tribal kin were not always united in their desire for schooling for

children of either sex, however. Charles Eastman's father had to overcome the strong objections of the boy's more traditional grandmother.
Irene Stewart (Navajo) told how a policeman one day took her to school
at Fort Defiance. Then she learned the full story. Her *father* had told the
agent to send the policeman, as her grandmother had been opposed to
schooling. "Years later," according to Stewart, "I was told that Gran-
mother took this very hard, and that her dislike for father increased."
Max Henley, another Navajo, remembered how for three years the
argument over whether or not he should attend school swung back and
forth between his traditional grandmother and his uncle, who wanted
him to learn English and get a job and earn money. He himself desired to
go, but the final decision seems to have evolved out of a group consensus;
perhaps his grandmother had finally accepted the idea.[21]

For a variety of reasons, therefore, tribal adults sent perhaps one half
of the narrators to school. Proficiency in English and the almost magical
skills of reading and writing could make both the young and their
families more competent in the new world growing up around them.
The children would also learn the knowledge of the whites, get to know
their customs, and thus become mediators between two worlds. Sometimes, as in the case of the Zuni, the motivations of an adult seemed
blatantly selfish; at all times they were highly pragmatic. These Indian
adults pushed upon their children the education of the Christian civilization for salvation in the present life—individual and tribal salvation.
Indeed the new skills could even be used to preserve the wisdom of the
past. Indians such as Joseph La Flesche, Geronimo, and the elders who
lectured Alford exhibited an adaptive, modern "tribal patriotism"; they
accepted certain elements of white civilization in order *to defend* tribal
identity, rather than to be assimilated into American society.

III

A number of those compelled to attend school claimed they had
wanted to go anyway.[22] About ten of the narrators made the crucial
decision themselves, with or, sometimes without parental consent. Considering that most were under ten years old at the time, knew little or no
English and almost nothing about the school itself and the white world,
why did these children so willingly embark on such an awesome adventure?

We come, in other words, to the question of *pupil* motivation, which will be a central concern throughout the rest of this book. Seven major clusters of influences—each cluster a complex and ever-changing mix in itself—influenced conscious pupil motivation: motivation for deciding to begin the school experience, and motivation for responding in such ambivalent ways to the school. These distinct but sometimes overlapping clusters are as follows: (1) a cluster of *personal motivations*, such as the hope of material gain or food or ambition or feelings of fear, bitterness, or curiosity; (2) a cluster of *kin* influences and pressures; (3) a cluster of motivations from the pupil's *cultural background*—the ways in which the values and patterns of tribal life influenced children against or for school; (4) a cluster of motivations from the school as a many-sided *institution*—the ways in which the discipline, clothing rules, sanctioned extracurricular activities, separation of the sexes, and other such official patterns of behavior influenced motivation; (5) a cluster of motivations emanating from the religious-academic-manual labor *curriculum*, including the broad knowledge school provided about American society; (6) a cluster of motivations produced by the *teachers, staff, and other whites*, including those met on "outing" experiences and elsewhere around and outside the school; and (7) a cluster of motivations produced by *peers*—other pupils, including those placed in positions of authority.[23]

Not all of the above factors always come into play. Few of the volunteers knew anything in advance about the schools to which they committed themselves, or about their curricula or staffs.[24] Their interest generally sprang from complex and changing blends of four of the "clusters": personal, kin, cultural, and peers (in the form of returned students or recruiting students). Indeed motivation for beginning school was often so mixed that it is most useful to consider a number of individual experiences.

Although Don Talayesva (Hopi) claimed that he volunteered for the local day school to avoid being caught by a policeman, he was also moved by a strong sense of curiosity. "I was willing to try it," he wrote. Later he accepted a move to the Keams Canyon boarding school for similarly personal reasons, which were stimulated by peer influence: he wanted to dress in white clothes like other boys. He was also "tired of working and herding sheep," with his father: in other words, kin and cultural background could work for, as well as against, the school."[25]

Curiosity, stimulated by recruiting Indian students, was also a factor in tempting Standing Bear to leave the Pine Ridge reservation in South Dakota for far-off Carlisle, Pennsylvania. In addition, the Lakota was anxious to please his father. Though the older man had come to see the need for some adaptation to white ways, he had reared his son in the traditional life-style. And Sioux cultural values, rather than any knowledge of school as such, also impelled the young Indian: "I had come to this school, merely to show my people that I was brave enough to leave the reservation and go East, not knowing what it meant and not caring." Thus personal motives, the influence of peers, respect for kin, and a passionate desire to excel according to tribal norms sent Standing Bear to Carlisle. Again, traditional cultural values worked *for* the recruiting school authorities. [26]

A similar curiosity initially propelled Zitkala-Sa into her new life. Other young Indians filled her head with stories of "the Wonderland" in the East. One friend told "of the great tree where grew red, red apples," Zitkala-Sa wrote. "I had never seen apple trees. I had never tasted more than a dozen red apples in my life; and when I heard of the orchards in the East, I was eager to roam among them." It is difficult to know whether she exaggerated her childhood experience, or employed the apple as metaphor for the mystery of the (American) East. But she also admitted that it was *not* an "ambition for Letters" which was stirring within her. And she powerfully conveyed a sense of excitement and curiosity—more credible in that her joy would turn to anguish even before she reached the school—as she begged her mother to let her enroll. "'Oh Mother, it is not that I wish to leave you, but I want to see the wonderful Eastern Land'." Her old aunt took Zitkala-Sa's side against her mother and brother, and the young girl achieved her wish. She began a successful but bitter school experience, one which prepared her to become an important spokeswoman for Indians in early twentieth century America, but which permanently shattered the relationship between herself and her mother. [27]

In the literature of Indian schooling, the term "runaway" usually refers to those who absconded *from* the classroom, but a number of these narrators actually ran the other way. Ernest Nelson's brother was already a student, spoke English to him, and thus "made me want to learn." When asked by a white man to enroll, the young Navajo just "went to Tuba city to attend school. It was like running away TO school, just the opposite of what was often done. It was my idea," he emphasized, "because I wanted to see how it was at school and I wanted to learn." [28]

Polingaysi Qoyawayma (Elizabeth Q. White), a Hopi, also fled to the classroom. She heard the Hostiles say that when a Hopi becomes a white man "'he no longer has a face. We want to be Hopis, not white men'." But she became fascinated by the local day school, noticing how the children seemed no worse for the experience when they came home in the evening; she even asked her "caught" sister to let her try on the school dress. Qoyawayma was especially impressed to hear that the school provided food! In the end the feeling of being excluded from "all this excitement" pushed her to disobey her parents and walk the short path from home to the day school at the bottom of the mesa. Later that day she suffered a bitter rebuke from her mother, who accused her of bringing grief to her kin, of having taken a "step away from your Hopi people," and of having set out on a road from which there was no turning back.[29] As with Zitkala-Sa and others, a powerful mix of personal drives motivated her, especially curiosity and a desire for the goods of white civilization, along with a degree of jealousy of peers at the school.

A similar sense of being excluded from adventure especially motivated Kay Bennett (Navajo). "The day before the children must return to school," she recalled of her siblings, "the boys got their school clothes out, and brushed them off. They started practicing English, much to the annoyance of Kaibah [Bennett] and her mother, who could not understand what they were talking about. . . . Kaibah wanted to go too. . . ." Small wonder, considering the excitement all around her, the proficiency of young kin in the new language, and the coming months of loneliness, herding sheep without companions. She would not leave without her mother's permission, however. After a family discussion, the older woman reluctantly acquiesced.[30]

One of the most memorable expressions of the desire for a school education came from a Navajo deprived of one. Like other narrators Ashie Tsosie recalled how his father hid him and his brothers from the tribal police: the father claimed he needed the boys to help him herd sheep and work on the farm. Instead of thanking him for preserving them from the corruptions of white society, Tsosie bitterly denounced his father: "To this day I regret his attitude," the sixty-four-year-old Navajo told an interviewer:

> Now, I am what I am—an uneducated man who does not know a word of English and who never has used a pencil. . . . I am recording my thoughts on tape in Navajo. . . . If I had been permitted to go to school and to have been well educated I might have been a teacher or a person sitting in an executive's chair as a director. . . . I would teach my children at home, along with their regular class work. I always will blame my father for my being held down in life. Many times when I go to the store or the Demonstration School the traders and teachers try to talk to me, but I can only stand dumb because I do not understand them. The best I can do is just smile.

It is difficult to know whether Tsosie projected present feelings of bitterness and jealousy onto his childhood. Comparing himself to those with schooling he felt "ignorant and envious." But his phraseology—"To this day"—suggests that even as a child he wanted to attend school. Indian peoples had for centuries been trading and exchanging cultural traits with other groups, including white Americans. If conservative Indians perceived school as an assault on traditional ways, other Indians could see it as an element to be utilized for personal and tribal needs. "What a change it might have made," concluded Tsosie, "if my father had let his boys go with the Little Policeman to the school! That makes the story of my life."[31]

"Kidnapped" by government police—to use Irene Stewart's expression[32]—sent by kin or other tribal adults, impelled by their own mixed and often shifting motivations, these narrators embarked on their radically life-changing experiences. For some the adventure began and perhaps ended at a local school. For others it included exciting, disorienting, and sometimes frightening journeys far away from home.

IV

"So one morning in September," wrote Don Talayesva, "I wrapped myself in my Navajo blanket . . . went down the Mesa barefooted and bare-headed . . . and reached the school late."[33] Fellow Hopi Polingaysi Qoyawayma also had but a short trip to make from Oraibi on Third Mesa to the day school at the bottom. But this journey was far more difficult for her, fearing as she did the inevitable family recriminations.

It was the trip to distant boarding schools that really brought young Indians face to face with white civilization. And few narrators conveyed more vividly the bewildered fascinaton of this experience than did Albert Yava. From about his fifth to eighth year, during the 1890s, the Tewa–Hopi had attended a day school and boarding school on the Hopi reservation. Then, at about thirteen, he defied his mother and father, and fled with other Hopis to the Chilocco Boarding School in Oklahoma—another case of a runaway *to* school. The trip began by team and wagon; at Holbrook, Arizona, the children took the train, and the adventure really began.

When offered plums by a man on the train, Yava was surprised to discover he had to pay for them—he thought it had been "just hospitality," and wondered at "how different the white man's ways were from ours." When his brother later bought him a strange, long yellow fruit, he discovered that "it was sweet inside, but the rind was tough." That was something else he learned: "How to eat bananas." But two things in particular preoccupied him on the long trip: pencils and spectacles. "It seemed to me that pencils had a lot to do with being educated," he wrote, because "teachers always carried a big bunch of pencils in their pockets." So he bought some, and left them sticking ostentatiously from his pocket. Glasses had fascinated him at the earlier schools: "If my teacher was wearing specs I would sort of get around in back of him and try to get a glimpse through them, but I was never successful in that." At a station he bought himself a pair, but was disappointed: "I couldn't see anything but the same things I'd seen before, it was just that they were darker." No doubt he had bought sunglasses. In a railway station restaurant, he kept falling off a stool because he felt like he was still "riding and swaying." With dispassionate humor Yava the narrator conveyed the embarrassed earnestness of his earlier self, when his enthusiasm for the new way ran far ahead of his understanding of it. Although his previous schooling provided some knowledge of white life, the trip to boarding school almost overwhelmed him with new experiences.[34]

"When I think about it now," wrote Frank Mitchell of his introduction to white clothes before he and his Navajo companions set out by wagon for Fort Defiance Boarding School, Arizona, in 1894, "I think about how ignorant we all were and how little we knew then about white people's ways of living. . . ." Yet because a number of tribal adults accompanied the children on the four-day trip, and along the way Navajo women sometimes provided food for the group, he was not unduly upset. "I did not feel lonesome or anything," he recalled, "I was glad to be going along." Besides, till then his family had been "always on the move." Food was the main thing on the mind of the boys most of the time. At night they slept or told jokes or funny stories, and the older men who had helped recruit them sat around the campfire discussing the plight of the people and the need for schooling. Mitchell's easy response to what might have been a shocking experience resulted from the fact that the trip blended the familiar with the unfamiliar in often positive ways. And, instead of being suddenly separated from all familiar tribal adults, like many other pupils-to-be, these Navajo boys traveled in the company of The People, turning the whole affair into a community outing.[35]

Luther Standing Bear and some of his Sioux companions were not so fortunate, and responded with more conflicting emotions. The trip from

Pine Ridge to Carlisle began in earnest with a boat ride down the Missouri. Suddenly cut from their society, many of the children began to cry, and two of the teenage boys threatened to jump from the vessel. Increasingly disorienting experiences assailed the children, and Standing Bear sharply recalled the details. A row of "houses" began to move— his first experience of a train. Then on-rushing telegraph poles frightened him, and he moved to the other side of the carriage. White people stared and laughed at the children at stations along the way, as though they were strange animals. And one morning they woke to find that the moon, which had been in front, was now behind them: "Apparently we had passed the place where the moon rose!" It took a while for them to understand that the train had merely reversed course at Harrisburg to make the last leg of the trip to Carlisle. By the time they arrived, many were truly worried; some thought they might fall off the edge of the earth or be killed, and the older boys sang to keep up the spirits of the rest. A tendency toward self-dramatization characterizes Standing Bear's two detailed accounts of the adventure. Yet he effectively communicated the oscillating feelings of the children as they veered between excitement and regret, fascination and fear. For many of these Sioux, ambivalence began with the trip to school.[36]

Their train journey to Carlisle in 1886 plunged some of the young Apache prisoners-of-war into similar spasms of awe and anxiety. Ramona Chihuahua, Asa Daklugie's future wife, asked him to kill her, should the army guards attack her, and he agreed to do so. He was later amazed to see "the earth covered with white stuff"—he had seen snow in the mountains before, but "not in big heaps, as it was here." When the train became bogged down, he remembered a story he'd been told about white people caught in the snow who resorted to cannibalism, and again he feared for the safety of his people. "If the food gives out," he wondered, "who would be eaten first?" It may seem hard to credit such extreme fears, and those of Standing Bear's companions. But these children came from tribes till then constantly at war. "Until I was about ten years old," wrote Apache James Kaywaykla, "I did not know that people died except by violence." There is little reason to doubt that Daklugie and his companions lived in a state of tension, if not fear, as they rode on a strange vehicle through mysterious lands to a more mysterious destination.[37]

These Indians at least traveled with large numbers of their companions. Charles Eastman walked alone the 150 miles to the Santee Normal Training School, Nebraska, in the 1870s. He presumed upon the generosity of a white family along the way. Somewhat suspicious of the young

Indian, they nevertheless took him in, fed him, allowed him stay the night, and refused his offers of payment. Their hospitality had a profound effect on him: "Then and there I loved civilization and renounced my wild life." One such experience hardly changed his life so dramatically; but it does suggest the importance of white Americans to later motivation.[38]

A veteran of local schools, and in possession of a letter written by a Quaker missionary, Thomas Wildcat Alford and another young Shawnee set out from Muskogee, Oklahoma, for Hampton, Virginia, in 1879—the same month and year that Standing Bear began at Carlisle. Instructions to the Shawnees were clear: "It was the business of train conductors to tell us what to do, and policemen were always to be trusted." The two boys were fascinated by "the marvellous passenger train, with its shrieking engine and grating noises," and were overwhelmed by the luxury of the cabins. "The train began to move," wrote Alford. "We were on our way! Wonderful! Wonderful! But soon our worries began."

Again fascination alternated with concern. These boys also faced inquisitive passengers. They were afraid to sleep, except at different times, and Alford's friend actually carried a pistol. At St. Louis they marveled at the immensity of Union Station, and understood enough English to enjoy hearing people talking about them. Time and time again they produced their "wonderful paper," only to be told to sit down and wait.

Finally, a conductor showed them to the train, and they were off. The journey released their tensions, and Alford thrilled to the new lands they passed through:

> I recollect the impression made on my mind as we travelled over the beautiful country, and through well cultivated fields, past beautiful homes, and through busy, bustling cities, and small towns. All was so strange to our eyes accustomed only to the western prairies and lowlands, or rolling timber hills. The deep, swift rivers, the beautiful mountain scenery, awe inspiring, marvellous. A wonderland indeed!

Yet anxiety again took hold when they arrived at Baltimore and the conductor put them into a cab, the driver of which "was not a conductor, nor a policeman, therefore he was not to be trusted." Alford's friend took the pistol from his pocket to be ready for the worst. Finally they reached a large, well-lighted building, and now began to worry that they would miss the boat to Hampton. Then

> there was the most terrible, ear-splitting sound. It was somewhat like the whistle on the train, but even more terrible. Then the whole building began

to move. Imagine our consternation. It began to dawn upon us that what we thought to be a building was a ship.

Next day they docked at Hampton, and entered the school in a carriage.

Thus two teen-age Indian boys traveled from Oklahoma to Virginia, by mule, train, boat, and carriage. "Even yet," wrote Alford decades later, "the memory of that long journey seems more like a dream than an actual occurrence."

Yet he gives the reader to understand that it *was* an actual occurrence, so impressive that it had imprinted itself onto his mind. Significantly, his account of the return trip is quite different, for by then he felt more at ease with white people, and "had grown accustomed to seeing well cultivated farms and beautiful country places, as well as thriving cities." Many of the western towns which had so impressed him on the way east now disappointed him.[39] And, although Alford's account is especially dramatic, in content it is similar to those of many other narrators, whose deep immersion in American life has just begun.

Notes

1. Katz, *Reconstructing American Education*, 50–53; Charles Burgess, "The Goddess, the School Book, and Compulsion," *History of Education Quarterly* 46 (May 1976): 199–216; David B. Tyack, "Ways of Seeing: An Essay on the History of Compulsory Education," *History of Education Quarterly* 46 (Aug. 1976): 355–89.

2. Kaywaykla, *In the Days of Victorio*, 199–200.

3. Betzinez, *I Fought with Geronimo*, 149.

4. Lame Deer and Erdoes, *Seeker of Visions*, 33.

5. Talayesva, *Sun Chief*, 89; Fred Kabotie, *Fred Kabotie: Hopi Indian Artist. An Autobiography told with Bill Belknap* (Flagstaff: Museum of Northern Arizona with Northland Press, 1977), 8–10. For a recent account of the intratribal conflict, Whiteley, *Deliberate Acts*.

6. Sekaquaptewa, *Me and Mine*, 8–12.

7. Belle Axtell Kolp, notarized affidavit, cited in Whiteley, *Deliberate Acts*, 95; Burton to commissioner of Indian Affairs, Feb. 9, 1903, cited in *idem*, 95–96; The Upheaval at Oraibi, ARCIA (1907), *Reports of the Department of the Interior* (Washington, D.C.: Government Printing Office, 1907), 82. Other tribes: J. A. Leonard to the commissioner of Indian Affairs, May 7, 1892, ARCIA (Washington, D.C.: Government Printing Office, 1892), 151; Report of Farmer in Charge of San Xavier Papago, ARCIA (1903), *House Document*

No. 5, 58 Congress, 2 session, serial 4645, 441–42; Walter McM. Lutterel to the commissioner of Indian Affairs, ARCIA (1901), *House Document* No. 5, 57 Congress, 1 session, serial 4290, 283; Gertrude Golden, *Red Moon Called Me: Memoirs of a Schoolteacher in the Government Indian Service* (San Antonio, Tex.: The Naylor Company, 1954), 17.

8. La Flesche, *Middle Five*, 127–28. The context was the boy's violation of the tribal ethic of generosity. On sending other children to Presbyterian school, David A. Baerreis, Foreword to *idem.*, xi. Cf. Clark and Webb, "Susette and Susan La Flesche," in Clifton, ed., *Being and Becoming Indian*, 140–41. Louis, the older brother of Francis, died while a pupil, Norma Kidd Green, *Iron Eye's Family: The Children of Joseph La Flesche* (Lincoln, Neb., 1969), 40. On the tribal police: Robert Burtt to Walter Lowrie[?], June 6, 1860, box 4, vol. 1, AIC (hereafter 4–1, AIC). Burtt was school superintendent while Francis La Flesche attended.

9. Grayson, *A Creek Warrior*, 36, 42; also Introduction by Baird, 3–11.

10. Charles Eastman, *From Deep Woods*, Chap. 2, and p. 45.

11. Daklugie et al., *Indeh*, 134–36; Chris, *Apache Odyssey*, 141. Also 68. See also Goodbird's grandfather: "It is their books that make the white men strong." Goodbird, *Goodbird the Indian*, 40–41; Carl Sweezy, *The Arapaho Way*, 20–21.

12. Jim Whitewolf, *Life*, 83.

13. La Flesche mentioned one such case, *Middle Five*, 132. See also Sekaquaptewa, *Me and Mine*, 120: "The year I was at home we never did have enough food." For an agent's comment, see Cyrus Beade, annual report from Osage Agency, Aug. 20, 1877, ARCIA (Washington, D.C.: Government Printing Office, 1877), 93.

14. Grayson, *A Creek Warrior*, 46–48; "Recollections of Peter Hudson," *Chronicles of Oklahoma* 10 (Dec. 1932): 517–18.

15. Alford, *Civilization*, 73–80, 89–90. It is impossible to discern the editor's influence on such prose. Alford eventually did convert to Christianity. Whites sometimes claimed that an Indian expressed interest in schooling: Jacob Vore, Omaha agent, July 29, 1878, in ARCIA (Washington, D.C.: Government Printing Office, 1878), 95; Elaine Goodale Eastman, *Sister to the Sioux*, 42–43, 123–24; report on Hampton Normal and Agricultural Institute, with ARCIA (1880), *House Executive Document* No. 1, part 5, 46 Congress, 3 session, serial 1959, 306–307—excerpts from letters to pupils of apparently satisfied kin. It is difficult to discern the influence of agents or others on the letters written to Washington (purportedly by Indians) asking for schools. See, for example, letter to "Our Great Father at Washington," which was "Signed by thirty-eight chiefs and headmen of the Winnebagos," Dec. 30, 1864, with ARCIA (1865), *House Executive Document* No. 1, 39 Congress, 1 session, serial 1248, 599.

16. FASISO47A (pseudonym), "Autobiographical Statements by FASISO47A, Monograph 1, *Zuni Kin Terms*, edited by John M. Roberts (1956; rpt., New Haven, Conn.: Human Relations Area Files, 1965), 107. Other cases of adults stressing the importance of English, Begay, in Johnson, ed., *Stories of Traditional Navajo Life*, 62; Moisés et al., *A Yaqui Life*, 37.

17. Highwalking, *Narrative*, 3; Mountain Wolf Woman, *Sister of Crashing Thunder*, 21, 26–30. Also, Mourning Dove, *Salishan*, 30–31.

18. Coleman, *Presbyterian Missionary Attitudes*, 95–97.

19. Zitkala-Sa, *American Indian Stories*, 40–41; Jones, ed., *Sanapia*, 24.

20. Shaw, *Pima Past*, 101–102; Elsie Allen, *Pomo Basketmaking: A Supreme Art for the Weaver*, edited by Vinson Brown (Healdsburg, Cal.: Naturegraph Publishers, 1972), 10. Also, Lilah Denton Lindsey, "Memories of the Indian Territory Mission Field," *Chronicles of Oklahoma* 36 (1958): 181; Lucille (Jerry) Winnie, *Sah-gan-de-oh: The Chief's Daughter* (New York: Vantage Press: 1969), esp. 21; Mourning Dove, *Salishan*, 24–27; Winnemucca Hopkins, *Life Among the Piutes*, 67; Little Bear Inkanish, *Dance around the Sun*, 23–24.

21. Eastman, *Deep Woods*, 24–25; Stewart, *A Voice in Her Tribe*, 15; Max Henley, in Johnson, ed., *Stories of Traditional Navajo Life*, 30–31. Also Goodbird, *Goodbird the Indian*, 40; Mitchell, *Navajo Blessingway Singer*, esp. 57; Zitkala-Sa, *American Indian Stories*, Chap.

7; Simon Pokagon, "Indian Superstitions and Legends," in *Native American Folklore in Nineteenth-Century Periodicals*, edited by William M. Clements (Chicago: Swallow Press/ Ohio University Press, 1986), 239–40. Pokagon was a Potowatomi.

22. For example, Pokagon, "Indian Superstitions," 238–39; Shaw, *Pima Past*, 102; Hanley, in Johnson, ed., *Stories of Traditional Navajo Life*, 30–31.

23. This is a modification of the six-category scheme in Michael C. Coleman, "Western Education, American Indian and African Children: A Comparative Study of Pupil Motivation Through Published Reminiscences, 1860s–1960s," *Canadian and International Education/Education Canadienne et Internationale* 18 (1989): 36–53.

24. But see Pokagon, "Indian Superstitions," 238–40, for a wildly enthusiastic expression of interest in school knowledge.

25. Talayesva, *Sun Chief*, 89–90, 94. Cf. Goodbird, *Goodbird the Indian*, 57–59; the rigors of the vision quest helped send him back to school. Also, Mitchell, *Navajo Blessingway Singer*, 43.

26. Standing Bear, *My People the Sioux*, Chap. 13, 135. His three accounts of the episode vary in details but are broadly consistent, see also Standing Bear, *Land of the Spotted Eagle*, 230–31; *My Indian Boyhood*, (1931; rpt., Lincoln: University of Nebraska Press, 1978), 157.

27. Zitkala-Sa, *American Indian Stories*, Chap. 7. See also Foreword by Dexter Fisher, "Zitkala-Sa: The Evolution of a writer," v–xx; Qoyawayma, *No Turning Back*, 51–59. Also La Flesche, *Middle Five*, 21.

28. Nelson, in Johnson, ed., *Stories of Traditional Navajo Life*, 231–32.

29. Qoyawayma, *No Turning Back*, 20–26. Also, 51–54.

30. Bennett, *Kaibab*, 156–59, 209.

31. In Johnson, ed., *Stories of Traditional Navajo Life*, 113–15.

32. Stewart claimed she was grateful for having been "kidnapped for education," *A Voice in Her Tribe*, 35.

33. Talayesva, *Sun Chief*, 89.

34. Yava, *Big Falling Snow*, 9–17.

35. Mitchell, *Navajo Blessingway Singer*, 59–61.

36. Standing Bear, *My People the Sioux*, 127–32. Zitkala-Sa also noticed the telegraph poles, *American Indian Stories*, 44–49.

37. Daklugie et al., *Indeh*, 140–41; Kaywaykla, *In the Days of Victorio*, xiii.

38. Eastman, *Deep Woods*, 34–40.

39. Alford, *Civilization*, 91–98.

CHAPTER 5

A Whole Different World

"ENTERING THE HOUSE, I stood close against the wall," wrote Zitkala-Sa of her fearful arrival at White's Manual Labor Institute of Wabash, Indiana, in 1884. "The strong glaring light in the whitewashed room dazzled my eyes. The noisy hurrying of hard shoes upon a bare wooded floor increased the whirring in my ears. My only safety seemed to be in keeping next to the wall." Like other narrators she graphically recalled the powerfully *sensual* nature of the arrival, which overwhelmed children used to natural illumination and sound-damping tepees or earth lodges or even small houses. "As I was wondering in which direction to escape from all this confusion," she recalled, "two warm hands grasped me firmly, and in the same moment I was tossed high in midair." She could only stare disapprovingly into the eyes of the well-meaning teacher—Zitkala-Sa did not yet speak a word of English—but the strange welcome continued: "she jumped me up and down with increasing enthusiasm. My mother had never made a play-thing of her wee daughter. Remembering this I began to cry aloud." [1]

Tribal children were accustomed to being educated and taken care of by others than natural parents. But little had prepared most of these autobiographers for the sheer strangeness of the school, with its echoing halls and electric lighting, and its staff speaking an unintelligible language and taking unacceptable familiarities with them. [2]

The present chapter will examine the responses of the children—first, to the arrival, then to institutional arrangements at the school, and to the staff. Chapter 6 will focus upon responses to the curriculum. And Chapter 7 will examine the ways in which the pupils responded to each other, and how they became brokers between two worlds. These three chapters are thus structured around the motivational clusters previously outlined: each new pupil brought *personal*, *kin*, and *cultural* influences to the new situation. The school presented itself as *institution*, *staff*, *curriculum*, and *peers*. The complex interplay among these motivational influences produced highly individual and ambivalent responses.

I

"This sudden change in my life was a shocking experience," wrote Irene Stewart of her arrival with a tribal policeman at Fort Defiance Boarding School. "From a primitive, wild, Navajo life into a strange place with strange people, food, clothing. I was homeless. No one cared for me as my old home folks had. I feared everything, especially the people and the strange facilities." Stewart's vocabulary reflects her later acceptance of many of the ideals of her new educators; but the fact that she came to like elements of the school only highlights her vivid memories of the first shock and loneliness of arrival.[3]

For those living near a day school, the shock could be less. But even the volunteer Qoyawayma remembered that "her heart pounded like a Hopi drum" as the red-faced, whiskered teacher at the local day school, his "hairy hand on his hips," spoke in a language she did not understand. And her bewilderment increased as she endured a bath and tried to copy marks from a board at the front of the room. Talayesva walked through the Hopi schoolyard and into a room full of baths. With characteristic boldness he got into one and began to scrub himself. A teacher entered, "threw up her hands," uttered an exclamation of surprise, and Talayesva fled. It was all a misunderstanding, however. The teacher had been impressed with the Hopi's voluntary arrival at the school. When he returned, she met him "with kind words which I could not understand," and called him a "Bright boy"—he, along with other supposedly reticent Hopi narrators, thrilled to such praise. For Talayesva the challenges continued. He was at first afraid to sit on a toilet: "I thought something might seize me, or push me from below. . . ."[4]

If the arrival bewildered even volunteers, the early days at school piled surprise on surprise and shock on shock. Few Euro-American children had to endure such extremes of culture shock—an incomprehensible language (or languages, in multitribal schools) and full-scale *deculturation*. Even most immigrant children shared far more with their American teachers than did these Indians.[5] The assault on traditional culture began symbolically, with the transformation of the outer child, and proceeded with a regimen and curriculum which would also, the teachers hoped, change the student mentally and spiritually.

II

On her first day at Fort Defiance, Irene Stewart also endured a bath. "I screamed and fought back but the big girl in charge was too strong. She got me in and scrubbed me. Then she put me into underwear and a dress with lots of buttons down the back. I remember how she combed my hair until it hurt. And the shoes she put on my feet were so strange and heavy. I was used to mocassins."[6] Stewart's discomfort was not surprising, coming as she did from a remote Navajo hogan. Lucille Winnie's part-Seneca and part-Cayuga parents, on the other hand, worked as BIA teachers. By the time Winnie arrived as a twelve-year-old at Haskell Institute in Kansas around 1912, others of her family had attended, and she had already visited the school. She was a veteran of day school, and was perhaps the most acculturated of these narrators as she began boarding school. Yet her first day at Haskell was "a never-to-be-forgotten experience," and her very "sophistication" in the ways of white America rebounded against her.

Although initially enthusiastic, she "was keenly disappointed" at not being allowed to room with her sister, and "wanted to go home at once." Then an "officer" (a senior female student) told the girls to take off their "home clothes":

> and I began to disrobe like the rest. Off came my blue serge skirt and blouse; then my Sunday lingerie, which I was so proud of. Mother had spent much time making the panties and slip to match, with a lot of embroidery and dainty pink ribbon running through the insertion. I was hoping everyone would see how elegant they were. A bundle was tossed at me and someone shouted "Put those on!"

The contents of the bundle "looked like prison garb." The heavy school shoes hurt her feet, but when she asked for another pair, the officer gave "a dirty look and said, 'Move on.'" Later that night she lay on her hard bed and wondered why she had "been so stupid" as to exchange her own room for the cold and impersonal dormitory. She gritted her teeth to keep back the tears. She would grow to like much about Haskell, but vividly contrasted her optimistic expectations with the tough reality of the school.[7]

Boys too experienced the forced transformation of the exterior person. At the schools attended by Francis La Flesche (Omaha) and by Jim Whitewolf (Kiowa-Apache), the garb of new arrivals was tied up in a bundle to be returned to the family—a powerfully symbolic rejection of the past. Standing Bear remembered the difficulties of getting used to the garments of "civilization." Those who took off their new trousers at night could not remember in the morning whether the fly buttons were on the front or the back! For Frank Mitchell (Navajo), buttons caused even greater distress. "A lot of us did not know how to work the buttons in front, and many just wet themselves. . . . They had to teach us all those things." Mitchell reflected to his interviewer that it was "embarrassing to talk about these things, but you ought to know them."[8]

Used as they were to the loin cloth and leggings, some Apaches rejected trousers. Ironically, one of the extracurricular activities at Carlisle temporarily allowed these Indians a sense of return to old ways. Asa Daklugie enjoyed athletics, and noted that "[t]here was one great advantage of running: we didn't have to wear trousers. Nobody knows how all Indian men hated those pants. The track team wore trunks, and we felt like Indians." Yet Jason Betzinez challenged Daklugie's claim that all Apaches hated trousers. "As I look today at our first photographs after we arrived at Carlisle, I realize what wild and unkempt-looking creatures we were." However:

> The school tailor shop turned out blue army-type uniforms for the boys while the dress shop made neat dresses for the girls. We wore these uniforms proudly. Never before had I owned such fine-looking clothing.[9]

These two Apaches disagreed on more than the virtues of white clothing: Daklugie was one of the most bitterly critical of the autobiographers, whereas Betzinez believed that Carlisle led him to Christianity. After the initial shock had dissipated, nevertheless almost all Indians quickly adjusted to scrubbed skin and to the often coarse "citizens clothes." Significantly, pupils such as Kay Bennett (Navajo) changed back into more traditional clothing upon return home for holidays, thus expressing her understanding that each type was appropriate for a particular setting.[10]

The narrators also adjusted to what might be termed "citizen's hair," but sometimes only after angry struggles. Girls did not often report the forced cutting of their hair, but Zitkala-Sa vividly recalled her humiliation. "Among our people," wrote the Yankton, "short hair was worn by mourners, and shingled hair by cowards." She tried to hide, but teachers and senior students found her under a bed:

> I remember being dragged out, though I resisted by kicking and scratching wildly. In spite of myself, I was carried downstairs and tied fast in a chair.
> I cried aloud, shaking my head all the while, until I felt the cold blades of the scissors against my neck, and heard them gnaw off one of my thick braids. Then I lost my spirit.

Zitkala-Sa enjoyed self-dramatization. But other Indian narrators described such use of force to impose the new standards, as did white Americans. Indeed, most teachers during these decades would have thrilled to the Yankton's last phrase as evidence that "savagery" had capitulated to "civilization." [11]

Boys more often suffered from the indignity of mandatory hair cutting. Some Carlisle boys wondered why, if long hair bred lice, girls were generally allowed to keep theirs? Obviously, because such hair on boys appeared uncivilized. "I can learn the white man's ways just as well with long hair," declared one resentful pupil. By taking the boys one by one from class, the staff defused such resistance. And Standing Bear perceptively noted the effect of group dynamics on himself. "When I saw most of them returning with short hair," he wrote "I began to feel anxious to be 'in style' and *I wanted mine cut too*" (emphasis added). But the loss threw him into a spasm of ambivalence—he immediately doubted his Indian identity. Nevertheless, as was the case with white clothing, he and other boys quickly got used to the new appearance. [12]

Into the twentieth century similar indignities awaited arrivals. James McCarthy a Tohono O'Odham (Papago) recalled how at Phoenix Indian School in 1906 "all of us boys with our bald heads were too ashamed to eat." Albert Yava explained the resistance to short hair, yet simultaneously implied his quick acceptance of it, this time at the Keams Canyon Boarding School in Arizona. "Our families didn't like our hair being cut," recalled the Tewa–Hopi. "Our traditional hairstyle was meaningful. The long hair we boys wore on the sides symbolized rain, you might say fertility, and it seemed to our parents that the whites were being pretty high-handed and insensitive, as well as being ignorant of our ways. Still, quite a few of the teachers were pretty nice people." [13]

Along with the new appearance went a "civilized" name—partly because Indian names were hard to pronounce, but more so because they were relics of a "savage" past. Although Ah-nen-la-de-ni's ancestors had taken the name La France, he recalled that "it made me feel as if I had lost myself" when teachers insisted that he henceforth be known as Daniel La France. "I had been proud of myself and my possibilities as 'Turns the Crowd' [Ah-nen-la-de-ni]," he wrote. "[B]but Daniel La France was to me a stranger with no possibilities. It seemed as if my prospect of a chiefship had vanished. I was very homesick for a time." Obviously he was also "identity sick"—how better to express the initial sense of alienation than to declare that the newly named boy was a stranger to himself? Yava lamented that not only did teachers shorten Nuvayoiyava (Big Falling Snowflake) to Yava. They also insisted he have a Christian name. One teacher liked to call him Oliver, but another took a personal interest in him, and demanded he be Albert Yava. Thus were new identities formed. Later, when he joined a Hopi ceremonial society, he gained yet another name: "But people still call me Yava."[14]

The Presbyterian teachers at La Flesche's school allowed *pupils* to select a new Euro-American name for each new pupil—a practice which implicated Omaha children in the destruction of their own culture, but also allowed them a small sense of participation in the affairs of the school. They generally enjoyed the exercise, and few ever complained about the names allowed them, which included George Washington, Philip Sheridan, and Ulysses S. Grant. Decades later Standing Bear's teachers at Carlisle also played at allowing a degree of choice to pupils. Each could pick his or her new name from a list on the blackboard. Still immersed in tribal culture, Standing Bear imagined the teacher's pointer to be a coup stick, and pretended he was "counting coup" (touching an enemy in battle) on the name. Again, the narrators soon became habituated to the new name; after all, in traditional society they would have been given a succession of names. "How proud I was to answer when the teacher called the roll!" declared Standing Bear.[15]

Many pupils adjusted to elements of the new way, then. But the first few days were startling, especially at boarding school, and often deeply imprinted on memory. Ah-nen-la-de-ni, who later grew to like school, left one of the most graphic descriptions of these early feelings of bewilderment. First came the bath, then the strange new clothes for the pupil. "Thereafter he was released by the tortures, and could be seen sidling about the corridors like a lonely crab, silent, sulky, immaculately clean and most disconsolate."[16]

III

Once the initial shock wore off, the pupils faced choices—obviously there were limited real choices in the early days, apart from the stark alternatives of acceptance or attempted flight. A few of these narrators did flee on their first day: Don Talayesva, as we have seen, and Charles Eastman, jeered at for his long hair and childish ways by more experienced students at a local day school. Had his father not insisted that Eastman return the next day, white America might never have known this most famous of all Indian spokesmen of the early twentieth century.[17]

But if they survived the initial shocks, choices began to present themselves to the young Indians. Should they continue to resist their teachers, or accept the regimen of the school? Should they learn enough merely to avoid punishment, or attempt to excel? Should they hold onto tribal culture, blending old ways and new, or attempt to forget kin and tribal life?

The ambivalence of their responses to such choices has already begun to emerge, and will continue to do so throughout this study. An ambivalent person, writes Christopher Boehm, "is torn between conflicting feelings, desires, or alternatives for action." We usually think of ambivalence as dualistic, or two-sided, but Boehm extends the term "to include inner conflicts that combine more than two conflicting impulses."[18] Occasionally a narrator recalled responding almost entirely without ambivalence: Mountain Wolf Woman (Winnebago), for example, seems to have thoroughly enjoyed her few years at school. Almost all of the other narrators remembered the good and the bad, and often produced tellingly ambivalent juxtapositions.

"I was tired of attending *any* school," wrote G. W. Grayson (Creek) of his attitude after many years as a student, "and longed to be free and out in the world where I would not have to attend school and pore over text books." Then his ambivalence suddenly surfaced. "No, I have always a warm nook in my affections for old Ashbury, for after all, have not some—indeed many of my happiest days been spent within her walls and on her campus?" Perhaps this was the ambivalence of retrospect; but he, like many narrators, described his boyhood reactions to school as conflicting. After four years at Haskell Institute in the early twentieth century, Irene Stewart had overcome her early shock, but conflicting feelings persisted: "I was anxious to go home, and at the same time reluctant to leave Haskell." The remembered ambivalence of another Navajo emerges even more starkly. Mrs. Bob Martin entered the Fort Lewis Boarding School in Durango, Colorado, about 1902:

> When first I got there it was frightening, I almost died of loneliness. It took a year for me to become accustomed. The teachers taught us what we had to learn, and we worked hard to be good students. We did what we were told to do. I enjoyed my school days. At times it was difficult, but I managed to get along well.[19]

Charles Eastman most strikingly conveyed the cultural ambivalence of the gifted, intellectually curious pupil. "At times I felt something of the fascination of the new life," he wrote of his early days at the Santee Normal Training School in Nebraska. But "again there would arise in me a dogged resistance, and a voice seemed to be saying, 'It is cowardly to depart from the old things!'"[20]

IV

As they became more familiar with the surroundings, the nature of the many challenges became clearer, challenges all the more awesome in those decades when the schools made so few concessions to Indian cultures. "It must be remembered," wrote Alford with that sense of cultural superiority which sometimes characterized the possessor of a school education,

> that Indian children of that time [1885] had to be taught the very rudiments of civilization, as well as to speak and read the English language. Such simple things as the use of chairs to sit on, the correct way to eat at a table, the use of knives and forks, the care of their beds such as spreading sheets properly . . . the habits of personal neatness, such as regular baths, the care of teeth, the brushing of their hair, and habits of decorum. In many cases it was more difficult to teach them these things than it was to teach them to speak and read English, for civilized manners were things considered utterly unnecessary by the parents of these children, and they were not encouraged to take up such ways.[21]

One of the first things many narrators learned about was "the bell." Pupil after pupil recalled the sensual impression of this instrument of regimentation. Although they got used to that too, it probably became for them what the alarm clock is for many twentieth-century Euro-Americans—a sound which, no matter where heard or when, startles the whole system. "At school we just went by the bell," recalled Frank Mitchell (Navajo). "Every time that bell rang, it meant that we had to get in line, or go to bed, or get up and get ready for breakfast, or dinner or supper." Zitkala-Sa recounted its even more exquisite use to divide the whole process of eating into smaller segments of time: when she sat down before the second dining-room bell, she received the disapproving stare of a teacher. Similarly La Flesche perceptively recalled its function at his school: "to call us to order." It is impossible to tell the extent to which a published autobiography reflects a spoken account, but the bell obviously made an impression on Jim Whitewolf (Kiowa-Apache): he mentioned it *ten times* on one page. And the young Fred Kabotie wondered how Hopis, without clocks or watches, could learn to tell time.[22] By means of the bell, obviously.

Looking back, an individual could even miss the structuring regularity of the bell. But the adjustment to such regimentation was not easy, even for one like Charles Eastman, who wanted to learn the new way. With a striking metaphor he conveyed the frustration of trying to live to the artificial segmentation of every day into short, discrete periods, each for one activity only. "I hardly think I was ever tired in my life until those first days of boarding school," he wrote of the Santee Normal Training School. "All day things seemed to come and pass with a wearisome regularity, like walking railway ties—the step was too short for me."[23]

Not every school attended by these narrators ran on military lines—the otherwise strict Omaha school of the Presbyterian BFM did not, for example. But Captain Pratt of Carlisle and Gen. Samuel C. Armstrong, head of Hampton Institute, were convinced of the validity of this approach. "The boys have been organized into companies as soldiers," wrote Pratt in 1880, "and the best material selected for sergeants and corporals. They have been uniformed and drilled in many of the movements of army tactics. This has taught them obedience and cleanliness, and given them a better carriage." A decade later Armstrong outlined and justified the rank system, military court, and army discipline imposed upon pupils at Hampton. "The military organization," he claimed, was

> the most potent factor in solving the problems of law and order which confront the [student] officers of the school, and is not only repressive, but directly and actively educative as well. It enforces promptness, accuracy and obedience, and goes further than any other influence could do to instill into the minds of the students what both negro and Indian sadly lack, a knowledge of the value of time.

Such a rationale is not surprising from old soldiers. But at other schools, too, educators became convinced that a military organization could teach young Indians of both sexes everything from obedience, to patriotism, to the Protestant work ethic.[24]

"It was a military school," wrote Helen Sekaquaptewa of the Phoenix Indian School, which she began to attend in 1915. "We marched to the dining room three times a day to band music. We arose to a bell and had a given time for making our beds, cleaning our rooms, and being ready for breakfast. Everything was done on schedule, and there was no time for idleness." Boys *and girls* lined up in uniform for inspection each Sunday morning. The boys saluted and the girls held out their hands to be checked; the "officers" noted every flaw in appearance. This school life, with its corporal punishment "as a matter of course," was "obnoxious to many students," claimed Sekaquaptewa, and some went to elaborate lengths to plan their escapes, despite the threat of harsh and humiliating punishments upon recapture. Yet Sekaquaptewa immediately noted positive sides: the government-issue dresses were of good material, for example, and individually fitted. And she "still loved to study."[25]

Lucille Winnie strongly objected to the military discipline at Haskell Institute. "All this shouting of commands and marching was a lot of nonsense to me. I felt *then* [emphasis added], and still do that the army is no place for a woman. Due to my firm belief I was never popular with the officers or matrons, and in seven years at Haskell my rank was 'buck private.'" She left a striking account of the cold and bullying staff, more like army superiors than mentors. Yet she obviously adjusted to the regimen, and her account of those seven long years is a classic of ambivalence. She progressed well in her studies, and remained convinced in later life that her education at Haskell had opened the world to her.[26]

Boys too chafed under the constant surveillance. "Whether at work or play, we were constantly watched," recalled Ah-nen-la-de-ni, "and there were those in authority over us." In the dormitory a student "captain" taught and enforced the rules, and reported all breaches of discipline to the teachers. Alford described the military regimentation at General Armstrong's school: "We dressed, we ate, we drilled, we studied and recited our lessons with a precision that left not even one minute without its duties." Pupils needed a pass to leave the campus, and were expected to salute teachers, officers, and fellow students "with proper respect." Yet although it was all very strange, wrote the Shawnee, "we liked it." And despite the difficulties of learning how "to keep immaculate our uniform of the school," he explicitly grounded his adjustment in his tribal education: "As I have said before, we had been trained to respect authority, and that is the secret of a successful apprenticeship to military life."[27]

Others who had much to criticize in the school could enjoy the drilling and the uniforms with shiny buttons and hats. "School was tough for us," noted James McCarthy (Papago), of life at Phoenix Boarding School after 1906. He remembered the language problems, homesickness, hair cutting, and the sometimes harsh whipping of students. Yet there is a strong sense of pride in his description of the military display at the school. "We had two rifle companies and our commander was Major Grestead of the 1st Arizona Infantry," wrote McCarthy:

> We had a very nice band with about twenty buglers and drummers. On Sunday we wore special blue uniforms for our parade and inspection. Many white people would come to watch.[28]

V

As in tribal society, negative incentives enforced discipline. Indeed, along with respect for kin, tribal conditioning to accept discipline, and personal factors such as ambition, *fear* was a major motivating factor in adaptive responses to the school. Frank Mitchell remembered the constant corporal punishment at Fort Defiance, along with less severe penalties meted out to girls, such as standing in the corner; a returned runaway might be made carry a heavy log around on his shoulder. "I was never naughty like that or punished that way," he claimed somewhat ingenuously. "I was always obedient because I was a little scared of them and so I always did what I was told." [29]

Zitkala-Sa remembered how one young girl "shrieked at the top of her voice" when beaten by a teacher, a description lent credence by the bitter Yankton's admission that the teacher then led the tearful girl from the room, "stroking her black shorn head." Perhaps, wrote Zitkala-Sa, it had occurred to the older woman that "brute force is not the solution for such a problem"—the girls had been lying in the snow, thus leaving the imprint of their young female forms on the whiteness. The approach of authorities at the Sherman Institute in Riverside, California, almost half a century later, was no more appropriate. Don Talayesva enjoyed the student debating society, but refused to participate in a debate in front of a large audience. The assistant disciplinarian, probably an Indian, led him to the basement:

> two strong boys let down my pants and held me. After about fifteen blows with a rawhide in a heavy hand, I broke down and cried. I slept very little that night and was sore for several days but was never again asked to debate in the auditorium. [30]

The account is reminiscent of Talayesva's childhood beating by the Hopi kachinas. But in this latter case he was a young man, and even in retrospect would hardly have admitted crying unless a severe beating took place.

Paul Blatchford (Navajo) left a graphic description of punishments at the Christian School in Rehoboth, New Mexico, about 1922. Recaptured runaways "had to pull their pants down, lean over a bench and receive 25 straps"—more if there were further violations. But even for the less serious offenses of being late for dinner or lineup, pupils faced a gauntlet of *their fellows*: "all those who could swing with their right arms, swung their belts at the person." For bed wetters the punishment was less brutal physically, but perhaps more so psychologically: the boy or girl had to carry the mattress around in the square . . . for a whole day.[31]

Even narrators who themselves strongly believed in the value of schooling described harsh punishments. A Navajo reported the constant use of a jail at the Albuquerque Indian School in the first decade of the twentieth century. Returned runaways might be incarcerated there for three days, but "even where you make a little mistake, they put you in jail too." If pupils talked in class, "they tie a piece of rag around the mouth and back of his head; in that way the school children used to mind and learn their lessons." Yet this was much better, the narrator believed, than the rowdiness of schools in his own day! Other narrators, such as Lucille Winnie, also exhibited nostalgia for the "order" of school life. But this did not prevent a critical recall of the harshness.[32]

Francis La Flesche wrote of the constant use of the rod at the Presbyterian school, and of the many rough shakings administered by Gray-beard, the teacher. Gray-beard once beat a dull pupil almost into unconsciousness—but this was unusual by school standards, and resulted in an apology from the perpetrator! Helen Sekaquaptewa remembered the use of the whip at Phoenix Indian School, and how the authorities devised special punishment for runaways: girls might be made to clean the yard and to cut the grass with scissors, while wearing a card that read "I ran away"; boys were put in jail and had to wear a dress to school. "Some of them forgot how to wear pants," she noted dryly. Qoyawayma claimed that most of the Hopi children at her day school were meek and "posed no disciplinary problems." Some of the boys became unruly, however: "Retaliation was prompt. A few of them were booted, others were slapped in the face." She "remembered vividly" the humiliating punishment of a friend who would not stop talking. The girl had to sit on an unheated stove:

> an eraser was shoved into her mouth. She sat there stiff with fright, head bent in shame and saliva dripping, until the teacher's sadistic appetite had been satisfied.[33]

On occasion such actions could be counterproductive: more than one narrator remembered pupils fighting back. Yet teacher harshness did not turn many of the narrators against school itself. For there were incentives to compensate for the rigid discipline and often capricious punishments.

VI

Some of these compensations should now be clear—the school uniforms, for example. And food. While some pupils complained about the quantity and quality of food, others were positively motivated. Anna Moore Shaw (Pima) enjoyed a new delicacy called "corn flakes." And Mildred Stinson (Oglala) admitted that she built up resistance against loneliness, at least partly because the pupils "ate pretty good." One thing she would remember to her dying day: "at four o'clock we got a big bun. . . . And everybody waited for this four o'clock time to come— just couldn't wait."[34]

The strongly ambivalent responses of many of the narrators require further explanation, however. There were a number of institutional factors—extracurricular activities built into the school systems—which positively motivated even students who were otherwise critical of the school.

At the larger schools, especially, sporting and musical activities, debating societies, and theater groups sprang up, apparently with full official approval. School newspapers often gave regular details on such activities. Indeed, pupils themselves in part prepared Carlisle papers such as *The Red Man* and *The Carlisle Arrow*. At the Santa Fe Indian School during World War I, Fred Kabotie joined an art club, helped organize a school orchestra, and acted in a play. During her third year at Haskell Institute, Irene Stewart began to like the place, partly because of new friends, but also because she joined the glee club and the basketball team. Schools sometimes planned outside activities for pupils: a trip to the circus at Gallup for Kay Bennett and her Navajo companions was "the greatest experience of their lives." And Alford would hardly forget one of his school trips to Washington, D.C., to witness the inauguration of President Garfield: "I was flag sergeant at that time, and had the honor of dipping the flag to the President."[35] A number of these sanctioned extracurricular activities especially appealed to narrators.

"The thing that pulled me through," wrote Asa Daklugie, "was the athletic training at Carlisle." Always ready to compare white to Apache culture unfavorably, he claimed that "the conditioning didn't measure up to my father's and Geronimo's training routine, but it kept me active and fit." And, significantly, although Daklugie regarded football as "silly," he took pride in the achievements of the Carlisle team: "We had the world beat. Our football players were fast and husky. They could outrun, outdodge, and outsmart the players of the big Eastern universities." The American phenomenon of loyalty to the college team had thus extended itself to Indians; no doubt Daklugie's pride was intensified when his team beat famous *white* universities.[36]

In an extraordinarily frank account, Pratt himself broadly corroborated Daklugie's claim. The principal recollected that, as a result of its roughness, he attempted to ban football against other schools. But he had to reconsider this at the insistence of pupils. "While they stood around my desk, their black eyes intensely watching me," wrote Pratt in his autobiography, "the orator gave practically all the arguments in favor of our contending in outside football. . . ." Pratt finally relented, and the incident demonstrates just how powerful a motivating force sports could become.[37]

Others such as Fred Kabotie and Albert Yava also recalled the importance of sports, and James McCarthy became especially active in baseball at the Santa Fe Indian School. The Papago took pride in the fact that the pupils themselves organized the team. And he reveled in his own status as sports star: "Many small boys came to see me; the boys liked to carry my baseball mask and my pitcher's glove when I played ball. Everybody seemed to like me." One of his great memories was of the day Santa Fe Indian School took on Albuquerque. "A big crowd was on hand to watch the game between the two Indian schools. . . . That afternoon we beat the champions 5 to 0." He fled and voluntarily returned to a number of schools, before the principal finally had him transferred back to Phoenix. McCarthy feared he would be punished, but the coach expressed satisfaction that McCarthy had returned to play for the school. It is difficult to know from the account exactly what happened; yet there is a strong impression that both the transfer and the lenient treatment for a runaway were the result of his sporting ability. The Meriam Report of a decade later would criticize the tendency of schools to pay too great attention to the "star" athlete.[38]

Although Irene Stewart enjoyed membership on a basketball club, female narrators appear to have taken less interest in sports. Anna Moore Shaw (Pima) was shocked at her first American football game: she could not understand why her male cousin and others were being so roughly treated. But Lucille Winnie wrote of the pride she took in the achievements of Haskell's football, track, and other teams—although at least one of her brothers died because of overexertion on the track. "Those 'Fast Winnie Brothers' whose speed and prowess on the athletic field was proclaimed far and wide are now buried on the family plot in Oklahoma," she wrote, "great Haskell althletes, whose hearts were not equal to the demand."[39]

Music too hath charms . . . With characteristic humor Luther Standing Bear described the bemusement of Carlisle pupils when first introduced to Western musical instruments—some blew into the wrong ends or spat into them—causing dismay in the tearful teacher. Standing Bear learned the bugle, but for him the charm lay as much in later being chosen to lead the school band as in the music. Fred Kabotie also remembered his introduction to this extracurricular activity. After its closing by the government, Carlisle's instruments went to the Santa Fe school. Kabotie hoped to be given the "shiny round one with tubes inside" (the French horn) but was near the end of the line and only got a B-flat clarinet. For this artist-to-be, a secondary career had begun: "As I improved, musical opportunities opened up."[40]

"Land of oranges. Land of perfume. Land of torture," wrote Polingaysi Qoyawayma, of the Sherman Institute in California. Even fifty years after the experience, emotions of suffering returned to her when the Hopi thought of the place. But there was "another, happier, memory of that time. Each day the schoolchildren sang. Song was Polingaysi's salvation." When asked to perform in public her "characteristic Hopi reticence" at first held her back. But soon she "began to receive pleasure from giving pleasure. . . . She found in this activity a way to express her pent-up yearnings, her uncertainties, and her loneliness, and to rise above them"—a way to survive the school, in other words.[41]

A group of white visitors—possibly government officials—unwittingly instigated a memorable incident in La Flesche's *Middle Five*. One of the visitors unexpectedly asked the pupils to sing an Indian song. "There was some hesitancy," wrote La Flesche with a nice touch of understatement. To sing such a song in class, and in the Omaha language, would, the students sensed, have been a violation of something sacred to the missionary teachers. But suddenly

> a loud clear voice close to me broke into a Victory song; before a bar was sung another voice took up the song from the beginning, as is the custom among the Indians, then the whole school fell in, and we made the room ring. We understood the song, and we knew the emotion of which it was the expression. We felt, as we sang, the patriotic thrill of a victorious people who had vanquished their enemies.

But the visitors only shook their heads: "'That's savage, that's savage!'" said one. "'They must be taught music.'" It speaks well both for their toleration of white ethnocentrism, and for the motivating power of Western music, that the young Omahas came to enjoy the "new study" almost as much as their own music.[42]

Christmas also caught the imagination of many narrators, especially those who spent long years at boarding schools without so much as a visit home. "One night in December we were all marched down to the chapel," recalled Standing Bear. "We stretched our necks to see everything. Then a minister stood up in front and talked to us, but I did not mind a thing he said—in fact, I could not understand him anyway. . . . we were all so happy." Although attending a local day school, Edward Goodbird also remembered the warmth of the Christmas party at the Hidatsa mission. But the good feeling did not last: miffed that they had not been given a magnet which had caught their eyes, Goodbird and a friend walked out of the school and refused to return for some time. In retrospect Goodbird blamed himself, rather than the teachers, for spoiling the otherwise enjoyable Christmas spirit.[43]

Missionary and government authorities prided themselves on the careful surveillance of the sexes at coeducational schools. Aware, nevertheless, that many students were young men and women of marriageable age, authorities sometimes allowed supervised activities between the sexes. Helen Sekaquaptewa claimed that Hopi adults objected to such school dances and parties "where boys and girls dance with their arms around each other." The Haskell authorities did not permit such familiarity, but for Lucille Winnie "socials" were "the biggest event of the week, as that was the only time we could visit with the opposite sex." Matrons and disciplinarians stood "eyeing us from the sidelines," the boys and girls sat around outside, ate lunch together, and listened to the school band—until the bell rang. Those with a "bad case" (romantically involved) were finally "driven into the fold by the matrons." At boarding school in Oklahoma, a Comanche girl invited Jim Whitewolf (Kiowa Apache) to a carefully organized "event," during which couples in their "Sunday clothes" were judged according to appearance and style. He and his partner actually won a large cake, and after the competition, the couples could talk together. Despite his nervousness he regarded the affair as a kind of rite of passage. "I was fifteen years old at the time. It was the first time I ever had a date with a girl and talked with her like that."[44]

Alford was especially impressed with the way coeducation at Hampton allowed for "a kind of good-fellowship between the sexes that was new to . . . me." Even in carefully segregated schools, boys and girls often sat in the same classrooms and dining rooms; and Hampton too had its "socials" with dancing, games, contests, and conversation— all "under proper supervision of teachers and officers." These activities took some getting used to: "The association with the opposite sex on a footing of equality was something new, and I am afraid we were very crude and awkward at first." But he believed that he learned how to act with girls, and, like Whitewolf, he and his school partner also won a large cake at a social. "I shall always remember with deep gratitude the kindly, pleasant efforts of my teachers to help me set myself right," wrote Alford.[45]

Vacations and days off also constituted deliberate softenings of the regimen. Although such breaks risked the recontamination of pupils in the "heathen" home environment, educators hoped that the returning pupils would begin the "uplift" of their kin. The practice could also assuage loneliness and provide a safety valve to dissipate pupils' frustrations, as autobiographers themselves sometimes suggested. When five-year-old Francis La Flesche cried for his mother on his first terrible day at the Presbyterian school, an older boy comforted him: "'You will see your mother soon, we can go home every bathing-day [Saturday]. It is only three days to wait, so don't cry.'" Throughout the book La Flesche recounted the happy visits to the village each Saturday—once school chores were completed. The visit did seem to serve as a kind of release, and the boys returned to school willingly in the evening. Thomas Clani conveyed well the pupils' sense of joy as Navajo parents arrived to take them home each June from Shiprock Boarding School in the 1920s: "That was one happy event." Despite the hard work at home with the family, "the summer was too short; September came and we returned to school in our government clothes." Kay Bennett, another Navajo, described how the new yearly rhythm of school life became superimposed upon the rhythm of the seasons. Child after child in her family began school, and returned each June to their happy mother—storing their government clothes until autumn. "The summer passed quickly," she wrote, *"and the children started thinking again about the school* [emphasis added]. Kaibah [Bennett] started practicing English."[46]

Some pupils could not wait to get back after breaks. "By the end of the summer I had had enough of hoeing weeds and tending sheep," wrote Talayesva of the strenuous Hopi life. "Helping my father was hard work, and I thought it was better to be educated." Others fulfilled the teachers' expectations by preaching the new way upon return, thus increasing the tension. It is impossible to tell whether such pupils would have been less or more content with school had they never been allowed home, but the vacation policy probably did serve to bleed off pupil frustrations at many schools, and unhappy summer holidays only made school more acceptable. A. A. Spencer, superintendent at the Montana Industrial School, certainly believed in the efficacy of periodic breaks.

"The privilege you gave me of allowing some pupils to go home in vacation . . . was highly prized," he informed the commissioner of Indian Affairs in 1895. "The pupils returned promptly at the end of the vacation, and they have seemed more cheerful and contented than ever before during the last school year."[47]

A variation on this approach, also a calculated violation of the quarantine principle, was to allow periodic kin visits to the school. Luther Standing Bear, for example, was especially impressed by the way Captain Pratt treated his father on a short visit to Carlisle. From Pratt's perspective, of course, two generations of an Indian family were now more satisfied with the school.[48]

VII

White school staff—principals, teachers, matrons, and other Americans met in relation to schooling—were of crucial importance for the initial and long-term responses of children to the new institution. Occasionally narrators mentioned being taught by Indian teachers of their own or other tribes: Anna Moore Shaw was fortunate to begin her study of English with a fellow Pima teacher, for example.[49] But few mention such occurrences. Apart from student "officers" and disciplinarians (see Chapter 7), white staff dominated the lives of these narrators.

Indians depicted white Americans they encountered as highly diverse. At the positive extreme was Rev. Alfred L. Riggs, the famous founder of the Santee Normal Training School. When so much new learning confused Charles Eastman, it was Riggs who explained "the reasonableness of it all." No mentor could have wished for a more affectionate portrait:

> The Doctor's own personality impressed us deeply, and his words of counsel and daily prayers, strange to us at first, in time found root in our minds. Next to my own father, this man did more than perhaps any other to make it possible for me to grasp the principles of true civilization.

Eastman implied that Riggs in part worked with, rather than clashed against, traditional upbringing: "He also strengthened and developed in me that native strong ambition to win out, by sticking to whatever I might undertake."[50]

In more mundane language Jim Whitewolf (Kiowa Apache) demonstrated the contrast possible at an Oklahoma boarding school. After

Whitewolf and other returned runaways had been given physical labor as punishment, the principal insisted that Mr. Bright, in charge of the barn, should whip them. He refused, saying the boys had paid enough for their crime, and called the principal "a little fellow." The principal then struck Bright, and a fight ensued, after which Bright dragged the crying principal around by the legs. Another member of the staff broke up this sordid fight, and the humiliated principal headed back to the sanctuary of his office. "Mr. Bright told us we were not going to get any whipping, and to go ahead and play." The personality extreme of staff is supported by the experiences of other narrators.[51]

One teacher remembered by G. W. Grayson "seemed to love the work of school teaching, as well as the pupils under him, and was always conscientiously desirous of benefitting those committed to his charge. . . ." But another gave the Creek such a severe flogging, "without sufficient cause," that for many years afterward Grayson hoped he might meet him again "and square accounts." Clinton Rickard remembered how a day-school teacher on the Tuscarora reservation in New York refused to allow his brother leave the class, and "the little fellow had to sit and relieve himself right there in his seat." When she attempted to slap him, Rickard fled, leaving his unfortunate brother to take the punishment; both later refused to return to the school. The teacher in another local school, however, was "very good to us."[52]

Helen Sekaquaptewa recalled one teacher who damaged her ear with a blow, and another who molested female students. While the Hopi girl stood at the top of the class, he attempted to rub his face against hers— she screamed and fled the room. But Sekaquaptewa formed such strong ties with the superintendent of the Phoenix school and his family, that she later offered to take care of his widowed wife in her old age.[53]

"The first teacher I remember," wrote fellow Hopi Fred Kabotie, "was Mr. Chipper, a fine man." This extraordinary teacher even played rough games with the pupils at the Shungapovi day school, "and he was always getting his clothes torn because we'd pile on him and hold him down. He was a wonderful guy, and while he was there we ate well." After he was transferred, however, "a fellow named Buchanan took over. He was the meanest teacher we ever had, and that was when I began running away from school." At Santa Fe Indian School, the Hopi formed a strong and affectionate relationship with the principal and his wife, who took special interest in his artistically talented pupil. "Of course," wrote Kabotie in a comment which holds good for many of the narrators, "in my years at many schools I'd had all kinds of teachers from the very worst best to the best—at least I knew what not to do."[54]

Narrators sometimes described teachers as neither fully good nor bad. Gray-beard, the teacher at La Flesche's school, emerges as a short-tempered old man, capable of outright violence, but one who could sometimes achieve a certain camaraderie with the pupils—as when he rushed out of the classroom with them to catch some bees. And a number of the pupils at Carlisle depicted Captain Pratt as a many-sided individual, demanding, self-righteous, but not without a sense of fairness and of humor. Even the unusually bitter Zitkala-Sa could grudgingly concede the good intentions of one of her supposed tormentors, who was nursing a dying pupil.[55]

At such times of sickness, staff could emerge as especially caring. While Brush, La Flesche's great friend, lay dying of tuberculosis, the superintendent and the doctor walked slowly up the steps to Brush's room "talking earnestly"—an impressive image of concern. Later, when a teacher dismissed school, he "gave special instructions to the scholars not to make any noise as they passed out, or while moving about the house, so as not to disturb the sick boy." With less drama, but as tellingly, Chris (Mescalero Apache) conveyed the dedication of a hard-working doctor during an epidemic at Albuquerque Indian School about the turn of the century. Similarly, Jim Whitewolf remembered how, during a measles epidemic, which killed one or two boys a day at his school, "the doctor and nurse were working day and night."[56]

VIII

If racist assumptions about inherent Indian inferiority became more characteristic of federal educational policies and practices in the early twentieth century, we might expect to find increasing evidence of this in the autobiographies. Indian children could have missed racism in their teachers, but the adult narrators were well-acquainted with the problems of living in or near American society. Surely in retrospect they would have remembered manifestations of racial prejudice from white staff?

Occasionally a narrator recalled possibly racist treatment. Mary McDaniel (Lakota Sioux) told her interviewer that during the 1930s the matron at her boarding school punished the "full bloods" more than the "mixed bloods," and that their English teacher called them idiots. But such memories are rare in the autobiographies, and the narrators suggest little change in interpersonal relationships at the schools from the 1850s to the 1920s. Teachers and staff were as harsh and as kind, as culturally intolerant but racially optimistic, in one decade as in another during this period. Occasionally a *narrator* gives forth with either native or acquired racism. "You may be surprised to learn," wrote Jason Betzinez with perhaps a touch of deliberate irony, "that the Apache has a strong feeling of racial superiority and regards others as being lesser creatures." [57]

Some narrators did meet racial prejudice, but it often came from whites other than teachers at the Indian schools. Standing Bear, for example, lamented that his "outing" work at Wanamakers, Philadelphia, came to a sudden end because as an Indian he could not find lodging— prejudice quite at odds with the ethnocentric but racially egalitarian behavior of Captain Pratt. These narrators, then, provide little sense of radical shifts in educational policy or practice toward greater racism at the missionary and government schools. For them the reality remained an educational system that strove to destroy every vestige of tribal heritage, but also to prepare young Indians for citizenship—admittedly of an ambiguous kind, mostly on the margins of white society. Don Talayesva succinctly expressed the sense of equality he believed he had gained with a school education: "I could talk with whites like a gentleman." [58]

Not surprisingly, the most explicit examples of racial prejudice emerge in the dozen or so accounts by narrators who attended public schools or other institutions with white children. Sarah Winnemucca and Annie Lowry, both Paiutes (the latter of part-white ancestry) told of separate incidents in which white parents complained about having their children educated with Indians. Winnemucca claimed that Catholic nuns capitulated and requested that she be removed from the school. When Lowry won a spelling competition, the defeated white girl's mother insisted Lowry be expelled. In this case the teacher did not surrender, possibly because Lowry's father was white and a major taxpayer in the district. In 1895 Zitkala-Sa moved from an Indian school to Earlham College, Indiana. As she was about to participate in a debating contest, a group of white pupils from an opposing school unfurled a banner ridiculing Earlham for choosing a "squaw" as its representative. Though bitterly resentful of this "worse than barbarian rudeness," she did not terminate her studies. At a previous debating contest, *white* pupils had given her flowers. [59]

Other narrators also had good experiences at white schools. When Fred Kabotie enrolled at the Santa Fe Public High School about 1920, he "felt lost, the only Indian among hundreds of white faces." But soon some older white students introduced themselves to him. Apparently they thought he might be another Jim Thorpe, and soon had Kabotie playing for the school football team. Whatever their motives, he was relieved to have made their acquaintance: "I was so glad to meet somebody that I still remember them." Ah-nen-la-de-ni, who attended Indian schools, a public school, and a nursing school with white students perhaps too easily absolved white America. "I have been asked as to prejudice against Indians among white people. There is some, but I don't think it amounts to much." Referring specifically to schooling among whites, he admitted that "Perhaps there were some in my Training School class who objected to being associated with an Indian. I never perceived it, and I don't think I have suffered anywhere from prejudice."[60]

In her later years Anna Moore Shaw (Pima) became increasingly concerned with racial discrimination in white society. But she recalled that as a student at Phoenix Union High School, graduating in 1920, she formed "dear friendships" with non-Indian girls. And she was appreciative of the teachers and "their special efforts to help me pass subjects which may have been a bit neglected in my education at the Indian school." In fact, she wrote, "throughout my days in high school I never noticed any prejudice directed at me because of my Indian blood."[61]

We can draw no general conclusions from such few incidents. But they do suggest that narrators could experience a greater sense of isolation at white schools, and were more likely to suffer explicitly racial abuse. For all their faults, then, the regimented Indian schools, with their paternalistic and sometimes harsh staff, may have served as buffers between tribal and American life.[62]

Notes

1. Chapter title ("A Whole Different World"), Shaw, *Pima Past*, 103, caption below illustration; Zitkala-Sa, *American Indian Stories*, 49–51. Despite her critical memories, Zitkala-Sa later strongly advocated "education" for Indians; see David L. Johnson and Raymond Williams, "Gertrude Simmons Bonnin, 1876–1938: 'Americanize the First American,'" *American Indian Quarterly* 12 (Winter 1988): 27–49.

2. Also, La Flesche, *Middle Five*, 4–5; Mitchell, *Navajo Blessingway Singer*, 61. Noise and light could impress even those beginning second schools: Winnie, *Sab-gan-de-ob*, 49; Sekaquaptewa, *Me and Mine*, 92–93. Standing Bear liked the bright light, *My People the Sioux*, 133.

3. Stewart, *A Voice in Her Tribe*, 16. Also Stinson, in Cash and Hoover, eds., *To Be an Indian*, 94–95, quoted in Chapter 2 of the present volume. Cf. Paul Blatchford (Navajo) in Johnson, ed. *Stories of Traditional Navajo Life*, 174; Blatchford's two cousins stopped crying once they saw other children in the school grounds. Golden, *Red Moon Called Me*, appended eight short essays "in the children's own style, with errors and other shortcomings," on "My First Day at School," which convey a similar sense of ambivalence and disorientation as autobiographical accounts written decades later, 189–93.

4. Qoyawayma, *No Turning back*, 24–25, and 61 on Hopi reticence; Talayesva, *Sun Chief:* 89–90, 96.

5. Nineteenth-century common school crusades also involved assimilationist attempts by elites to impose Protestant, democratic education on supposedly deficient lower classes and immigrants, see, for example, Katz, *Reconstructing American Education*, 16–23.

6. Stewart, *A Voice in Her Tribe*, 15–16.

7. Winnie, *Sab-gan-de-ob*, 44–47.

8. La Flesche, *Middle Five*, 28; Jim Whitewolf, *Life*, 84; Standing Bear, *My People the Sioux*, 142; Mitchell, *Navajo Blessingway Singer*, 58–59, 67–68. Also Ah-nen-la-de-ni, "An Indian Boy's Story," 1783; Hyer, *One Heart*, 9.

9. Daklugie et al., *Indeh.*, 146; Betzinez, *I Fought with Geronimo*, 153.

10. "Citizens clothing": Mountain Wolf Woman, *Sister of Crashing Thunder*, 28; Bennett, *Kaibab*, 221. Others who liked the new clothes: Rogers, *Red World and White*, 6, 15; Sekaquaptewa, *Me and Mine*, 134; McCarthy, *Papago Traveller*, 29.

11. Zitkala-Sa, *American Indian Stories*, 52–56.

12. Standing Bear, *My People the Sioux*, 141–42, and *Land of the Spotted Eagle*, 189. Cf. Pratt, *Battlefield and Classroom*, 232.

13. McCarthy, *Papago Traveller*, 28–29; Yava, *Big Falling Snow*. 12. Also La Flesche, *Middle Five*, 75, on the changing emotions of a new student shorn of his hair and the acceptance by more senior pupils of "civilized" hair; Daklugie et al., *Indeh*, 144; Eastman, *Deep Woods*, 21–23; Jim Whitewolf, *Life*, 83. The braids of this Kiowa Apache were returned to his father.

14. Ah-nen-la-de-ni, "An Indian Boy's Story," 1783; Yava, *Big Falling Snow*, 3. Also Daklugie et al., *Indeh*, 144.

15. La Flesche, *Middle Five*, 28, 74–75. Cf. critical comments in Preface, xvii–xviii; Standing Bear, *My People the Sioux*, 136–38. Cf. Alford, *Civilization*, 103.

16. Ah-nen-la-de-ni, "An Indian Boy's Story," 1783.

17. Charles Eastman, *Deep Woods*, 23–25.

18. Christopher Boehm, "Ambivalence and Compromise in Human Nature," *American Anthropologist* 91 (Dec. 1989): 921.

19. Grayson, *A Creek Warrior*, 44–45; Stewart, *A Voice in Her Tribe*, 30; Mrs. Bob Martin, in Johnson, ed., *Stories of Traditional Navajo Life*, 121. Also, Bennett, *Kaibab*, 228; Rogers, *Red World and White*, 90–92; Qoyawayma, *No Turning Back*, 59–66; James, *Chief of the Pomos*, 40–41; and Yava's general comment: "We sometimes cuss and praise the white man in the same breath," *Big Falling Snow*, 137. See also Sally J. McBeth, *Ethnic Identity and the Boarding School Experience of West-Central Oklahoma American Indians* (Lanham, Md.: University Press of America, 1983), esp. 116–17.

20. Charles Eastman, *Deep Woods*, 46–47.

21. Alford, *Civilization*, 126. Alford was then a teacher in the Shawnee Boarding School, and the demands were those facing his own pupils. See also Sweezy, *Arapabo Way*, 5–7.

22. Mitchell, *Navajo Blessingway Singer*, 63; Zitkala-Sa, *American Indian Stories*, 53; La

Flesche, *Middle Five*, 78; Jim Whitewolf, *Life*, 85; Kabotie, *Hopi Indian Artist*, 10–11. Also, Winnie, *Sa-gan-de-ob*, 49.

23. Juanita (Cherokee) missed the bell, K. Tsianina Lowawaima, "Oral Histories from Chilocco Indian Agricultural School," *American Indian Quarterly* 11 (Summer 1987): 246; Eastman, *Deep Woods*, 46–47. Also, Zitkala-Sa, *American Indian Stories*, 66; Institute for Government Research, *Indian Administration* (Meriam Report), 577–78.

24. Training School for Youth, Carlisle Barracks, ARCIA (1880), *House Executive Document*, No. 1, part 5, 46 Congress, 3 session, serial 1959, 302; Report of Hampton Normal and Agricultural Institute, Hampton, Va., ARCIA (1900), *House Document No 5*, 56 Congress, 2 session, serial 4101, 319.

25. Sekaquaptewa, *Me and Mine*, 134–38, also 105; Trennert corroborates much of the account, *The Phoenix Indian School*, 47–48, and *passim*. Even outside Phoenix school, girls couldn't help but march in step if they heard a band: "how embarrassing it was!" Shaw, *Pima Past*, 133. Institute for Government Research, *Indian Administration* (Meriam Report), 395.

26. Winnie, *Sah-gan-de-ob*, 48–49, all Chap. 2.

27. Ah-nen-la-de-ni, "An Indian Boy's Story," 1783; Alford, *Civilization*, 99–100.

28. McCarthy, *Papago Traveller*, 26–30. Standing Bear did not object to military discipline, and was "proud" when he led the Carlisle band across the newly opened Brooklyn Bridge, *My People the Sioux*, 145, 148–49, 171. See also neutral description by Ernest Nelson, in Johnson, ed., *Stories of Traditional Navajo Life*, 232–33 (note illustration).

29. Mitchell, *Navajo Blessingway Singer*, 67–68. Mitchell was not *always* obedient. Also Jim Whitewolf, *Life*, 94.

30. Zitkala-Sa, *American Indian Stories*, 57–59; Talayesva, *Sun Chief*, 130.

31. Paul Blatchford, in Johnson, ed., *Stories of Traditional Navajo Life*, 175. Also, Myrtle Begay, in *idem*, 63.

32. Anonymous Navajo, in Alexander H. Leighton and Dorothea C. Leighton, eds. *The Navajo Door: An Introduction to Navajo Life*, (Cambridge, Mass.: Harvard University Press, 1944), 125–27. Nostalgia: also Noah White, in Cash and Hoover, eds., *To Be an Indian*, 105; Lowawaima, "Oral Histories," 245–46.

33. La Flesche, *Middle Five*, 46, 121, for example; violence, Chap. 15. See also Coleman, "Credibility"; Sekaquaptewa, *Me and Mine*, 136–38: the "training" of a perennial runaway helped him outsmart the Japanese during World War II; Qoyawayma, *No Turning Back*, 27–28. Also, Robert A. Trennert, "Corporal Punishment and the Politics of Indian Reform," *History of Education Quarterly* 29 (Winter 1989): 595–617.

34. For complaints: Ernest Nelson and Thomas Clani, in Johnson, ed., *Stories of Traditional Navajo Life*, 233, 244; Winnie, *Sah-gan-de-ob*, 50. Positive comment: Shaw, *Pima Past*, 126; Stinson, in Cash and Hoover eds., *To Be an Indian*, 95. Also, Chris, *Apache Odyssey*, 83; La Flesche, *Middle Five*, 71; Qoyawayma, *No Turning back*, 63; W. Mh. Whiteman to commissioner of Indian Affairs, in ARCIA (1879), *House Executive Document* No. 1, part 5, 46 Congress, 2 session, serial 1910, 180.

35. See, for example, *The Carlisle Arrow* 12 (Nov. 19, 1915), ("A weekly newspaper printed . . . by the students"). Also, Trennert, *The Phoenix Indian School*, 127–33; Stewart, *A Voice in Her Tribe*, 30; Kabotie, *Hopi Indian Artist*, 27–29, 32–33; Bennett, *Kaibah*, 244–47; Alford, *Civilization*, 107; Winnie, *Sah-gan-de-ob*, esp. 55.

36. Daklugie et al., *Indeh*, 146–47. Football would not teach him survival skills. Betzinez also played American games, but in the early days played shinny, an Indian game, *I Fought with Geronimo*, 155–56. Pratt corroborates Daklugie's claim that the Carlisle team beat many of the best and Betzinez's claim that initially some Indians played traditional games, *Battlefield and Classroom*, 319, 316. The organized sports generally were Euro-American games, another example of the assimilationist thrust of Indian schools. See also Peter Mählmann, "Sport as a Weapon of Colonialism in Kenya: A Review of the Literature," *Transafrican Journal of History* 17 (1988): 172–85.

37. Pratt, *Battlefield and Classroom*, 317–18. On pupil initiative and the growth of sports at white American high schools, Tyack and Hansot, *Learning Together*, 193.

38. Kabotie, *Hopi Indian Artist*, 34; Yava, *Big Falling Snow*, 18; McCarthy, *Papago Traveller*, 40–41, 47, 49–52, 61–67; Institute for Government Research, *Indian Administration* (Meriam Report), 394–96.

39. Shaw, *Pima Past*, 127–28; Winnie, *Sah-gan-de-oh*, 53–55. Also, Institute for Government Research, *Indian Administration* (Meriam Report), 395, on the desire of girls at a major school for more "play space" for sports; for illustration of girls playing basketball, Trennert, *Phoenix Indian School*, 129.

40. Standing Bear, *My People the Sioux*, 147–49, 171–72. Pratt also noted the origin of the band, Training School for Youth, Carlisle Barracks, ARCIA (1880), *House Executive Document* No. 1, part 5, 46 session, 3 session, serial 1959, 302; Kabotie, *Hopi Indian Artist*, 32. Also Stewart, *A Voice in Her Tribe*, 30; Myrtle Begay, in Johnson, ed., *Stories of Traditional Navajo Life*, 65; Daklugie et al., *Indeh*, 144; Shaw, *Pima Past*, 134, illustration 182.

41. Qoyawayma, *No Turning Back*, 59–61.

42. La Flesche, *Middle Five*, 99–100. Cf. Standing Bear, *My People the Sioux*, 166–67.

43. Standing Bear, *My People the Sioux*, 146–47; Goodbird, *Goodbird the Indian*, 39–40. Also, Shaw, *Pima Past*, 129; Jim Whitewolf, *Life*, 92–93; Sekaquaptewa, *Me and Mine*, 102–103; Eastman, *Deep Woods*, 104; Mrs. Bob Martin, in Johnson, ed., *Stories of Traditional Navajo Life*, 131; Lindsey, "Memories," 183; Nathan Kakianak, *Eskimo Boyhood: An Autobiography in Psychosocial Perspective*, edited by Charles Hughes (Lexington: University of Kentucky Press, 1974), 61–70. Cf. Coe, *When the Grass Was Taller*, 287: Christmas "plays such an important part in childhood reminiscence."

44. Sekaquaptewa, *Me and Mine*, 117–18; Winnie, *Sah-gan-de-oh*, 2; Jim Whitewolf, *Life*, 91–92. Cf. D. W. Eaves, Report of School at Fort Lapwai: "the sexes, while carefully guarded, should not be separated, as the defining of a proper relation of the sexes is a most important branch of civilization," ARCIA (Washington, D.C.: Government Printing Office, 1889), 355.

45. Alford, *Civilization*, 101–103. A number of Indians married and lived "in model housekeeping cottages" at Hampton, Elaine Goodale Eastman, *Pratt*, 67. See also Charles Eastman, *Deep Woods*, 59, 73.

46. La Flesche, *Middle Five*, 3–4. On visits home, for example, 16–21, 123–29, 141–45; Thomas Clani, in Johnson, ed., *Stories of Traditional Navajo Life*, 244; Bennett, *Kaibah*, 223, 235. Also, Jim Whitewolf, *Life*, 93; pupil essays on vacations in Golden, *Red Moon Called Me*, 193–95.

47. Talayesva, *Sun Chief*, 100; ARCIA (1895), *House Document* No. 5, vol II, 54 Congress, 1 session, serial 3381, 188.

48. Standing Bear, *My People the Sioux*, 149–53, 167–70. McCarthy's uncle once visited him at Santa Fe Indian School, and stayed on as a baker, *Papago Traveller*, 45. See also Report of Superintendent of San Carlos School, with ARCIA (1896), *House Document* No. 5, vol. II, 54 Congress, 2 session, serial 3489: "Pupils do not visit their homes excepting in vacation times, but parents visit freely on Saturdays. . . ."; Woodruff, *Indian Oasis*, 56–61.

49. Shaw, *Pima Past*, 107–108. Also, Highwalking, *Narrative*, 10. By explaining the lesson in Cheyenne, her teacher uncle helped her learn more effectively.

50. Eastman, *Deep Woods*, 48.

51. Jim Whitewolf, *Life*, 90.

52. Grayson, *A Creek Warrior*, 42–43, 45; Clinton Rickard, *Fighting Tuscarora: The Autobiography of Chief Clinton Rickard*, edited by Barbara Graymont (Syracuse, N.Y.: Syracuse University Press, 1973), 8–9.

53. Sekaquaptewa, *Me and Mine*, 104–105, 106–107, 139–140.

54. Kabotie, *Hopi Indian Artist*, 11, 27–29, 65.

55. La Flesche, *Middle Five*, Chaps. 5, 15; on Pratt, see Chapter 8, in the present volume, and Coleman, "Credibility"; Zitkala-Sa, *American Indian Stories*, 66–67.

56. La Flesche, *Middle Five*, 146–47; Chris, *Apache Odyssey*, 89–90; Jim Whitewolf, *Life*, 97.

57. Mary McDaniel, in Earl Shorris, *The Death of the Great Spirit* (New York: Signet, 1971), 158; Betzinez, *I Fought with Geronimo*, 143. Alford did not mention black students at Hampton; perhaps he did not wish to acknowledge the racial segregation, see: Elaine Goodale Eastman, *Sister to the Sioux:* 19–20; Wilma King, "Multicultural Education at Hampton Institute—The Shawnees: a Case Study, 1900–1923," *Journal of Negro Education* 57 (1988): esp. 527. Cf. Abraham Makofsky, "Experience of Native Americans at a Black College: Indian Students at Hampton Institute, 1878–1923," *Journal of Ethnic Studies* 3 (1989): 140–42.

58. Standing Bear, *My People the Sioux*, 189; Talayesva, *Sun Chief*, 138: he referred to a discussion with the Keams Canyon agent.

59. Winnemucca Hopkins, *Life Among the Piutes*, 70. Cf. Canfield, *Sarah Winnemucca*, 30–31; Annie Lowry, *Karnee: A Paiute Narrative*, by Lalla Scott (Greenwich, Conn.: Fawcett, 1966), 66–67; Zitkala-Sa, *American Indian Stories*, 76–80. Cf. bitter experience of Qoyawayma in Newton, Kansas, *No Turning Back*, 101.

60. Kabotie, *Hopi Indian Artist*, 34; Ah-nen-la-de-ni, "An Indian Boy's Story," 1787.

61. Shaw, *Pima Past*, 141–42, 147.

62. For a study that demonstrates the complex, ambivalent, symbolic importance of the Indian boarding school in the memory of ex-pupils, see McBeth, *Ethnic Identity*; also Hyer, *One House*.

CHAPTER 6

Half-and-Half: The Curriculum

W ITHIN THE HIGHLY regimented framework of the school, learning was supposed to take place. And the curriculum at most of these government and missionary schools fell into the then-celebrated half-and-half pattern. Details varied from decade to decade and from school to school, but generally the pupils spent part of each day in the classroom, and part working at manual labor intended to prepare them for life outside the school. This chapter will first examine pupil responses to the academic part of the curriculum, beginning with the English language, then to the manual labor requirements, and finally to the religious proselytizing that permeated all activities at mission schools and to some extent at government schools.

I

Many tribal adults sent their children to school to learn English, and individual narrators claimed that, from observing student siblings, they became interested in the white man's language. Such linguistically ambitious children quickly discovered that most school learning was closed to them until they achieved a degree of proficiency in English. Although missionaries sometimes utilized tribal languages in their schools, especially to communicate religious "truths," the government decided by the 1880s that English should be the language of the schools. "There is not an Indian pupil whose tuition and maintenance is paid for by the United States Government," declared J. D. C. Atkins, commissioner of Indian Affairs in 1886, "who is permitted to study any other language than our own vernacular—the language of the greatest, most powerful, and enterprising nationalities beneath the sun." Even before this, however, government and missionary schools had often forbidden pupils the use of tribal languages. English was both a part of the curriculum and the tool through which all other "official" learning took place; further, it was a symbol of the whole enterprise of "uplift."[1] In multitribal schools, it became the lingua franca of the pupils.

"For me it was very hard," said Belle Highwalking (Northern Cheyenne). "No one spoke English and we couldn't understand the white people when they spoke to us." The rule against using tribal languages intensified the sense of frustration. The new student, wrote La Flesche, "was obliged to walk about like a little dummy until he had learned to express himself in English." Many probably fled because they never achieved proficiency in the medium of instruction; others spent endless imcomprehending hours each day in class (such students could gradually learn to perform many of the manual duties around the school). Of all who faced these problems, none was more isolated that Elsie Allen at the Covelo Boarding School in California, during the early twentieth century. She knew no English, learned almost none at the school, and found herself "unable to follow simple dressing and eating chores." At first only *one* other pupil spoke her dialect of Pomo—and the two rarely met. Thus Allen understood and spoke to no one for most of the year. "My stay at Covelo was not very fruitful because of the language barrier," she wrote, "and I often cried at night with homesickness." She bore no grudge, however. At the next school a "kind and patient" teacher helped her with English, which she later insisted on speaking to her own children.[2]

Even students desirous to learn found the new language difficult. At a local day school Anna Moore Shaw progressed faster when taught English by a fellow Pima through the Pima language. But after he left "it was hard for us to understand the strange sounds of the English language" spoken by the new American teacher. Ah-nen-la-de-ni (Mohawk) recalled that his day-school teacher taught only pronunciation and memory work. After a while the pupils could pronounce all the words in the Fifth and Sixth McGuffey readers, "but we did not know what the words meant." Although Mary Inkanish (Cheyenne, of part-white ancestry) felt that she had begun to speak English fluently at the Darlington mission school in Oklahoma, her poor pronunciation embarrassed her in front of more linguistically accomplished Cheyenne children: "*Doctor* always came out . . . *noctor*." Don Talayesva also remembered his embarrassment, sitting in a class with smaller boys at the Keams Canyon Boarding School. Within a few days he had begun to understand simple words, but soon "grew tired of school and thought of running away."[3]

Luther Standing Bear poignantly described how, at Carlisle, he had initially hoped that merely by sleeping in a white man's house he would awake speaking English. But the Dakota soon realized that he "must learn one word at a time." Because Jason Betzinez was in his late twenties when he began at Carlisle, this Apache also had language difficulties. But he credited much of his final achievement to the effort of teachers, who "patiently went over with me again and again the words I was trying to say." Perhaps the most eloquent cry of anguish came from Charles Eastman, when remembering how the mere recitation of English words caused such problems. "For a whole week we youthful warriors were held up and harrassed with words of three letters, like raspberry bushes in the path, they tore, bled, and sweated us—those little words rat, cat, and so forth—until not a semblance of our native dignity and self respect was left." He remained diffident about using the language for some time, developing fluency, he believed, but not accuracy.[4]

Even resentful pupils made progress. "Within a year I was able to express myself somewhat in broken English," wrote the ever-bitter Zitkala-Sa. "As soon as I comprehended part of what was said and done, a mysterious spirit of revenge possessed me." Almost as bitter against "white eyes," Asa Daklugie nevertheless attributed much of his progress to a dedicated teacher. "Learning English wasn't too bad," wrote the Apache. "There was a necessity for memorizing everything because we could neither read nor write. Before the winter was over I was learning to read." His teacher was "very patient and kind . . . and she was not bossy like most white ladies are. She seemed to know without being told *that I wanted desperately to be able to read* [emphasis added] and she helped me." Ironically, only through reading did he learn the fate of his own people, by then sent to Florida after Geronimo's surrender in 1886. Reading also got him into trouble: using a dictionary, Daklugie took the first meaning of the word "ferment," "to work," and wrote the sentence, "I will not ferment in the house," which led to a confrontation with his teacher and to the even more dramatic one with Captain Pratt, described below.[5]

The learning of English could thus became both a challenge and pleasure. Future Commissioner of Indian Affairs Ely S. Parker (Seneca) remembered his humiliation at being unable to understand fully some jokes made at his expense by English officers he met in Canada; a desire for "personal gratification" motivated him to return to the mission school. Benefiting from the help of Brush, his more senior friend, La Flesche thrilled as he advanced in the language, for personal ambition, learned from childhood in status-conscious tribes, powerfully motivated many of these narrators. "I felt proud of his [Brush's] praise and worked all the harder," the Omaha wrote. "We had gone through the alphabet swimmingly. . . . When I was able to read short sentences, I felt sure that I should soon take my place among the advanced pupils." At night school Refugio Savala (Yaqui) also threw himself into the enterprise. "I started writing and became a word hunter in English and Spanish," he recalled in a memorable passage. "The dictionary was my hunting ground." And when Irene Stewart moved to a school *without* a rule against speaking Indian languages, she voluntarily continued to use English."[6]

Jim Whitewolf (Kiowa Apache) could not remember how long he had been at school before teachers took away his playing bricks and insisted he learn English. But his vivid account highlights a number of significant factors that influenced learning: the help of senior pupils; the "object method" used to teach the language; and, especially, the enthusiastic initiative of the pupil himself. Logan, an older student appointed to help the newcomer, explained that Whitewolf should repeat the words used by the teacher as she pointed to objects—some of the words he knew because Logan had already taught them to him. After class, moreover, he began to *apply* what he had learned: "When we went to play I would see real birds and call out 'bird.'"[7]

II

As they struggled with English, pupils also faced a whole new organization of knowledge, which fragmented the world into discrete "subjects," each to be grappled with for a specific number of minutes and then dropped on the hour for a new subject.

Younger pupils encountered a fairly basic curriculum: "they taught us the ABCs and 1, 2, 3 and all that," Frank Mitchell (Navajo) recalled somewhat facetiously of his first year at Fort Defiance Boarding School. "As soon as you got up to ten you knew you were qualified as educated. We never had tests or grades. We never knew who was on top of anyone else." Had Mitchell stayed beyond a few years, his curriculum would have become more demanding, as many government and missionary schools by then taught a variety of academic subjects, such as English, arithmetic, algebra, geometry, history, geography, and biology.[8]

In the late 1850s at Asbury Manual Labor School, run by the South Carolina Methodist Conference, G. W. Grayson (Creek) "struggled through long division to the unraveling of the binominal theorem, the digging out of Latin roots and kindred work." Presbyterian missionary correspondence and Francis La Flesche's memory both testify to the variety of academic subjects taught at the Presbyterian boarding school on the Omaha reservation—and at other BFM missions—and to the use of the famous McGuffey series of readers with their increasingly demanding English. At this school students could develop an acute sense of just "who was on top" of the pupil hierarchy. "What do they know," La Flesche scathingly asked of his own friends. "They're all way back in the Second Reader, and you [Brush] are in the Fifth, and I am in the third."9 Many narrators easily accepted the grading of students according to academic achievement, which mirrored the competitive ethos in their tribes.

The content of the new knowledge could also be intensely motivating. After four years at mission and government day schools, Thomas Alford (Shawnee) believed he had "mastered the first four rules of arithmetic to the complete satisfaction of my teachers," and had "a smattering knowledge of geography, physiology, grammar, and had taken a peep into the fascinating study of natural philosophy and other branches of higher learning and science." But more important, both for himself and for those who would teach him at Hampton Institute:

> I had only glimpsed the wonders of education. I had only tasted the joy of knowing things, and had a consuming thirst for more knowledge.10

If, during the decades covered by this study, the government and mission schools rarely achieved a full high-school curriculum, some did offer an impressive academic curriculum. This intellectually stimulated ambitious students like Alford, Grayson, La Flesche, Eastman, Winnie, Shaw, Sekaquaptewa, and others, and allowed them to build what they considered to be successful lives.

Yet even enthusiastic students remembered their experiences with various degrees of ambivalence. La Flesche vividly conveyed the boredom of the classroom, the endless rote learning, and the tiredness that crept over not only pupils but the *teacher* too. During one recitation a girl read to the class

> in a tone that made it difficult to resist the drowsiness that attacked everyone in the room. She came to a hard word, and, according to our custom, she spelled it. Gray-beard, who was sitting with eyes shut, pronounced it for her with a suppressed yawn.

After his experiences at Carlisle, Standing Bear became a teacher for a period. He boasted how, in contrast to another group of students, his own students could not merely repeat English words, but could *understand* them—a criticism of the white teachers who taught the other pupils "like a bunch of parrots." Shaw (Pima) actually enjoyed memory work, perhaps because of the religious subject matter; but she found arithmetic "a dull subject."11

The narrators do not provide detailed insight into how they responded to subjects such as arithmetic or history. When important visitors arrived at La Flesche's school, the students faced a barrage of purely factual questions such as "Who discovered America?" Perhaps La Flesche was having a little joke at the expense of the school and of the reader: this question was asked of a dull student named Abraham Lincoln, who haltingly answered "George Washington." An account by the ten-year-old Brush of events leading to the American Revolution suggest that after a few years at the school the boys had picked up a certain amount of American mythology. After the Boston Tea Party, according to Brush,

> the old king sat still for a long time; then said to his soldiers, you go and fight those 'Mericans, and they did fight, and had the Rev'lution. That war lasted eight years, and the king's soldiers got licked. Then the 'Mericans made General George Washington their President because he couldn't tell a lie.

The language sounds contrived, perhaps, but in both his preface and in correspondence La Flesche insisted that he carefully reproduced the kinds of language (English and Omaha in English translation) spoken by the children at school. Further, the simple, cliché account of the American Revolution is hardly different from what white contemporaries of that age would have given.[12]

Obviously most of the exchange of information, as in schoolrooms elsewhere, was one-way. But Alford suggested that a teacher at Hampton may momentarily have opened himself to knowledge brought by a student. During a class in natural history, the Shawnee told the teacher of a "freak of nature" he and his father had witnessed years earlier: "A huge rattlesnake . . . with dried leaves protruding from every scale! It went slowly towards a ledge of rock and disappeared from sight with its load of leaves' . . ." Rather than dismiss the story as savage nonsense, the teacher appears to have thought about it and remarked that, being a cold-blooded creature, the rattler built a leaf nest as a hiding place, and not for warmth.[13]

Few things shocked young Indians more than the information received in geography class: "when the teacher placed before us a painted globe," wrote Eastman,

> and said that our world was [round] like that—that upon such a thing our forefathers had roamed and hunted for untold ages, as it whirled and danced around the sun in space—I felt that my foothold was deserting me.

All my savage training and philosophy was in the air, if these things were true.

Edward Goodbird endured a similar ordeal, and he too claimed that the revelation of the Copernican theory caused him to doubt his tribal learning. More than that, the new knowledge proved to him that he had to choose between Hidatsa and white ways. It also gave Goodbird a sense of superiority over supposedly more ignorant kin. An uncle insisted that the earth was flat, but this "I would in no wise admit, and I came home daily with new proof that the earth was round." Luther Standing Bear claimed that he and his schoolmates were equally shocked until a teacher accurately predicted an eclipse.[14]

It was also in geography class that one of the most joyous discoveries took place. The bitter Asa Daklugie began his reminiscence of the Carlisle experience with ominous words: "desperate to the extent that we [he and his future wife] did not care whether we lived or died, we were thrust into a vicious and hostile world that we both hated and feared." As should already be clear, his actual responses to Carlisle were far more ambivalent. And, when introduced to a geography book, they were overwhelmingly positive. One day the teacher who had helped him learn English

> opened a big book to show me Arizona, and for the first time in my life I saw a map. I was fascinated. When she showed me mountains and rivers I could tell their names in my language. I knew the Spanish for some of them and a few in English. She let me take that geography book to the dormitory and Frank Mangus and I almost wore it out.[15]

At moments such as this, a whole new way of looking at the world suddenly opened up before a young Indian.

Although in retrospect Standing Bear wondered why tribal perspectives had no place in the academic curriculum, nowhere in these accounts did an Indian claim that *as a pupil* he or she objected. They accepted without question the entirely Euro-American curriculum, with its deliberate rejection of "savage" knowledge. When Don Talayesva became homesick to the point of tears at the Keams Canyon Boarding School, the older student explained to him the rationale for being there: "to learn the white people's way of life."[16] If Hopis lived among Navajos, they would not expect to be taught Hopi values; why, then, would they expect to be taught Hopi values at a white school? Indeed, to the extent that Indian adults exercised choice, they sent their children to school to learn *white* ways; they themselves would teach the old ways. In depicting the easy acceptance by pupils of the totally foreign curriculum, the adult narrators have credibly reentered the mind of the Indian child encountering the strange new knowledge of the white tribe.

Although few of even the gifted achieved as much academic success in the white world as did Dr. Charles A. Eastman, his memory of struggle and acceptance applies to the developing experiences of many, especially the most talented and adaptive. Impelled by mixed and changing motivations, they moved from incomprehension, to grudging or anxious acceptance of English and the new learning, to sometimes enthusiastic acceptance of the intellectual challenge—without necessarily denying all of their own traditions. "I was now a stranger in a strange country," Eastman recalled of himself at eighteen, after three years of schooling, "and deep into a strange life from which I could not retreat." Despite some "nerve-trying moments," he soon recovered his balance. "I absorbed knowledge through every pore. The more I got, the larger my capacity grew, and my apetite increased in proportion." [17]

III

These narrators also responded in diverse and often changing ways to the second part of the school curriculum, the manual labor element. Almost every narrator mentioned his or her duties in this area, and government and missionaries were proud to boast of the supposed wisdom of the half-and-half system. Not only would manual labor, including "outings" with white families, help teach Indian boys farming, blacksmithing, or tinsmithing, and girls the domestic arts. But such things, along with military discipline, would develop "civilized habits," Western concepts of time, and a Christian respect for work. Occasionally whites admitted or implied another benefit of the system (for the school authorities), one later criticized by the Meriam Report: the widespread use of pupils in farming and other enterprises contributed massively toward the financial support of many schools. [18]

By sixth grade, recalled Irene Stewart, "[I] was a well-trained worker." Although generally positive about her schooling, the Navajo left a harsh condemnation of the system at Fort Defiance, noting how it could turn pupils against the school:

I have never forgotten how the steam in the laundry made me sick; how standing and ironing for hours made my legs ache late into the night. By

Above The Presbyterian boarding school on the Omaha reservation in northeastern Nebraska, which opened in 1858. Here Francis La Flesche began his schooling in the early 1860s.
Nebraska State Historical Society

Left Francis La Flesche as a young man of about twenty-two in 1879, with his sister Susette La Flesche *Nebraska State Historical Society*

Above First Indian students (girls) of Carlisle Indian School, on arrival in October 1879 *J. N. Choate, photographer/Cumberland County Historical Society, Carlisle, Pennsylvania*

Right Capt. Richard Henry Pratt, legendary founder and superintendent of the Carlisle Indian Industrial School, Pennsylvania, the first government off-reservation boarding school, ca. 1898 *Cumberland County Historical Society, Carlisle, Pennsylvania*

Left Charles A. Eastman (Ohiyesa), Santee Sioux, ca. 1887 *Dartmouth College Library*

Above left Francis La Flesche ca. 1908 *Nebraska State Historical Society*

Above First Indian students (boys) of Carlisle Indian School, on arrival in October 1879. Luther Standing Bear (Brulé Sioux) is in this group, possibly sixth full figure from the right, sitting, with white stripes on trousers. *J. N. Choate, photographer/Cumberland County Historical Society, Carlisle, Pennsylvania*

Right Luther Standing Bear (at back, center) and family *Cumberland County Historical Society, Carlisle, Pennsylvania*

Carlisle Indian School band   *Cumberland County Historical Society, Carlisle, Pennsylvania*

Tinner's apprentices, Carlisle Indian School   *J. N. Choate, photographer/Minnesota Historical Society*

Left Jasper Kanseah (left) at Carlisle Indian School, with fellow Apache boys Alfred Kateh (standing) and Joseph Ezhuna *Cumberland County Historical Society, Carlisle, Pennsylvania*

Apache group at Carlisle Indian School in 1891: Jason Betzinez is in the back row, fifth from the right; Asa Daklugie is sixth from the right. The small boy sitting at the front is James Kaywaykla; sitting above him to the left is Ramona Chihuahua, future wife of Daklugie. *Cumberland County Historical Society, Carlisle, Pennsylvania*

Geronimo (third from the right, front) and Apaches after surrender in 1886; the boy at the top left is Jasper Kanseah. *National Anthropological Archives, Smithsonian Institution, Washington, D. C.*

Left Thomas J. Morgan (second row, fifth from left), Commissioner of Indian Affairs (1889-1893), with the faculty of the Carlisle Indian School, ca. 1891; Captain Pratt is on Morgan's left. *Cumberland County Historical Society, Carlisle, Pennsylvania*

Below Art class of Miss Elizabeth Forster at Carlisle Indian School *Cumberland County Historical Society, Carlisle, Pennsylvania*

Bottom left Class at Carlisle Indian School, 1903   *Cumberland County Historical Society, Carlisle, Pennsylvania*

G. W. Grayson, principal chief of the Creek Nation (1917-1920) *Western History Collections, University of Oklahoma Library*

Above Pupils at Carlisle Indian School, 1884 *Cumberland County Historical Society, Carlisle, Pennsylvania*

Right Chilocco Indian School in Oklahoma *Western History Collections, University of Oklahoma Library*

Above Edward Goodbird (Hidatsa) with
parents, Son of Star and Buffalo Bird
Woman, in 1906 *Gilbert Wilson, photographer/Minnesota Historical Society*

Left Thomas Wildcat Alford (center), as
a member of a Shawnee delegation to
Washington *Hampton University's
Archival and Museum Collection, Hampton
University, Hampton, Virginia*

Above left Anna Bender, first Chippewa
(Ojibway) woman graduate of Hampton
Institute in 1906 *Hampton University's
Archival and Museum Collection, Hampton
University, Hampton, Virginia*

Helen Sekaquaptewa (Hopi) in 1980 *Helga Teiwes, photographer/Arizona State Museum, University of Arizona*

Indian students gardening at Santee Normal Training School, Nebraska, ca. 1885
Minnesota Historical Society

evening I was too tired to play and just fell asleep wherever I sat down. I think this was why the boys and girls ran away from school; why some became ill; why it was so hard to learn. We were too tired to study.[19]

Belle Highwalking (Northern Cheyenne) "gradually got used to" such labor. And Kay Bennett (Navajo) remembered how at Toadlena Boarding School Navajo pupils accepted having to tidy their rooms before inspection, but resented cleaning the washroom, showers, and toilet. All received this chore periodically, but those who broke a rule got it as an extra duty, for physical labor could also be used as punishment. At Sherman Institute, girls especially disliked scrubbing the dining hall on their knees. Yet Qoyawayma claimed that the Hopi children did not mind peeling potatoes—which they liked eating raw—and she enjoyed learning about farming and about the cultivation of vegetables and fruits. Again, there was carryover from traditonal life: the girls "were following a set pattern," wrote Qoyawayma, "much as they had done on the Mesas." Moreover, a positive new element had been added: "their field of knowledge was gradually expanding."[20]

Similarly, Luther Standing Bear discriminated between different kinds of physical labor. Again and again he requested that Captain Pratt reassign him from tinsmithing, a job he felt would be useless on the reservation and which took excessive time from his studies. Pratt refused, and the Dakota's decision to leave Carlisle after five years may in part have been a result of this. Yet Standing Bear enjoyed his "outing" at Wanamakers of Philadelphia, where he worked in a number of departments and lived in the city. When an Indian companion quit the job, Standing Bear "worked all the harder, just let them know that not all Indians were quitters."[21]

A number of other students noted that manual labor duties delayed their academic progress. The ambivalence of Betzinez emerged in his account of "outings." The Apache worked for a Quaker farm family, "warm-hearted people, who tried numerous times to help me improve myself." But after three summers of such labor, he decided to stay at Carlisle: "I realized that my education as well as my efforts to learn English were being retarded by being absent so long from the school." During the next summer he spent more time in the classroom, but he had to continue blacksmithing, carpentry, plumbing, and general construction work. A carriage he made won a prize in the annual school exhibit—evidence that a pupil could put effort into the work forced upon him at school.[22]

Other narrators reported with even less complaint how the manual labor demands interfered with their studies. Ah-nen-la-de-ni remembered how at his government school there were "shoemakers, black-smiths, tinsmiths, farmers, printers, all sorts of mechanics among us." He spent over two years at the tailoring trade and "outed" with farmers. Later he transferred part-time to a local public school and felt he would have graduated quicker except for his many industrial duties at the Lincoln Institute. And Helen Sekaquaptewa merely noted in passing how the half-and-half requirements at Phoenix Indian School actually prevented her from graduating.[23]

Such lack of resentment was in part due to the fact that young Indians sometimes received payment for their labor. Sekaquaptewa took charge of the school laundry one summer (about 1912), at a salary of $15 a month. "What I earned myself was the only money I ever had," she wrote, conveying the thrill which many narrators experienced at the sudden possession of money, although most of it went immediately into a school bank. She established a number of financially profitable "outing" and houseworking arrangements while she was a pupil at the Phoenix school. "I had to earn all of my spending money, and my hands were never still," she wrote. "I was always doing embroidery or crochet or tatting, making things to sell." Indeed her account reads like a success story of the Protestant work ethic—or a blending of it and the equally demanding Hopi work ethic. "In the three years that I was in Phoenix," she wrote, "I never bought candy or pop but bought thread to make things so I could earn more."[24]

Although members of one of the least acculturated Indian peoples in the early twentieth century, other Hopis were similarly motivated. Polingaysi claimed that she "had her father's desire to learn and to earn money." When teachers agreed to pay her for housework, "she was overwhelmed with happiness." Even the small sums earned gave such pupils a feeling of recompense and of power—if only the power to buy candy from the school canteen or, in the case of Don Talayesva, a second-hand pistol, for he "thought a man with a gun in his holster looked important." A payment of $2 per day made "outing" labor in the Colorado beet fields more bearable for James McCarthy (Papago). And Lucille Winnie (Iroquois) worked on Saturday mornings for a teacher at Haskell. "The dollar she paid me was a small fortune," wrote Winnie, "and I would make it stretch to at least four trips to The Shack [an off-campus eating place]."[25]

Moreover, pupils experienced a special sense of pride at being given responsibility—in their own societies they would also have been re-warded with more demanding tasks as they grew older; cultural influences reinforced personal motivations. Standing Bear thrilled to every such "burden" placed upon him at school, from the Wanamaker challenge, to being chosen to recruit for the school on his reservation. More than the salary motivated Sekaquaptewa. At Keams Canyon the school authorities made a policy of placing particular pupils in positions of trust: "The teachers and matrons gave us responsibility and depended upon us as we grew older." She proudly noted that, when working for the principal's wife at Phoenix, "she let me run the whole house when she saw I could do it." James McCarthy delighted in picking up jobs, even when not all of them paid. Indeed he stressed that he was too busy to feel homesick, and in his account there is no sense of exploitation: "They had me doing everything around there—stage driver, mail carrier, night watchman, fireman, milker, and captain of the baseball team. I did not mind it."[26]

But, again, there was a further form of personal motivation influencing many narrators: fear. Jim Whitewolf (Kiowa Apache) experienced almost every job in his school, and even enjoyed working in the employees' building—or at least enjoyed the good food the pupils got there. But he succinctly expressed a major reason for acceptance of the work regimen. "I didn't like the jobs they gave me," he wrote. "But I knew that if I did them all right they wouldn't bother me. But if I didn't they might whip me."[27]

IV

Christian proselytization suffused the educational effort during these decades. Missionaries, of course, attempted to indoctrinate denominational creeds into young Indians. But even as the government edged the mission societies to the margin, its teachers also sought to imbue pupils with some form of Christianity. For most secular as well as missionary educators, "civilization" was inconceivable unless grounded in Christian—especially Protestant—values.

As might be expected, the young Zitkala-Sa bitterly rejected Christianity. Guilt about deserting her mother, bitterness over what she saw as prejudice against Indians, a fierce ambition to gain the respect of the whites she loathed—all fused to produce an autobiography of intense anguish, and all colored her responses to Christianity. Once she scratched out the eyes of a devil depicted in a religious book. If at that time she did not regard this as a rejection of Christianity, her teachers would have seen such defacement of a holy book as an act of rebellion. Later, during a tension-filled visit home, her mother tried to comfort her by offering the only book in the house, an Indian Bible, the gift of a missionary. "I took it from her hand, for her sake," wrote Zitkala-Sa, "but my enraged spirit felt more like burning the book, which afforded me no help, and was a perfect delusion to my mother."[28]

Others paid little serious attention to the proselytizing. At the Carlisle school, freedom of religion meant that all students "had permission to choose" a Christian denomination, according to Standing Bear, and his memory is confirmed by Captain Pratt in his 1882 annual report. The Lakota became an Episcopalian, and later an assistant to a missionary on the reservation; but Christianity received little attention in his autobiography, and he appears to have neither resented nor enthused over his new denominational allegiance.[29]

Frank Mitchell remembered the ineffectiveness of missionaries who preached to the Navajo children in English. "They talked about God and most of us did not understand it. So I guess they were just talking to themselves." One missionary did make an effort to begin his address in Navajo; but his pronunciation was incorrect, so while he thought he addressed them as "my dear children," he in fact called them "abalone shells." Don Talayesva was only mildly disappointed when he prayed to the Christian God for oranges and candy, and received nothing. Later, at riverside government school in California he unwittingly joined the YMCA, gave at least one sermon at a meeting, and won a prize for learning the names of the books of the Bible. Yet Christianity appears to have little affected him, either mentally or in terms of behavior. Indeed it was a deeply frightening dream-vision, brought on when he talked badly of a Hopi "two-heart" (a witch), which decided him to return permanently to Hopiland. And Ida Damon (Navajo) just "left Christianity at school. I didn't take it too serious."[30]

With a flash of resentment quite out of character in an otherwise forgiving autobiography, Sekaquaptewa complained that at a government school in the early twentieth century pupils had to attend Sunday School, along with day and evening services:

> I couldn't understand a thing [the preacher] talked about, but had to sit and listen to a long sermon. I hated them and felt like crying. If I nodded my head going to sleep, a teacher would poke me and tell me to be good.

Every time the preacher reached an oratorical climax, pupils thought he would at last finish but he would start all over again. The Hopi recalled dismissively how the "different sects were always urging and bribing us with little presents to join their church. It didn't appeal to me and I didn't join any of them."[31]

Other narrators mentioned the mixed pleasure and confusion of listening to the narrative traditions of Christianity. Sanapia, the Comanche, "really did enjoy" the mission school she briefly attended in Oklahoma, and the teachers "were really nice people." But this did not make the Bible stories any easier to understand or accept at face value:

> they question [sic] us out of the bible to see if we really read it. . . . When she tells us how Jesus was born, we just laugh and act silly and our matron would say, "Don't laugh." Then we ask her, "Did you see the baby?" You know, things like that. . . . All the time we thought it was silly for them not to go and see the baby when it was born.

Mary Little Bear Inkanish (Cheyenne) had never seen lions, so she did not know why Daniel was afraid of them. She thought that Judith, who cut off a man's head, "'was a real mean woman . . . as mean as a Sioux'"—a comment which suggests how Indian children would begin to interpret Old Testament stories in terms of their own experience.[32]

Some narrators did open to the new religion. Although an adult when sent to Carlisle, Jason Betzinez believed that the most powerful influence on his life was his "introduction to the teachings of Christianity." He felt no sense of resentment that he had been required to attend church, and also joined the YMCA. Although he provided few details, the Apache left the reader in no doubt as to the importance of his conversion. "This influence became stronger and stronger as I came to understand English better. It changed my whole life." Indeed his autobiography is an example of what H. David Brumble calls the "Carlisle made me" narrative.[33]

Thomas Alford's account might be termed a "Hampton made me" narrative. He too embraced Christianity, but not without a powerful struggle between different truths and clashing loyalties to kin, culture, teachers, and peers.

"Hampton was not a sectarian school," he wrote, "yet there was a strong moral and religious influence ever working among the students." He enjoyed the study of the Bible and found many compatibilities between Christianity and Shawnee beliefs. Although his tribal elders had encouraged him to take up the learning of the whites, but not their religion, influences mounted upon him to convert. "Under the continual pressure and interest of my friends and teachers, this question of religion became a paramount issue in my mind," and he "became conscious of a deep soul hunger to know the truth." A conversion experience followed:

> Then came the conviction of truth, the dawn of knowledge, when I knew deep in my soul that Jesus Christ was my savior. . . .
>
> This struggle went on continually. There was no rest from these thoughts and no quieting of the insistent voice that was ever calling in my heart, calling me to the feet of Jesus. In the end that voice won, and I was happy in the love of God, although very well I knew that my hope of earthly glory was over—my dream had been in vain. I could work for people, I might even teach them the truth about Christianity, but they never would accord me the honor and respect they gave to their chief. Time has proven this true.

The experience produced a powerful sense of release—and also a strongly ambivalent reaction as Alford contemplated his future among the Shawnees. Neither in his or other accounts, however, is there any hint of guilt about previous life; tribal cultures did not instill such a sense of personal "sin." And once the moment passed, Alford does not seem to have anguished much about the new faith. "The question of religion being settled to my satisfaction, and to that of my teachers and friends," he wrote, "I was able to concentrate on my studies."[34] Despite the obviously Christian form of the "rebirth," Alford's reversion to everyday affairs suggests a strongly surviving Indian sense that the goal of spiritual help was to make easier the way of this world, rather than to achieve salvation in the next.

V

Although they do not deny the wholehearted acceptance by individual Indians of Christian spiritual beliefs, scholars have also noted the often mixed and pragmatic motives for conversion. At times of cultural and personal stress, some tribal men and women came to believe that Christianity could serve personal and ethnic needs, just as did their own instrumental religions.[35] Young pupils may not have accepted aspects of the new faith for quite the same reasons as did their adult kin. But these narrators also had mixed motives for becoming interested in Christianity.

The influence of kin was often important: Anna Moore Shaw's Pima family was already attending church when she began school. Further, the careful distinctions impressed upon Alford were unusual. Tribal children sent to school by adults were accustomed to seeing all life holistically, and generally considered Christianity an inextricable part of the new way to be learned. As Alford showed, peers too influenced individuals. Brush, La Flesche's friend, preached his understanding of Christianity to schoolmates. Brush's own motivations were highly mixed, however, and would not have completely pleased the missionaries: he wanted to be a preacher and wear a black coat and "a pair of boots that squeaks and reaches to my knees. . . ."[36]

The short account in Edward Goodbird's autobiography indicates how many-sided were the factors for one narrator. The Hidatsa strongly respected his teacher—as a pupil he never swore, he claimed, "because Mr. Hall told me it was wrong." Goodbird also enjoyed Bible stories. And he suggests the importance of what we might call institutional factors in conversion: the sense of habit and identification brought about by being a member of a particular institution. "As I grew older and began to read books," he wrote, "I thought of myself as a Christian, but more because I went to the mission school, than because I thought of Jesus as my savior." There were also kin influences: a father sympathetic to the new way, and a cousin who wrote encouraging Goodbird to become a Christian. Further, although the Copernican theory shocked him into a claim that white and Hidatsa world views were exclusive, he also saw possible similarities in tribal and Christian beliefs. Once when the missionary teacher told the class that he "had seen the light," Goodbird thought the man was referring to a vision. He never quite rejected all of Hidatsa belief, and often lived a heavily traditional life outside the classroom, yet Goodbird came to accept Christianity as a true faith, one to which he was drawn for a complex mixture of reasons.[37]

Other Indians also saw compatibilities between tribal and Christian beliefs, which allowed them to accept more easily some elements of white culture. When Jim Whitewolf heard a Catholic priest preach, the boy thought that "[t]he only thing he was doing that I knew was good was the praying because we had always had such praying in the Indian way." Don Talayesva's hope for material answers to his prayers also indicates how young Indians could see the Christian God as yet another spirit being to be propitiated through ritual. Tribal prophecies that allowed them to perceive Americans as long-awaited white "brothers," who would return from the East, also facilitated conversion for some Hopis.[38]

Many narrators thus adopted a *syncretic* understanding of tribal and Euro-American beliefs, first at school and then in later life. Moreover, since Indian religious values were intertwined with other areas of life, such religious syncretism in fact constituted a broader pattern of cultural fusion.

At the Presbyterian school, Francis La Flesche resented boring sermons, but he enjoyed Bible stories, especially when Brush read them out to him and made them seem like traditonal stories. He also hinted that Omaha values helped him better understand Christianity: a lecture from his father on the need for generosity later moved him to think about the meaning of a Christian prayer, which the pupils "had said a hundred times before." 39

Pupils at the Omaha mission continually blended two cultures. In regular contact with their villages, they sometimes left school for the yearly tribal buffalo hunt. La Flesche himself attended tribal dances while a pupil, and actually attempted to flee school for the annual hunt. At night pupils enjoyed tribal myths, occasionally interrupted by Graybeard. Having accepted white stories by day, they found no obvious cultural conflict in enjoying Omaha stories at night, especially as they saw many compatible ideas. After one such session Brush interjected, "'That's just like the Bible story of Adam and Eve,'" and attempted to lecture them on the importance of attention in the schoolroom and chapel. Another boy ventured that the devil was "like some of our big medicine men," in that he could change his form into that of an animal. La Flesche conveyed how the boys had absorbed, compared, and easily blended the two traditions. Their openness to new ideas was a product of Omaha practicality and of the examples given by many of their acculturating families. Culture, kin, and personal flexibility allowed them to syncretize both traditions. 40

Almost half a century later at the Albuquerque Indian School, the Mescalero Apache companions of Chris also told traditional stories at night in the dormitories. "Even when we were in school, we used to think about our own people and our own ways," he recalled. "Someone in the dormitory would start telling a Coyote story. While it was being told, everyone would be quiet. Then, at the end of the story all would break out laughing." On other occasions groups stole out of this dormitory too, and went back to camp to listen to the old men telling stories, then returned to the school. Chris also described visions that took place at school. Thus young Apaches remained heavily committed to their home culture, no matter how carefully the school attempted to quarantine them. 41

Blending or casually compartmentalizing different traditions was not always so easy. No matter how accustomed she became to the Fort Defiance school, Irene Stewart retained her Navajo fear of *chindi* (spirits of the dead) and would not go near the hospital: "I had been told that lots of people died there, and that there must be a lot of children-ghosts." At church John Rogers had learned much that was different from Chippewa (Ojibway) beliefs: "It was very confusing to me and I did not try to straighten it out." On returning to school after a period at home, he noted that he was learning many things he would never have been taught by his own people:

> But I knew *then* [emphasis added], as I have since, that no amount of such learning that came to me in these schools would keep me from loving the things of nature. . . . But now I must do as the white man said, and I did not rebel. So schooling went on as usual.[42]

Vine Deloria Sr., an Episcopal minister, eloquently expressed similar cultural tensions, but felt he needed both traditions. At fourteen he entered a military school. "By this age, I must have absorbed a [Lakota] culture that was never going to leave me," he wrote. "I am a good actor in seeming to be perfectly at home in American society. There is constantly a slight strain in my associations with white people. From time to time, I have to go off by myself and relive that early culture to get refueled, so to speak, for refreshment, recalling the ways of the Standing Rock people sixty years ago." Howard Whitewolf, a Comanche—not to be confused with Jim Whitewolf, the Kiowa Apache—described how he gave up white clothing upon return to his people after three years at Carlisle: "Even though I had been trained at school, my mind was still 'wild,' and I thought the Indian way better." In his case the tension temporarily resolved itself in favor of the old ways, until he later underwent a Christian conversion—but still strongly advocated Indian self-reliance.[43]

The adaptive, syncretic responses of many of these narrators indicates the degree to which the school succeeded in changing them. But it had failed in its goal of total transformation. Even the most anxiously "progressive" of the Christian Indians, such as Alford, Betzinez, Goodbird, and Shaw, retained elements of traditional culture well into adulthood. For Rogers and Qoyawayma the attempt to blend old and new ways led to continual tension or anguish. For many the effort was ultimately less difficult than might have been expected. Unlike their culturally *exclusive* teachers, these Indians sprang from culturally *inclusive* tribes, and many succeeded in achieving personally satisfying blends of tribal and white cultural traditions.

VI

In these last two chapters we have seen how, due to complex motivational influences, Indian pupils responded in strikingly diverse and often ambivalent ways to the institutional and curricular sides of the school and the the staff. Responses also changed. While Zitkala-Sa's trail was from joy to shock to continual misery, she obviously adjusted enough to master the academic curriculum and become a major voice in American Indian reform. The experience of Jason Betzinez was in part the reverse: from resentment and shock at compulsory attendance to acceptance of much, though not all, of the Carlisle program to joyful conversion to Christianity. Fellow Apache Asa Daklugie also began his school experience in fear and resentment; yet he adjusted to Carlisle and even managed—despite himself—to enjoy some of his school experience. Ironically, Lucille Winnie's relative sophistication in white ways made her initial adjustment to Haskell more difficult.

Despite the shocks, they got used to it. Indeed narrator after narrator used just such a phrase to indicate his or her adjustment, sometimes reluctant, sometimes enthusiastic. And significantly perhaps two-thirds willingly continued at more schools. "We caught onto it," were the words used by Sanapia (Comanche). Max Henley (Navajo) was happy to begin school, and "pretty soon . . . got used to the place." Another Navajo began less enthusiastically, but arrived at a similar point: "After one year and a half, that much time, we kind of forgot we were lonesome. We can get along better then." And Fred Kabotie (Hopi) remembered that "[o]nce we settled into the routine, classes and military life weren't so bad. . . ." Few of these Indian boys and girls adjusted more easily than the once-reluctant Apache "volunteered" for Carlisle by Captain Pratt. "I suppose that some of the young Indians, who had had little discipline, fretted under this military discipline," wrote Jason Betzinez,

> But we conformed. I am happy to say that for my own part I took to this regulated life quite naturally. From the outset I made up my mind to be a true young man, to obey the rules, and to try to please the warmhearted man who had brought us here. This was my great good fortune, to have determined to take full advantage of this opportunity to make something of myself, to lift myself to a more useful life than the old pitiful existence to which I had been born.

Betzinez thus scornfully minimized the effects of tribal education on his willingness to adjust to new forms of discipline and knowledge at Carlisle. His adjustment, also a product of his own personality and resolve, was nonetheless impressive.[44]

One motivational factor only touched so far, was of major importance both in multiplying the suffering of new arrivals, or in helping them adjust to the school: the peer group. Perhaps nothing was as important to pupils as other pupils.

Notes

1. ARCIA (Washington, D.C.: Government Printing Office, 1886), xxiii. See also Francis Paul Prucha, *American Indian Policy in Crisis: Christian Reformers and the Indian, 1865–1900* (Norman: University of Oklahoma Press, 1976), 283–85. The government reluctantly continued to permit some use of Indian languages in mission schools; Coleman, *Presbyterian Missionary Attitudes*, 116–19.

2. Highwalking, *Narrative*, 3; La Flesche, *Middle Five*, xvii. Cf. Robert Burtt, superintendent of the BFM school, Annual Report of the superintendent, Oct. 29, 1861, 4:1, AIC (third page); Allen, *Pomo Basketmaking*, 11–13. Teachers did not always agree with this rule, Golden, *Red Moon Called me*, 143.

3. Shaw, *Pima Past*, 107–108; Ah-nen-la-de-ni, "An Indian Boy's Story," 1781; Inkanish, *Dance Around the Sun*, 38–39. My experience teaching English in Finland corroborates her reference to shame in front of student peers, rather than teachers; Talayesva, *Sun Chief*, 96.

4. Standing Bear, *My People the Sioux*, 155–56; and see *Land of the Spotted Eagle*, 242: as a teacher, Standing Bear encouraged his Sioux pupils to use both languages; Betzinez, *I Fought with Geronimo*, 154; Charles Eastman, *Deep Woods*, 46, 54.

5. Zitkala-Sa, *American Indian Stories*, 59; Daklugie et al., *Indeh*, 144–47, 150–51. And Chapter 8 in the present volume. See also James, *Chief of the Pomos*, on his joy at improving in English: "I became so proud of myself when walking home from school you could see my little humming bird chest sticking out like a pigeons breast," 19.

6. Ely S. Parker, "Writings of General Parker: Extracts from His Letters, and an Autobiographical Memoir of Historical Interest," *Publications of the Buffalo Historical Society* 8 (1905): 530–31; La Flesche, *Middle Five*, 13; Refugio Savala, *Autobiography of a Yaqui Poet*, edited by Kathleen M. Sands (Tucson: University of Arizona Press, 1980), 44–45. Stewart, *A Voice in Her Tribe*, 34.

7. *Jim Whitewolf, Life*, 85–86. See also Sekaquaptewa, 128–29; Alford, *Civilization*, 87; Griffis, *Tahan*, 237–40. On the "object method," Woodruff, *Indian Oasis*, 166–69; Report of the Superintendent of Indian Schools (Estelle Reel), ARCIA (1903), *House Document* No. 5, 58 Congress, 2 Session, Serial 4615, 384: "The Indian teacher must deal with conditions similar to those which confront the teacher of the blind and deaf." Reel then describes the "object method."

8. Mitchell, *Navajo Blessingway Singer*, 63. Letters and reports appended to ARCIA

often contained information on government and missionary school curricula. It is difficult to tell how accurately such reports reflected practice in the classroom, but autobiographers and government or missionary teachers generally agree on the variety of the academic curriculum. For a basic government-school academic curriculum, Report of School at Fort Lapwai, Idaho, ARCIA (Washington, D.C.: Government Printing Office, 1889), 354; for the ambitious academic curricula of off-reservation schools, see yearly reports, appended to ARCIA, for example: Report of Carlisle School, ARCIA (Washington, D.C.: Government Printing Office: 1883), 162–64; Report of Hampton Normal and Agricultural Institute, Hampton, Va., ARCIA (1890), *House Executive Document*, No. 1, part 5, vol. II, 51 Congress, 2 session, serial 2841, 315–166; also detailed "Course of Study," CLVI–CLXII; Trennert, *Phoenix Indian School*, esp. 119–20, note 9.

9. Grayson, *A Creek Warrior*, 43; La Flesche, *Middle Five*, 62. On the curriculum, also 13–14, 68, 76–77; Annual Report of the Superintendent, Oct. 29, 1861, 4:1, AIC (2d page): Coleman, *Presbyterian Missionary Attitudes*, 153–55. See also John H. Westerhoff, III, *McGuffey and His Readers: Piety, Morality, and Education in Nineteenth-Century America* (Nashville: Abingdon, 1978), 111–61, for lessons from the first editions of the first to fourth readers.

10. Alford, *Civilization*, 80.

11. La Flesche, *Middle Five*, 45; Standing Bear, *My People the Sioux*, 239; Shaw, *Pima Past*, 126–27. Also, Ah-nen-la-de-ni, "An Indian Boy's Story," 1781. Contemporary educators could criticize the overmechanical teaching: for example, W. M. Hailmann, Report of the superintendent of Indian Schools, ARCIA (1897), *House Document*, No. 5, 55 Congress, 2 session, serial 3641, 337. In reports appended to ARCIA teachers sometimes provided details on their methods.

12. La Flesche, *Middle Five*, 50–52, xviii; Francis La Flesche to Herbert Small, 1899[?], Box 12, 4558 (38), Fletcher and La Flesche Papers, NAA. All the correspondence in 4558 (39) relates to *Middle Five*. For a sense of how older students at Haskell Institute answered history and other examinations, see Examination Papers, 1915 (Haskell Institute), Records of the Education Division, RG 75, NA. It would be hard to tell that the writers were Indians.

13. Alford, *Civilization*, 72. On how Yuma pupils taught their teacher not to mention the dead, see Golden, *Red Moon Called Me*, 77.

14. Eastman, *Deep Woods*, Goodbird, *Goodbird the Indian*, 43; Standing Bear, *My People the Sioux*, 155.

15. Daklugie et al., *Indeh*, 141, 144–45.

16. Standing Bear, *Land of the Spotted Eagle*, 236; Talayesva, *Sun Chief*, 95.

17. Charles Eastman, *Deep Woods*, 54.

18. For "civilized habits," J. W. Perit Huntington, Superintendent Indian Affairs in Oregon, to commissioner, ARCIA (1863), *House Executive Document* No. 1, 38 Congress, 1 session, serial 1182, 172. Huntington noted that the labor of Indian children "is indeed made to contribute to their support . . ." Also, for example, Report of Salem Indian School, Chemawa, Oreg., ARCIA (Washington, D.C.: Government Printing Office, 1887), 253; Report of Superintendent of Indian Schools, ARCIA (1890), *House Executive Document* No. 1, part 5, vol. II, 51 Congress, 2 session, serial 2841, 268–69; CIA William A. Jones, ARCIA (1900), *House Document* No. 5, 56 Congress, 2 session, serial 4101, 30–32; M. Friedman, Annual Report," *The Red Man* 3 (1910): 50–62. For every dollar spent by the government on a Carlisle student, wrote Friedman, "the students produce nearly a dollar in return," 62. Also Coleman, *Presbyterian Missionary Attitudes*, 97–104; Institute for Government Research, *Indian Administration* (Meriam Report), 375–77, for example.

19. Stewart, *A Voice in Her Tribe*, 17. The strenuous demands of the Indian school upon the *staff* is a major theme of Minnie Braithwaite Jenkins, *Girl from Williamsburg* (Richmond: The Dietz Press, 1951).

20. Highwalking, *Narrative*, 3; Bennett, *Kaibah*, 218, 227; Qoyawayma, *No Turning Back*, 63.

21. Standing Bear, *My People the Sioux*, 147, 175–90. Quotation 183.

22. Betzinez, *I Fought with Geronimo*, 154–59.

23. An-nen-la-de-ni, "An Indian Boy's Story," 1783–84. While attending high school, he was still enrolled at the Lincoln Institute; Sekaquaptewa, *Me and Mine*, 142.

24. Sekaquaptewa, *Me and Mine*, 124, 138; and 188, on Hopi work ethic.

25. Qoyawayma, *No Turning Back*, 62; Talayesva, *Sun Chief*, 109; McCarthy, *Papago Traveller*, 43, 45; Winnie, *Sah-gan-de-oh*, 50. Also Kabotie, *Hopi Indian Artist*, 30, 32; CIA Atkins, ARCIA (Washington, D.C.: Government Printing Office, 1887), XVII, on the board and "fair wages" received by "outing" students. Cf. Coleman, "Western Education," 43–44; African narrators who did not receive payment were more resentful.

26. Standing Bear, *My People the Sioux*, 171, Chaps. 16, 18; Sekaquaptewa, *Me and Mine*, 139; McCarthy, *Papago Traveller*, 45.

27. Jim Whitewolf, *Life*, 94–96.

28. Zitkala-Sa, *American Indian Stories*, 62–64, 73.

29. Standing Bear, *My People the Sioux*, 144–45, 203; Indian Training School, ARCIA (Washington, D.C.: Government Printing Office, 1882), 180; M. Friedman, Annual Report, *The Red Man* 3 (1910): 63, quoted in present volume, Chapter 3.

30. Mitchell, *Navajo Blessingway Singer*, 65–66. He was a Catholic and a Blessingway singer, 332; Talayesva, *Sun Chief*, 96, 116–17 (YMCA), and 119–34 (on dream vision); Ada Damon, "'That's the Way we Were Raised': An Oral Interview with Ada Damon," edited by Yvonne Ashley, *Frontiers* 2 (1977): 61. Also McCarthy, *Papago Traveller*, 164–84.

31. Sekaquaptewa, *Me and Mine*, 129. In later life she syncretized Hopi and Mormon beliefs, 224–44.

32. Jones, ed., *Sanapia*, 24; Inkanish, *Dance Around the Sun*, 50–51, 53.

33. Betzinez, *I Fought with Geronimo*, 156; Brumble, *American Indian Autobiography*, 141, all Chap. 6. Also Shaw, *Pima Past*, 119–20, 127.

34. Alford, *Civilization*, 76–77, 104–107.

35. See, for example, Axtell, *The Invasion Within*, esp. 280–86, 332. Also, Ann Fienup-Riordan, *The Real People and the Children of Thunder: The Yup'ik Eskimo Encounter with Moravian Missionaries John and Edith Kilbuck* (Norman: University of Oklahoma Press, 1991); Kenneth M. Morrison, "Baptism and Alliance: The Symbolic Mediations of Religious Syncretism," *Ethnohistory* 37 (Fall 1990): 416–37; Rebecca Kugel, "Religion Mixed with Politics: The 1836 Conversion of Mang'osid of Fond Du Lac," *idem.*, 37 (Spring 1990): 126–57; Van Lonkhuyzen, "A Reappraisal of the Praying Indians."

36. Shaw, *Pima Past*, 119; La Flesche, *Middle Five*, 62–63.

37. Goodbird, *Goodbird the Indian*, Chap. 5. Quotations 43, 44. Also 68–69, on the pragmatic motivations which, Goodbird believed, influenced many Hidatsas to become Christians. Also suggestive of Goodbird's syncretism: Chaps. 3, 4, and 8; and Introduction by Mary Jane Schneider, XXVII–XIX.

38. Jim Whitewolf, *Life*, 44; Talayesva, *Sun Chief*, 96. On Hopi prophecies: Sekaquaptewa, *Me and Mine*, 227; Qoyawayma, *No Turning Back*, 8; Whiteley, *Determined Acts*; Loftin, *Religion and Hopi Life*; Armin W. Geertz, "Hopi Prophecies Revisited: A Critique of Rudolph Kaiser," *Anthropos* 86 (1991): 199–204; Geertz, "A Container of Ashes: Hopi Prophecy and History," *European Review of Native American Studies* 3 (1989): 1–6.

39. La Flesche, *Middle Five*, 7, 14, 129–30. Also, Sweezy, *Arapaho Way*, 64–65, Chap. 8, and 76: "There are many ways to God"; Woodruff, *Indian Oasis*, 208–209.

40. La Flesche, *Middle Five*, 29–31, 58–64, 129–30, Chap. 10. Also 56–57, 94–95, on dreamlike visions experienced at school; Joan Mark, "Francis la Flesche: The American Indian as Anthropologist," *Isis* 73 (1982): 498–99; Michael C. Coleman, "The Mission Education of Francis la Flesche: An American Indian Response to the Presbyterian Boarding School in the 1860s," *American Studies in Scandinavia* 18 (1986): 67–68, note 3.

41. Chris, *Apache Odyssey*, 87–89, 122–24. See also Standing Bear, *Land of the Spotted Eagle*, 235.

42. Stewart, *A Voice in Her Tribe*, 18–21. Stewart also recalled the telling of traditional

stories at school. On Navajo fear of the dead, Vecsey, *Imagine Ourselves*, 120–22. See also, Dalkugie, et al., *Indeh*, 116. Cf. 273; Rogers, *Red World and White*, 45, 73–74. Also 86.

43. Deloria, "Standing Rock Reservation," 194. Cf. Raymond J. DeMallie and Douglas R. Parks, eds., *Sioux Indian Religion* (Norman: University of Oklahoma Press, 1987), 14–15; Howard Whitewolf, "A Short Story of my Life," *The American Indian Magazine* 5 (Jan.–March 1917): 29.

44. Jones, ed., *Sanapia*, 24; Henly, in Johnson, ed., *Stories of Traditional Navajo Life*, 31; Anonymous Navajo, in Leighton and Leighton, eds., *Navajo Door*, 125; Kabotie, *Hopi Indian Artist*, 27; Betzinez, *I Fought with Geronimo*, 153. Also, Stewart, *A Voice in Her Tribe*, 18; Kaywaykla, *In the Days of Victorio*, 200; Ah-nen-la-de-ni, "An Indian Boy's Story," 1784.

CHAPTER 7

Peers and Mediation

"RED FEATHER AND WHITE FISH spoke both together, while I listened attentively, for everything was strange to me," wrote Charles Eastman of his fortunate encounter with two more experienced Santee Sioux pupils on his first journey to the local school. Mediating between him and the white world, the boys explained some of the mysteries of school. They told him how white people counted the days and divided them into amazingly small pieces, and had "everything in their books." Later that same day, however, Eastman fled the school, to the jeers of other less helpful older pupils: "'Hoo-oo! Hoo-oo! There goes the long-haired boy!'" [1]

In these two images Eastman caught much of the effect pupils could have upon each other. Some pupils *of both sexes* picked on, bullied, or even terrorized their companions; not all of the suffering endured at the school was imposed by the authorities. [2] On their own initiative, however, other young Indians reached out, in a kind of "unofficial" mediation, to help fellow pupils adapt and survive. In addition, the authorities utilized both willing and reluctant older pupils as "official" mediators: they helped administer the schools and maintain discipline, and served as links between school and tribe, and between school and white society.

Historians have recently emphasized the importance of mediators or "brokers," who straddled the divide between Indian and white cultures and helped interpret each to the other. Further, according to Margaret Connell Szasz, the greatest inroads upon native culture were made through their young people. Yet the mediatory role of Indian children both inside and outside the school has not been sufficiently examined by scholars, and the present chapter will demonstrate the crucial role of school pupils in these complex confrontations. [3]

I

The optimism and nostalgia that pervade Francis La Flesche's *Middle Five* do not conceal the harsh picture the Omaha presents of pupil relationships. The only distinction that counted among the boys, wrote

La Flesche, was cowardice: "the boy who could not fight found it difficult to maintain the respect of his mates, and to get a place among the different 'gangs' or groups of associates the boys had established among themselves." La Flesche did fight, and established a measure of security, augmented when he joined "the middle five" gang, between the bigger and smaller boys. One dull, childish student who could not fight, however, "became the butt of every trick a schoolboy could devise, and there was no one who would do battle for him"—La Flesche did not except himself from the general unwillingness to protect this large but pathetically vulnerable orphan.[4]

La Flesche somewhat romanticized an actual fight between one of his friends and a school bully, rendering it in prose acceptable to a Victorian audience: "Then followed an exciting scene. Gideon rushed at Warren, and aimed blow after blow at his face, but our boy skilfully parried each attack. . . ." There was nothing romantic, on the other hand, about the fight between Clinton Rickard and a bully at the local day school on the Tuscarora reservation in New York state; nor did the narrator claim a very impressive role for himself:

> When this big boy came in I hit him. He hit back and I grabbed his head and held on, all the while punching and scratching him. He kept gnawing at my wrist and every time he did so the blood spurted out, but he could not make me quit. . . . I would not let go of the boy because I knew he would give me a beating if I did.

The bully finally gave up, and Rickard recalled with satisfaction that the bigger boy was "all black and blue with lumps and bruises."[5]

John Rogers (Ojibway) recounted a more ritualized form of testing that took place at White Earth Boarding School in Minnesota around the turn of the twentieth century. Two of the pupils had older brothers at the school, "and that made them think they could run all over the smaller boys." These bullies sent an intermediate to challenge Rogers and his friend, and Rogers endured the taunt of "coward," as other boys tried to egg him to fight. Some students put chips of bark on Rogers's shoulder and on the shoulder of one bully. Each knocked off the other's chips, and the fight was on. Rogers won, but later had to fight the second bully. The quaint chivalry—indicative, as we shall see, of the kind of pupil subculture that developed at many schools—should not detract from the seriousness of the encounter. Rogers faced the jeering encouragement of other boys, the likelihood of even greater contempt had he refused to fight, or of domination by a bully had he lost.[6]

Girls did not necessarily have it much easier. Although Helen Seka-quaptewa believed that schooling opened a new and rich life to her, she also recalled how the bigger and stronger preyed upon the weak, the different, or even the more studious. Her complaint that Navajo girls and boys at the Keams Canyon Boarding School always got full plates of food, whereas small girls like herself never got enough, might suggest the bias of a Hopi narrator. But Hopi girls were just as much of a problem to each other. The Friendly girls teased Hostile children: "tormentors would take our native clothes from the boxes and put them on and dance around making fun of them." When she tried to comb her long, thick hair, the other girls laughed at her. Before helping comb her hair, one bigger Hopi girl extorted some of the food that Helen brought from home; another combed it so roughly Helen was reduced to tears, and she wondered why bigger girls had to be so mean to little ones.

Ambivalence strongly characterized her responses to the new institu-tion. "I enjoyed school and was eager to learn. I was a good reader and got good grades. The teachers favored me and whenever visitors came they always called on me to recite." But immediately she continued: "I was not the most popular girl in school and my ability did not help me socially, it only made others jealous." Dispassionately she told of argu-ments with less studious girls, suggesting Hopi ostracism of a too-ambitious peer: pupil cruelty did not always involve physical abuse. She was lonely, and nobody asked her to dance at school socials. But she still could feel sympathy for Ella, an especially unfortunate girl denounced for being a witch—a deadly serious accusation in Hopi society. The other girls ganged up on Ella and beat her, and she "ran screaming downstairs to the matron." Again defying the group, Helen did not participate in the attack, and experienced even greater isolation after-ward: "My, I felt little that night. I got into bed right away and covered up my head so they wouldn't stare at me."[7]

Kay Bennett also remembered bullying by a girl. Before the pupils set off on their marvelous circus trip to Flagstaff, one of the bigger girls demanded that Bennett steal a lipstick for her or face a beating upon return. Bennett might have done so, but the opportunity did not present itself. So later the bully "grabbed one of her [Bennett's] hair braids, and jerked her back, then slapped her hard." Bennett gave as good as she got, "and soon the girls were on the ground wrestling and hitting each other." Finally a teacher separated them, and, when nei-ther would tell the cause of the fight, sent both to face a wall until bedtime.[8]

II

Many narrators recall warmer experiences, however, as other pupils sought them out, to assuage their loneliness or offer them information or help against bullies. Often such "unofficial" mediators were kin. Mildred Stinson remembered how two aunts (in the Lakota kinship system aunts need not have been older women) tried to comfort her during the first lonely days at boarding school. But "they were lonesome too, and I was lonesome—we were all lonesome." That Stinson could finally "build up a resistance against this sort of thing" may have in part been a result of the concern shown by those aunts. James McCarthy was mightily relieved to find an older Papago relative would be accompanying his group to boarding school and would "look out" for them. One would expect a relative to do just that, but Lucille Winnie's brothers and sister were disgusted when she began at Haskell, as they felt she would be a burden upon them. "Sis" was a student officer, assigned to help Lucille and had no alternative but to do her duty. The assistance later offered by Lucille's brother, however, was most likely against school rules. A privileged member of the Haskell football team, he ensured that she got "good eats," or at least better food than ordinary students did.[9]

Don Talayesva recounted the strange method a cousin used to lift his spirits when he was contemplating running away. As the Hopi was "sitting sad and still," his cousin "asked me if I were lonesome and I almost cried." The older boy took him to the pig pen, and Talayesva remembered the effect the strange domestic animals of the white man had upon him:

> They were funny animals—like dogs with hooves. They looked horrible with their little eyes, sharp mouths, and dirty faces. . . . He caught one by the tail and I clambered upon its back and rode it about the pen. It was great fun. I felt better when I got off, and thought to myself that if my homesickness returned I would ride a pig again.

Some time later Talayesva noticed the telltale signs of loneliness in a Hopi clan relative, and he took the younger boy to see and ride the same pigs. As he watched, Talayesva hinted at the kind of personal satisfaction to be gained by helping a younger pupil: "I felt grown up as I sat there in my long pants, looking down at him."[10] Kindness was no doubt its own reward; but a sense of satisfaction from acceptance of adult responsibility also played a part in such mediating. As did cultural factors: in Hopi society kin looked out for kin. Brokers thus perpetuated this deeply ingrained tribal ethic at the schools.

Pupils other than kin or clan relatives, such as the strangers who met Eastman, also offered themselves as mediators between school newcomer. On the train to the Tucson Indian Mission School, Anna Moore Shaw (Pima) met a girl hardly much older than herself, but more experienced in the ways of the white world. "'Ann, you are going to like the mission school,'" the girl assured her, and explained that only naughty pupils might be whipped. Authorities assigned the two girls to the same room at the school, and her new friend showed her around and explained the workings of a shower. Shaw did not remember all pupils so fondly, noting that some informed on their fellows who spoke Pima at the school. But the little mediator she met on the train obviously made adjustment easier for her, and helped her respond more positively to the school.[11]

Asa Daklugie described how a mixture of surprise, compassion, and perhaps tribal solidarity moved him to assist the young James Kaywaykla, who burst into tears at dinner when he got no syrup for his pancakes. "It was the first time that I'd seen one of the Apache children do that," wrote Daklugie. "I felt sorry for him. I knew that it was not just being deprived of the syrup, though we loved sweets and seldom got any. It was because he was the youngest child at Carlisle, and lonely." Although it was against school rules, Daklugie got more of the syrup for his young companion.[12]

If constant bullying features as one major theme of La Flesche's autobiography, another relates to the help and encouragement pupils gave to newcomers. The boy who reminded him that he could return to his mother each Saturday did so spontaneously. Soon Brush became his constant mediator, mentor, and best friend. When Omaha twins arrived at the school, La Flesche himself helped Brush continue the mediating process: "we lost no time in helping them along in their English." Later, members of "the middle five" gang actually enticed a curious Omaha child to join the school. Brush constantly lectured his younger friends on the importance of learning the new ways; and on his death bed exhorted La Flesche to "tell the boys I want them to learn; I know you will, but the other boys don't care. I want them to learn, and to think. You'll tell them, won't you?"[13] One might suspect that La Flesche romanticized Indian childhood camaraderie in these passages, if he had not also given such a chilling picture of the other side of student life.

Occasionally, as we shall see, older students induced younger ones to resist or flee—another way of helping them avoid the demands of the school. But much of the unofficial brokering by older pupils involved helping the younger ones survive against predators and adjust to the school, thus contributing toward more positive responses to the new institution.

III

Had such unofficial mediation been the only help that students gave to each other, it would have greatly alleviated the task of the school staff. The authorities also employed pupils as official mediators, however, and as controllers of other pupils, and as mediators between the school and tribal and white societies. Older pupils knew the ropes, understood the curriculum and regimen; it made good sense to groom them as officers, disciplinarians, interpreters, and general helpers. For those so honored, there were compensations for the burdens of responsibility.[14]

After the unofficial mediator whom she met on the train introduced Shaw to the mysteries of the school, the official mediator took over. "All the little girls sat at one long table," wrote the Pima, "with an older girl as monitor at the head. She helped us to learn table manners and dished out the food for us." And, most important: "Before we sat down to eat, we repeated the Grace in unison." Reluctantly but efficiently the sister of Lucille Winnie did her duties as a student officer at Haskell. She washed the newcomer's face, and briefed Lucille on school protocol. And at Toadlena Boarding School the matron assigned an older student as helper to Kay Bennett. This official mediator kept close to the young Navajo, sleeping in the next bed. She explained school rules and the meaning of sermons. She also introduced Bennett to an invention which was new to a girl from a remote hogan: the radio. La Flesche's Presbyterian boarding school used willing older pupils in many roles—from helping name newcomers, to outfitting them in new clothes.[15] And it is likely that some of the fellow-students who helped pressure Thomas Alford into his Christian conversion did so at the behest of the school authorities.

Jim Whitewolf (Kiowa Apache) spent a few years during the 1880s at boarding school in Oklahoma, and provided one of the most detailed accounts of the ways in which a school could utilize a senior pupil. Whitewolf responded to the school experience with typical ambivalence. He resented the hard work, the punishments, and "the bell," and actually fled a number of times. Ultimately he accepted the school, gained satisfaction from learning English, and acknowledged the later usefulness of the agricultural skills he absorbed there. Whitewolf arrived with only a few words of English, and the school assigned Logan, a distant relative, as his personal guide and interpreter (the authorities assigned interpreters for each tribal language at the school). From the beginning Logan took care of him: "He told me that when the first bell rang, we would go to eat. He said that when we got down there he would tell me what to do." And he did. "You're on your own now," Logan informed him after the first day, but maintained his official role as mediator long after that. "All my first year in school I continued to feel like a stranger," Whitewolf recalled, but Logan's help eased the transition to full participant. Logan even sat behind Whitewolf in class, explaining how he was to play with bricks until he learned more English. And, as we have seen, Logan instructed him in *how to learn* the new language by repeating the words of the teacher when she pointed to objects.

Whitewolf suggested some of the demands such a role placed upon Logan, who also went to school half a day and worked in the barn. In addition he performed jobs less likely to win him popularity among his peers, such as hunting down runaways. He and another senior pupil came after Whitewolf and his friends on one of their attempts to escape: the older boys "were afraid that we might freeze somewhere or maybe die. They were responsible for us and had to find us"—a heavy burden for boys perhaps no older than teenagers. Yet Logan appears to have accepted easily these heavy duties, which probably appealed both to his personality and to his tribal and kin sense of responsibility.[16]

Narrators appreciated the help they got from school-appointed mediators, but as often they resented the way older students lorded it over them; this prefect system could easily become officially sanctioned bullying. Although later she conceded that they probably had the interests of pupils at heart, Winnie left a very negative image of the gruff, short-tempered Indian disciplinarians and officers at Haskell, including her own sister. Narcissa Owen, who attended a small country school in the 1840s, remembered how the pupil "at the head of the spelling class" might be allowed to administer punishment: he used to give a stroke of the ruler on the hand to those who missed the spelling. "The consequence was," wrote Owen, "that the pupils were always trying to get even with the head of the class." The assistant disciplinarian and the boys who thrashed Don Talayesva for refusing to take part in a debate were probably Indians. Hoke Denetsosie (Navajo) left an especially bitter account of the abuse of pupil power at the Tuba City Boarding

School. Details, such as the state of the pupils' pockets, remained sharp in his memory:

> I want to say that some of the student officers were very mean to their squads. Most of the time our desserts were not eaten by us. Instead, apples or pieces of pie or cake were sneaked out in our coat pockets to be given to our captains. That happened so much that our coat pockets would be so stiff and messy that they hardly would bend and we would have a hard time keeping our hands warm on cold days. Those who disobeyed the wishes of the captains usually got a kick in the behind or some other form of punishment, but those things never were reported for fear of reprisals.[17]

IV

The official mediatory tasks of senior students extended far beyond the school compound. The federal government and missionary societies clearly intended their schools to send out a light into the "darkness of heathenism," a goal expressed in characteristic language by E. Painter, agent for the Omahas in 1872. Noting the "quick perceptions" and "accuracy with which they have answered the questions propounded to them," he believed that the young Omaha pupils could contribute greatly to the prosperity of the tribe. "This is an encouraging aspect in the future of these people," Painter wrote to the commissioner of Indian Affairs, "as the little flock of boys and girls now undergoing the process of intellectual training must soon become active and leading men and women in their little community, and the influence of their good examples and cultivated minds cannot be otherwise than salutary." On the questionnaire sent out to ex-pupils of Carlisle in the early twentieth century sometimes appeared the ominous question: "Have you done anything for the betterment of your people?"[18]

But even while still pupils, young Indians could begin to spread the light beyond the school to their own peoples. "I remember when some of our boys came home from school back east," wrote George Webb (Pima), "[h]ow nicely they were dressed in dark blue uniforms with yellow stripes on the arms and down the side of their pants!" When his mother told him that the boys were from the Carlisle school, Webb "joined the others standing around admiring these boys' uniforms, and made up my mind that I would like to go to school too." Captain Pratt also employed this tactic in seeking volunteers for Carlisle from among the captive Apaches at Fort Marion, Florida. "He brought with him, as a testament of the value to the Indians of attending this school, a Carlisle student, an Apache boy, who happened to be my favorite second cousin," wrote Jason Betzinez. The tactic "had no effect on me nor on the other prisoners. No one volunteered." Not a man to let this complication prevent him doing good to Indians, Pratt coopted a group anyway. Chris, also Apache, remembered an even more aggressive use of pupil recruiters: the Mescalero boarding school sent out some of the older boys "to catch" Apache girls who refused to come to school.[19] The hunting down of runaways by older pupils was merely an extension of such a policy at many schools.

Recruiting students at Pine Ridge in 1879 also sparked Luther Standing Bear's interest in Carlisle. A few years later he himself temporarily returned to the reservation, chosen by Captain Pratt to become a recruiter to his own people. He had difficulty persuading the Sioux to send more children, especially as so many had already died at the school from various illnesses. But the young Lakota finally prevailed, and there is little hint that he felt exploited by the school. He enjoyed the responsibility, and the word "proud" appears regularly in his account of the episode. Although first educated in traditional society, he no longer seemed sensitive to the radical reversal of roles involved in the disturbing spectacle of a mere child lecturing to older men. Despite this part-rejection of tribal values, his heavily personal motivations were also influenced by a Lakota sense of pride in achievement.[20]

Thus one generation of young Indians returned to the village or reservation to entice the next generation into the school. Sometimes the recruiters had finished their own schooling and were returning at last to share the benefits with their peoples. On other occasions they were still students, with the new duty of recruiter added to their other responsibilities. They were crucial mediators in the on-going task of convincing other Indian children, and their kin, of the value of the school, no doubt explaining to them the nature of the strange place, and perhaps helping them in their initial problems of adjustment.

Other brokering duties also linked the more promising pupils to the home culture. Brush, the friend of La Flesche, interpreted for the school superintendent at the Omaha village. And Jim Whitewolf reported how those at a local mission school liked his brother, "and they would always take him along when they went around making visits to the people. . . . He would interpret for them when they went around to the camps." During breaks from school, the brother told the family about what he had learned; it was he who persuaded the parents to be baptized at the local Presbyterian Church. It is likely that many other students competent in English did such translating and relaying of their new knowledge to those at home. Merely by speaking English at the hogan, the Navajo siblings of Kay Bennett piqued their sister's interest in the school.[21]

Further, to ensure continuing financial, legislative, and executive support for the crusade, educators needed to convince Americans on the home front that the schools were efficiently pacifying the Indians. Thomas Alford's trip to Washington to attend the inauguration of President Garfield was part of such a campaign. In his senior year, the Shawnee and three other students accompanied General Armstrong as representatives of the school to other large cities. The object of the trip, Alford believed, "was to interest people in the education of the Indians and in helping Hampton Institute in a financial way." Alford himself made speeches on the educational needs of his people. The trip netted about $60,000, he believed.[22]

Captain Pratt was especially aware of the need for favorable press in the East, and lost no opportunity to parade his charges in front of white society. The Carlisle superintendent was "always very proud to 'show us off' and let white people see how we were progressing," wrote Standing Bear. "Sometimes we were drilled for days before starting out on an invitation for dinner, so that our deportment should be all correct and proper." In his own autobiography Pratt strongly and unapologetically corroborated Standing Bear's description of exploitation. "Carlisle's contribution to the parade in New York [in 1892] was 270 boys and 52 girls," wrote Pratt proudly. Some of these boys carried

A large and most elaborate silk banner . . . on which was emblazoned in large letters "United States Indian Industrial School, Carlisle, Pennsylvania," and conspicuously under that "Into Civilization and Citizenship."

The educator went on to quote "some of the many encomiums in the great newspapers" about the display of Indian capacity for citizenship.[23]

If in retrospect Standing Bear exhibited a degree of resentment, there is no indication that he objected to such exploitation while he was a pupil. Ah-nen-la-de-ni recalled his own anger *as a student*, however, when the staff at Lincoln Institute, Philadelphia, refused him permission to transfer to Carlisle. "The reason why I and others like me were kept at the school," the Mohawk believed, "was that we served as show scholars—a result of the system and evidences of the good work the Institute was doing." The Mohawk claimed that the institute fraudulently exhibited as two-year students those who had been eight years at the school, and exhibited goods bought in Philadelphia as samples of students' work. A veteran of many years' schooling, the Mohawk himself became a prime exhibit:

I was good for various show purposes. I could sing and play a musical instrument, and I wrote essays which were thought to be very good. The authorities were also fond of displaying me as one who had come to the school a few years before unable to speak a word of English.

Perhaps the writer exaggerated the cynicism of the authorities, but he conceded that an earlier principal had not been so dishonest. Further, Ah-nen-la-de-ni was no opponent of education. His frustration developed because these authorities prevented him from continuing his education at what he believed to be a better school.[24]

As in their responses to the ethnocentric curriculum, the narrators generally accepted the one-sided nature of their official mediating tasks, which explained the school to younger students, to tribal adults, and to white society. Only rarely do we find a pupil attempting to convey understanding of Indian life to a non-Indian. Annie Lowry once showed a white classmate how Paiutes extracted rubber from rabbitbrush and used it for gum, which both enjoyed chewing. A teacher at La Flesche's school asked the Omaha pupils why they rubbed snow on their faces. "'All boys do that,'" Brush explained. "'The old folks tell them to do it because then their faces and hands won't get frozen.'" La Flesche did not convey the response; the usually ethnocentric missionaries would hardly have been impressed, although in such a practical matter the "savage" knowledge might have been accepted. The early twentieth century incorporation of Indian arts and crafts into certain school curricula could also imply some willingness to learn from Indians, especially when Carlisle appointed Angel de Cora (Winnebago) as a teacher. At Santa Fe School in the second decade of the twentieth century, Mr. de Huff, the principal, and his wife became interested in the Hopi character and themes of Fred Kabotie's painting. But this principal was soon transferred because, Kabotie believed, "he was reviving Indian culture rather than eliminating it, as the schools had been ordered to do."[25]

Apart from the unofficial mediation in which pupils took care of each other, then, most of the mediating inside and outside the schools was decidedly one way, as the authorities utilized their charges efficiently and sometimes cynically to convey to others the message of the educational crusade, and to help toward the efficient running of the school. In a sad commentary on the one-sidedness of his experience with whites—a comment applicable to most of the other narrators, most of the time, at most of the schools—Standing Bear concluded: "Never once were they intelligent enough to concede that they learned anything from us."[26]

Of course the teachers and missionaries generally believed that a fair exchange was taking place. For their efforts on behalf of the school, pupils gained the inestimable riches of Christianity and "civilization." Further, the teachers believed with some degree of justification that young Indians thus developed a new sense of responsibility, along with American ideas of systematically ordered hard work which would enable them and their people to survive in modern America. And the authorities could validly claim that the designation of older pupils as helpers to the young was a major factor in alleviating some of the shock of entry to the schools: the practice contributed both to easier student adjustment and to better pupil-to-pupil relationships. It also, of course, created bitterness among those on the receiving end of pupil power. Whatever can be said in defense of the policy, it often involved gross exploitation of young Indians, who had little choice but to accept the duties given.

Moreover, the children sometimes experienced a double dose of exploitation. Although some kin thought of the child's own need for schooling, more often they thought of the family's or the people's need for the knowledge of the whites. Thus, these Indian children bore at least two heavy burdens of responsibility as they struggled to satisfy both their new educators and their own peoples.

V

Why did most narrators readily accept both the unofficial mediatory roles and the official duties thrust upon them to help run the schools? Some of their reasons have already emerged in this chapter; the motivations were complex, and ran the full gamut of the seven motivational clusters earlier introduced.

Kin relationships were crucial. Many of the narrators left for school with kin admonitions to obey and learn ringing in their ears—therefore the ready acceptance of school rules and responsibilities. Further, all of the narrators came from cultural environments in which education and the protection of the young was a kinwide and often communitywide responsibility, and in which the acceptance of both greater responsibility as well as greater privileges was a mark of manhood or womanhood. Had Logan, Jim Whitewolf's school-appointed mediator, remained with his people, he might have been apprenticed to a warrior, and might later have taken a younger boy under his wing. Once again we see how, despite the different forms, tribal and white practices could be compatible.

Motivational factors relating to the school as an institution also influenced young mediators. Standing Bear, Alford, and others sent to represent their schools in the great cities or among the tribes definitely exhibited a sense of institutional identity. This pride in alma mater probably existed more at the large schools, with their myriad student activities and their highly developed sports. Affection and respect for teachers also motivated pupils. The special treatment given to Brush by the Presbyterian superintendent—"who liked the boy, favored him in various ways, loaned him books to read, and talked with him about them"—was clearly a factor in Brush's passionate espousal of the goals of the Omaha school. Luther Standing Bear deeply respected Captain Pratt, and also claimed that "we would do anything for Miss Burgess."[27] An interest in elements of the curriculum, especially English and perhaps Christianity, also impelled more experienced pupils to influence other Indians in these areas.

Clearly, personal factors were also powerful motivators. Student officers at Winnie's and other schools gained a great sense of satisfaction lording it over their fellows. Logan seems to have been little corrupted, however, or surely Whitewolf would have complained about mistreatment. Obviously, placing pupils in positions of authority could appeal both to the most, and to the least, admirable sides of the human personality.

Finally, the pupils too were exploiters of the school, and this accounted for some of their readiness to do its work. Once they adjusted, many were quite happy to learn English, make money, rise in the ranks, and gain knowledge of the white world, both for their own use and for that of their kin and peoples. We must not minimize the degree to which these young Indians suffered exploitation by others. But in their own instrumental approach to the school, many of the narrators developed a degree of counterexploitation.

An individual student such as Standing Bear acted because of a complex mix of motivational influences: loyalty to staff and school; obedience to his father's command to learn the ways of the whites; cultural conditioning to accept responsibility as one grew older; the Lakota encouragement of the quest for personal glory. Thus, although critical of many aspects of school life, he had no compunction about accepting every duty the school imposed upon him. An equally egotistical but less glory-seeking pupil such as Don Talayesva, on the other hand, accepted responsibility for a younger clan member, and explicitly enjoyed the sense of being more grown-up as he watched the boy ride the pigs; but Talayesva neither sought, nor apparently got, major mediatory tasks thrust upon him by the schools he attended.

VI

Another aspect of pupil relationships remains to be discussed in this chapter: the effect upon young Indians of coming face to face with members of other tribal groups, especially at the larger, multitribal boarding schools. The first effect, of course, was the Babel effect; to speak to each other, as well as to their teachers, the young pupils had to learn a lingua franca. Initially this was not always English. At Carlisle, James Kaywaykla and other Apache children first learned the sign language—"which our people had never used"—a form of communication then becoming obsolete among the Plains Indians. By 1911 about twenty-seven tribal groups were represented at the Wahpeton Boaring School in North Dakota, and Sam Writer (Ojibway) had to speak *Sioux* to his girlfriend there. Some of the other Sioux pupils "used to gad around and laugh at me," he recalled, "for how I pronounced those words. . . ."[28] Although pupils often persisted in speaking tribal languages, English soon became the major and official medium of communication at most schools.

Young Indians faced challenges beyond the linguistic. Exposure to other tribal groups at the Lincoln Institute in Philadelphia was disturbing yet ultimately mind-broadening for Ah-nen-la-de-ni. "Till I arrived at the school," he claimed, "I had never heard that there were any other Indians in the country other than those of our reservation." Further, he did not know he was a "Mohawk," for his people called themselves "Ga-nien-ge-ha-ga," meaning "People of the Beacon Stone." The greater the surprise, then

> when I found myself surrounded in the school yard by strange Indian boys belonging to tribes of which I had never heard, and when it was said that my people were the "civilized Mohawks," I at first thought that "Mohawk" was a nickname and fought the boy who called me by it.

Soon he was living without difficulty with non-Mohawks. Albert Yava (Tewa–Hopi) was equally surprised to find that not all the pupils at the Chilocco Boarding School in Oklahoma were dark-skinned and dark-haired. He later found out that such pupils "were Indians, all right," Cherokees and other tribes. "It was the first time I ever knew that

Indians came in different colours," he remarked, but drew no invidious racial distinctions.[29]

At some schools, however, tribal antagonisms appeared. When a group of Ponca boys, whose people lived on the reservation of the related Omahas, came to the windows of La Flesche's school, they and the Omahas traded insults, especially about different hairstyles. "We could not help laughing at their appearance," wrote La Flesche. The tribal division was made more stark by the fact that "the little savages" outside the windows were unschooled. Had the Poncas been brought into school, it is likely that, after further insults, fights, and gang building, they and the Omaha children would have come to accept each other, as pupils did elsewhere. James McCarthy also remembered tribal antagonisms at his school. "The Pima boys were real mean to the Papagos," he wrote of his experiences at Phoenix. Yet at the Santa Fe school he claimed that "[k]ids from all the tribes were like brothers now." Except for those brushes with Pimas, intertribal tension did not seem to bother him much at any of the many schools he attended.[30]

The most striking examples of intertribal antagonism reported in these autobiographies occurred between Hopis and Navajos. The Hopis complained about Navajos; possibly because of their larger population and smaller sense of vulnerability, the Navajos complained less about the Hopis. Such prejudices appear to have caused some trouble at school, as evidenced by Helen Sekaquaptewa's account of being bullied by the physically larger Navajo girls and boys. Don Talayesva admitted that at his day school, on the other hand, he was the bully: "We Hopi hated Navajos, and decided to make this one miserable." Talayesva jerked the boys' ears—only to be caught by a teacher and slapped "right and left." But at schools containing pupils from both these tribes, no pattern of rigid hostility is apparent; most of the time the children seemed at least to coexist peacefully.[31]

Many of the narrators got to know and make friends with members of different tribes. Jim Whitewolf, the Kiowa Apache, had a Comanche friend, and the girl who asked him on his first "date" was also Comanche. Mountain Wolf Woman, a Winnebago, made friends with the Oneida matron at her school. Charles Eastman noted in passing how at the Santee Normal Training School he became friends with a Mandan, "one of our ancient enemies." Similarly, Standing Bear met a Pawnee at Carlisle—and suddenly remembered that he had earlier seen the same boy as a Sioux prisoner. Standing Bear did not claim that he and the Pawnee boy became friends, but significantly there is no indication that they renewed tribal rivalries at the school. Other narrators such as Winnie and Alford made references to the tribal heterogeneity at their schools, but also leave us with a strong impression that the various tribal groups learned the common language and accepted each other very quickly.[32] Thrown into an environment in which similar demands were made of all pupils of the same age and sex, and in which the staff was usually white, this result is hardly surprising. As we shall see in the next chapter, resistance to school authorities was rarely monolithic, but probably increased the sense of broad pupil identification, rather than merely tribal.

The narrators provide little indication, however, that as pupils they had begun to go much beyond such intertribal coexistence to a broader conception of themselves as "Indian," rather than Sioux or Hopi. Some probably did leave school with such an enlarged sense of identity. Charles Eastman wrote about the culture of his own tribe, but saw himself as a spokesman for "the Indian." Eastman later helped found the Society of American Indians in 1911. Zitkala-Sa for a time served as secretary of this Pan-Indian organization, before founding her own political organization, the National Council of American Indians. And Lucille Winnie's self-proclaimed "mission" was to work for all Indians, not just her Iroquois forebears.[33] Indians such as Don Talayesva and Frank Mitchell were also deeply changed by school. But they were less affected by such broadening of Indian identity, and remained far more focused upon their own Hopi and Navajo peoples after school.

In 1891 Commissioner Morgan characteristically exaggerated the success of multitribal schools in the "blending together of many tribes." The children, he claimed, "learn to respect and love each other, and there is thus broken down those tribal animosities and jealousies which have been in the past productive of so much harm and a fruitful source of so much trouble both to the Indians and the nation."[34] Yet there is some truth to Morgan's claims. If children often victimized each other at the schools, they could also extend mutual help and support. Further, considering the centuries of intertribal antagonisms, or merely the linguistic and cultural differences among many pupils, the school did provide an environment in which young Indians from a great number of tribes learned to adjust to each other in a remarkably short time.[35]

Notes

1. Charles Eastman, *Deep Woods*, 18–23.
2. See also Haig-Brown, *Resistance and Renewal*, 75; Rosalie Wax, "The Warrior Dropouts," in Howard M. Bahr, et al., eds. *Native Americans Today: Sociological Perspectives* (New York: Harper & Row, 1972): 148–50. Reprinted from *Trans*-action (May 1967).
3. Nancy L. Hagedorn, "'A Friend to Go Between Them': The Interpreter as Cultural Broker During Anglo–Iroquois Councils, 1740–70," *Ethnohistory* 35 (Winter 1988): 60; Szasz, *American Colonies*, 23. Her comment is good for centuries beyond the colonial period; Clifton, ed., *Being and Becoming Indian*; Daniel K. Richter, "Cultural Brokers and Intercultural Politics: New York—Iroquois Relations, 1664–1701," *Journal of American History* 75 (June 1988): 40–67. Cf. Tamara Hareven, "The History of the Family and the Complexity of Social Change," *American Historical Review* 96 (Feb. 1991): 124.
4. La Flesche, *Middle Five*, 11, 134.
5. *Ibid.*, 40–41; Rickard, *Fighting Tuscarora*, 6.
6. Rogers, *Red World and White*, 69–72.
7. Sekaquaptewa, *Me and Mine*, 93–95, 103–104, 125–27. Fear of witchcraft is a major theme of Talayesva, *Sun Chief*. Also, Whiteley, *Deliberate Acts*, 68–69. Dorothy Eggan emphasizes the interdependency and conformity of traditional Hopi life, "Instruction and Affect."
8. Bennett, *Kaibah*, 245–47. Also, Zithala-Sa, *American Indian Stories*, 30.
9. Stinson, in Cash and Hoover, eds., *To Be an Indian*, eds. Cash and Hoover, 95; McCarthy, *Papago Traveller*, 38–39; Winnie, *Sah-gan-de-oh*, 40, 46, 50; Also Bennett, *Kaibah*, 214–15.
10. Talayesva, *Sun Chief*, 96–97, 102.
11. Shaw, *Pima Past*, 125–27.
12. Dakulgie et al., *Indeh*, 147–49. Editor Eve Ball notes that the school appointed Daklugie to assist Kaywaykla, 144; but here his mediation was definitely unofficial.
13. La Flesche, *Middle Five*, 3–4, 13–14, 22, 72–74, 151.
14. In the pre-Civil War decades, some mission schools utilized the English Lancastrian system: teachers picked more experienced pupils as classroom monitors and instructors of large numbers of younger pupils. These autobiographers did not experience this system. See Ronald Rayman, "Joseph Lancaster's Monitorial System of Instruction and American Indian Education, 1815–1838," *History of Education Quarterly* (Winter 1981): 395–409; Berkhofer, *Salvation and the Savage*, 25–27.
15. Shaw, *Pima Past*, 126, 131; Winnie, *Sah-gan-de-oh*, 46; Bennett, *Kaibah*, 216–20; La Flesche, *Middle Five*, for example: 21, 28, 75. Also Eastman, *Deep Woods*, 40.
16. Jim Whitewolf, *Life*, 39, Chap. 3. Quotations, 84–86, 94. Even linguistically inexperienced pupils served as interpreters; Mitchell, *Navajo Blessingway Singer*, 66; Shaw, *Pima Past*, 131. Sekaquaptewa's husband also brought back runaways, *Me and Mine*, 137.
17. Winnie, *Sah-gan-de-oh*, 45–49, 58; Narcissa Owen, *Memoirs of Narcissa Owen, 1831–1907* (1907; rpt. Owensboro, Ky.: McDowell, 1980), 53; Talayesva, *Sun Chief*, 130; Denetsosie, in Johnson, ed., *Stories of Traditional Navajo Life*, 94. Also Trennert, "Corporal Punishment," 606, 609–10.
18. ARCIA, (1873), *House Executive Document* No. 1, part 5, 42 Congress, 3 session, serial 1560, 604; the "ominous question" can sometimes be found in School Records, Records of Graduates and Returned Students, Records of the Carlisle Indian Industrial School, RG 75, NA. There is a folder on each student. Around 1911 Lambert Istone (Apache) answered: "I have taught the boys to farm and to be clean and honest."

19. George Webb, *A Pima Remembers* (1959; rpt. Tucson: University of Arizona Press, 1982), 85; Betzinez, *I Fought With Geronimo*, 149; Chris, *Apache Odyssey*, 83.

20. Standing Bear, *My People the Sioux*, 123–24, 161–66.

21. La Flesche, *Middle Five*, 61; Whitewolf, *Life*, 58; Bennett, *Kaibah*, 156–59. See also Tom Ration, in Johnson, ed., *Stories of Traditional Navajo Life*, 309; Michael C. Coleman, "American Indian School Pupils as Cultural Brokers: Cherokee Girls at Brainerd Mission, 1828–29," in Margaret Connell Szasz, ed., *The Cultural Broker: Link Between Indian and White Worlds, 1690s–1990s* (Norman: University of Oklahoma Press, forthcoming). Two pupils who wrote essays for Gertrude Golden indicated how, while on vacation home, they attempted to communicate their new knowledge to kin, see Golden, *Red Moon Called Me*, 194–95.

22. Alford, *Civilization*, 107–108.

23. Standing Bear, *My People the Sioux*, 167; Pratt, *Battlefield and Classroom*, 294, and all Chap. 26. Also, 283–85. Pratt declared: "Every report, speech, and publication Carlisle was able to put out was made to present these facts [of the school's mission] to administrative and legislative heads and to the public," 273.

24. Ah-nen-la-de-ni, "An Indian Boy's Story," 1784–85. He quotes samples of his own poetry.

25. Lowry, *Karnee*, 65; La Flesche, *Middle Five*, 105. On BFM ethnocentrism, see Coleman, *Presbyterian Missionary Attitudes*; De Cora, "Angel de Cora," 285; Friedman, Annual Report, *The Red Man* 3 (Oct. 1910): 57; Kabotie, *Hopi Indian Artist*, 27–29. When a Zia schoolmate painted ceremonial scenes, his own people ostracized him. Also, Golden, *Red Moon Called Me*, 33–34: while accepting the ethnocentric educational policy, individual government teachers could appreciate elements of Indian culture. Also Jenkins, *Girl from Williamsburg*.

26. Standing Bear, *Land of the Spotted Eagle*, 242.

27. La Flesche, *Middle Five*, 14; Standing Bear, *My People the Sioux*, 161.

28. Kaywaykla, *In the Days of Victorio*, 200; also Standing Bear, *My People the Sioux*, 143. The sign language was initially used at Hampton too, Paulette Fairbanks Molin, "'Training the Hand, the Head, and the Heart': Indian Education at Hampton Institute," *Minnesota History* 51 (Fall 1988): 86. Oscar Good Shot (Oglala Sioux) noted how Oglala young people no longer much used the sign language by the 1920s, "Oscar Good Shot: the Narrator of a Sioux Visitor," in Thomas B. Marquis, ed., *The Cheyennes of Montana* (Algonac, Michigan: Reference Publications, 1978), 272; Sam Writer, in Cash and Hoover, eds., *To Be an Indian*, 210, on poor Sioux pronunciation.

29. Ah-nen-la-de-ni, "An Indian Boy's Story," 1782. There is some ambiguity in this passage; Yava, *Big Falling Snow*, 18. Cf. surprise of Rose (Shingobe) Barstow, an Ojibway, when a nun told her that she was "an Indian," S. Carol Berg, "Memories of an Indian Boarding School: White Earth, Minnesota, 1909–1945," *Midwest Review* 11 (Spring 1989): 33.

30. La Flesche, *Middle Five*, 107–10. On Ponca-Omaha relationship, Milner, *With Good Intentions*, 175–76; McCarthy, *Papago Traveller*, 29, 45.

31. Talayesva, *Sun Chief*, 107. For recent accounts of continuing Hopi–Navajo tensions, see Loftin, *Religion and Hopi Life*, 90–92; Catherine Feher-Elston, *Children of Sacred Ground: America's Last Indian War* (Flagstaff, Ariz.: Northland Publishing, 1988).

32. Whitewolf, *Life*, 90–92, 116; Mountain Wolf Woman, *Sister of Crashing Thunder*, 27–28; Eastman, *Deep Woods*, 41–42; Standing Bear, *My People the Sioux*, 57; Winnie, *Sah-gan-de-oh*, 44; Alford, *Civilization*, 99. Also, Stewart, *A Voice in Her Tribe*, 29–30; Sweezy, *Arapaho Way*, 40. See Betzinez, *I Fought with Geronimo*, 165–66: at Fort Sill, Oklahoma, in 1894, Apaches, Kiowas, and Comanches "each shoved forward a Carlisle graduate who conversed in English" and helped the tribes overcome old animosities. Betzinez carefully noted that other Apaches told him of this example of ex-pupil brokering.

33. Wilson, *Ohiyesa*, 154–58; Dexter Fisher, Foreword to Zitkala-Sa, *American Indian*

Stories, xv–xvi. See also Johnson and Wilson, "Gertrude Simmons Bonnin," 27–40; Winnie, *Sah-gan-de-oh*, esp. Chap. 10. Clinton Rickard also saw himself as a spokesman for all Indians, and founded the Indian Defense League of America in 1926, *Fighting Tuscarora*, 76–77, 161. Also Standing Bear, *My People the Sioux*, 183.

34. ARCIA (Washington, D.C.: Government Printing Office, 1891), 70. Two decades later Superintendent Friedman of Carlisle validly claimed that the members of about ninety tribes were "given a wider horizon and a broader conception of life. They form lasting friendships." But he was overambitious in claiming that this process achieved "the nationalizing" of Indians, in the sense of detribalizing them, Annual Report, *Red Man* 3 (Oct. 1910), 63–64.

35. McBeth also found that pupils from different tribes got along well at Oklahoma boarding schools in the twentieth century. She noted that although tribal identity survived, Pan-Indianism increased, *Ethnic Identity*, 120–22. Also 141.

CHAPTER 8

Resistance

THE SOMETIMES PARADOXICAL behavior of Zitkala-Sa epitomizes the meaning of "resistance" in this chapter. As a pupil at a number of schools, she often bitterly resisted her teachers. Yet, after her initial adjustment, the Yankton gave no indication that she wanted to flee the schools. She continued her studies, emerging in 1897 from Earlham College, Indiana, as a highly educated young woman by contemporary white American standards, and taught for a period at the Carlisle Indian School.[1]

Resistance, then, should be distinguished from *rejection*, to be examined in the following chapter. Resistance means those forms of pupil opposition to the school and its staff that were compatible with continued attendance, often compatible with impressive achievement as a student. Playing truant to attend a village ceremony implied resistance rather than rejection, for example, if the pupil intended to return, as some autobiographers did. An individual pupil could pass through resistance into rejection, and permanently flee or refuse all cooperation; or could continually oscillate between the two forms of response. But resistance and rejection embodied different responses to the school.

I

Certain forms of resistance may be universal among schoolchildren. Just like contemporary Euro-American pupils, these Indian narrators delighted in all kinds of pranks, disobedience, and defiance of authority. At the day school which Ah-nen-la-de-ni attended on the Mohawk reservation in New York during the late nineteenth century, the teacher could not preserve discipline over the bigger boys and girls, and the children spent much of their time drawing pictures of themselves and the teacher, and exchanging insults, which later led to schoolyard fights. The Mohawk did not defend or romanticize such unruliness, complaining that he had learned little after six years at the school. Clinton Rickard also criticized such a teacher at a day school on the

Tuscarora reservation in the same state, who was harsh and guilty of favoritism toward her relatives, but similarly failed to control her class.[2]

The generally diligent La Flesche was sometimes among those who resisted. He once tied a wasp under his desk, and the pupils delighted in the mystified response of Gray-beard to the sudden emission of a buzzing sound in the classroom. When the teacher went to investigate, the wasp stung him. The timely entry of visiting dignitaries probably saved La Flesche a thrashing. This Omaha narrator especially conveyed a strong sense of good-humored yet defiant resistance in Gray-beard's classroom, which rarely passed into real rejection of the school, any more than it does in many classrooms throughout the world.[3]

La Flesche and Omaha children temporarily turned the tables on Gray-beard as he struggled with the Omaha name of a new pupil: his pronunciation "set the whole school laughing." During the same episode a pupil accidentally hit Gray-beard in the face with a wad of paper from a small blowpipe: "We covered our faces to suppress the giggles that bubbled up at this mishap," wrote La Flesche. "The teacher looked serious, then we became scared." But Gray-beard exhibited his more tolerant side, and the danger passed. Frank Mitchell's companions made up all kinds of descriptive nicknames in the Navajo language for teachers whose names *they* could not pronounce. One skinny teacher, who at times "got mean," became "Miss Chipmunk"; another became "Miss Red Corn," because of her complexion; one of the kitchen staff, "an awful looking thing," was known to the pupils as "The Woman Who Makes You Scream."[4]

Conspiring to get the better of teachers or of the system constituted an important form of resistance. Standing Bear and his friend so hated the itchy red flannel underwear provided at Carlisle that they secretly bought more comfortable underclothes. But each Sunday morning they had to change quickly into the red flannels for inspection; only after that could they rush to the dormitory and change back. The Lakota similarly enjoyed telling how, by cleaning their own food onto the plates of other students, he and some friends repeatedly rejoined a food line. A Creek who attended the Chilocco Boarding School from 1927 to 1935 caught a major part of the motivation for such actions: "There's no other way you could survive in that kind of an environment," he recalled. "We, we used to *deliberately* do things . . . just to show 'em that we could do it and get away with it. It wasn't . . . *malicious*, we did it for the fun of it, just to let them know that, that we could still outwit them."[5]

Oscar Good Shot's sense of satisfaction at winning a prize in a national essay competition on the subject of tuberculosis was likewise heightened by the deceptive way in which he did it—at least he recounted the story without a hint of guilt. While a student at the Pine Ridge Boarding School in South Dakota during the early twentieth century, the Oglala Lakota (Sioux) exploited his school duties to research the project:

> According to our school rules all books had to be left in the desks at the end of each day. But I was the janitor, so every night I got my tuberculosis book from my desk and went to the basement and studied it while the other boys were playing. Then I put back the book, so nobody knew it had ever been taken out. After some weeks, the government gave me five dollars as third prize.

Ah-nen-la-de-ni also gained great satisfaction from circumventing the lady directress of Lincoln Institute, Philadelphia, who refused to let him apply for admission to nursing school. "She made the mistake of return-ing the application to me," he wrote with a clear sense of having outfoxed the woman. He then sent the completed application "through a secret channel," as all regular mail was examined by school authorities. Later the Mohawk made his escape from the school jail to the nursing school. He had been incarcerated, he believed, for complaining about conditions at the school to the Indian Rights Association, a respected reform group—a particularly courageous act of resistance.[6]

As an ethnologist, Francis La Flesche had a keen memory of carefully planned pupil conspiracies to outwit and even manipulate the school authorities. "There were times when the pupils became very tired of their books, and longed to take a run over the prairies or through the woods," recalled the Omaha. "When this longing came upon them, *they sought for ways and means to have the school closed, and secure a holiday*" [emphasis added]. Knowing they would be called from class to help in the round-up, members of the Middle Five allowed some pigs to escape. The plan worked perfectly: "We ran down the hill with wild shouts and cries. All the afternoon we chased pigs, and had a glorious time, while the girls had to stay in school and be banged at by Gray-beard." The misfortune of the girls no doubt intensified the pleasure, but the final triumph occurred in the evening when the superintendent thanked the boys publicly for the service they had rendered the school in recapturing the pigs! We must not exaggerate the significance of such small victories; most of the time Superintendent Burtt and his staff called the shots. But the pupils no doubt gained much pleasure from doubly outwitting the authorities.[7]

Although they permitted boys and girls to share the same classrooms and dining rooms, and might arrange carefully chaperoned socials, dances, and outings, in general the school authorities strove to separate the sexes. As boys and girls would in Western society, Indian children, especially adolescents, often tried to circumvent such restrictions. La Flesche's school had a barrier across the playground, yet "little romances were going on right under [the teachers'] eyes." Lilah Lindsey, also a pupil at a Presbyterian mission school in the post-Civil War period, conveyed how the sexual segregation only stimulated more curiosity. The two doors leading to the boys' hall and the girls' hall were "forbidden ground" for the other sex. "How often when a teacher opened a door to go over to the boys' side, would a girl peek over to see if she could see a boy. If the teacher was coming over on the girls' side, it was the boys' turn to peek. This forbidden friendship was indeed sacred and mysterious." Among older students, moreoever, attempts persisted to communicate through notes, despite the rules." [8]

Six decades later, the self-proclaimed Christian and dedicated scholar Anna Moore Shaw became an equally dedicated resister of similar rules of segregation. "Although the girls and boys were separated at the Phoenix Indian School," wrote the Pima, "we could not help but notice each other." This was especially true in the case of teenagers and young adults who were old enough for marriage. The "first and only romance" of Shaw's life began in 1912 when at the age of fourteen she met Ross Shaw:

> We wrote notes because the matron was very strict and only let us see each other at social functions. But sometimes Ross would sneak over to the girls' side of the campus, where we could play croquet until the matron discovered us and shooed Ross back where he belonged. Soon we were going together. We were childhood sweethearts.

As the two Pima later married, perhaps it was easier for the otherwise obedient Anna to relate such resistance. But her casual and unapologetic account suggests that such violations were widespread at the school— and at other schools, as narrators and later historians have noted. [9]

Don Talayesva engaged in a number of affairs at various schools; the Hopi also indicated how on some occasions the violations of the segregation rule involved large numbers of pupils, apparently acting in concert. The assistant disciplinarian of the Keams Canyon Boarding in Arizona climbed through a window into the girls' dormitory one night "to sleep with his sweetheart," as the earthy Talayesva recalled. Another Hopi who attempted to do the same was caught and locked in a room all night in nothing but underwear. After questioning by the matron, the boy broke down and gave her a long list of names. Each boy and girl received a whipping, and the boys were then locked up for the day and given bread and water. The pupils must have realised the severity of the punishment should they be caught, yet they had persisted in resisting this rule—obviously far more than a single instance had been involved.[10]

Sometimes anger and even violence erupted against teachers or other school staff. "When my father was ready to leave me, I screamed, kicked, and clung to him, begging to go home," wrote Mourning Dove (Salish). "[W]hen the sister tried to calm me, I screamed all the louder and kicked her. She picked me up off the floor and marched me into a dark closet under the long stairway to scream as loud as I could. She left me to sob myself to sleep. This cured my temper." After equally violent protests at having her hair cut, Zitkala-Sa subsided into bitter accommodation at boarding school in Indiana. Later sent to work in the kitchen, she angrily drove the wooden mixer through the bottom of a jar of turnips, and watched with pleasure as "the paleface woman" lifted the jar and the pulped contents fell to the floor. "I felt triumphant in my revenge," she wrote. But ambivalence immediately surfaced: "deep within me I was a wee bit sorry to have broken the jar." When she noticed the absence of turnips from the school dinner, her mood changed again: "I whooped in my heart for having once asserted the rebellion within me."[11]

Such resistance could be more than irritating to a teacher. Sekaquaptewa (Hopi) reported how, at the Phoenix school, "a big Yuma girl" who was about to be punished "grabbed the strap and chased both the matron and the disciplinarian from the room." The incident conjures up an amusing image, but at Lilah Lindsey's Presbyterian boarding school in the Creek Nation, a girl broke two ribs and wrenched the wrist of a female teacher.[12]

Asa Daklugie described an incident of violent resistance, which at first reading is hard to credit for the picture it provides of the extraordinary tolerance of Captain Pratt. After the misunderstanding in English class, when Daklugie unknowingly misused the word "ferment," his teacher sent the young Apache to the Carlisle superintendent. Pratt locked the office door and then took a whip from behind a bookcase. "I thought that he might be armed," wrote Daklugie, the plausible response of a boy who had spent most of his life until then with Geronimo's band:

> I took the whip from him and tossed it up on the book case. As I did so he grabbed my collar. I turned, seized his, and jerked him off his feet. I held him at arm's length and shook him a few times, then dropped him to the floor.
>
> "If you think you can whip me," I told him, "you are *muy loco*. Nobody

has ever struck me in all my life; and nobody ever will. I could break your neck with my bare hands."

The response of Pratt, Civil War and frontier veteran, was even more surprising. "Strangely," wrote Daklugie, "he did not get mad. Politely he asked me to sit down, and I did." When the boy explained the misunderstanding which had caused the classroom confrontation, Pratt *laughed*, and quietly instructed Daklugie of the need for courteousness toward teachers.[13]

The whole episode might be discounted as the empty boasting of an aging Apache, but the picture of Pratt as a man who mixed strong convictions with a surprisingly tolerant sense of humor is consistent with other accounts. It is also consistent with the self-image Pratt conveys in his own autobiography.[14] Further, the Carlisle principal himself described how a Lakota girl slapped the face of a matron at the school; just like Pratt in Daklugie's description, the matron defused the situation by a calm and unviolent response. Other whites also recorded isolated incidents of student violence against teachers. In 1895, for example, a superintendent wrote with satisfaction about the absence of corporal punishment at his school for Arapaho children, except on one occasion: "a teacher in a fit of passion slapped a boy in the face and in return received a severe blow on the forehead with a slate." The two offenses, according to the understanding writer, "were about equally censurable under all circumstances."[15]

Much of this resistance was a form of escape without escaping, and little different from what white children did in their schools at the time. Other forms of resistance, however, were more specific to children from tribal backgrounds.

II

All cases of syncretic blending of traditions should be seen as cultural resistance to school demands for total rejection of the tribal past and total acceptance of the Christian civilization. Pupil insistence upon speaking the tribal language in violation of school rules was both an example of such syncretism and a major form of cultural resistance— especially when the student *could* use English.

Ah-nen-la-de-ni recalled how pupils at the Lincoln Institute in Philadelphia often violated the language rule, and were punished by being made to stand in the public hall or march about the yard while the other pupils were at play. "Most of the time we talked Navajo, our own language, to each other," recalled Frank Mitchell of his period at Fort Defiance Boarding School. "They did not understand us and we did not understand them." And Kay Bennett remembered how at the Toadlena Boarding School after the holidays, the authorities imposed penalties on those speaking Navajo, to force them into a *resumption* of using English. But few violators were caught "as the children stayed some distance from those in authority, or whispered, covering their mouths, when they wished to use their native tongue." [16]

It is particularly difficult to speak a second language to companions who speak one's mother tongue. We should not, therefore, make too much of the natural tendency of children to lapse into Omaha or Navajo when out of the earshot of teachers, especially when they spoke English poorly. But whether done by choice or because of incomplete mastery of English, this form of resistance diluted the effect of "civilization" upon pupils, and perpetuated tribal thought processes and values.

La Flesche, Chris (Mescalero Apache), and Irene Stewart (Navajo) participated in the telling of tribal mythology within the dormitory. In La Flesche's account the pupils were aware they were violating school rules and on occasion suffered the rod. It is less clear whether they believed that their resistance was a form of cultural subversion of the aims of the schools, or whether they merely enjoyed the defiance of telling stories after the lights went out. Whatever the case, such actions also helped perpetuate tribal cultures within the walls of the school.

Cultural resistance took many other forms. When Peter Hudson began as a six-year-old at the Stockbridge School in Oklahoma during the 1860s, he refused, "like any good Choctaw," to give his name. The teacher was a daughter of Peter Pitchlynn, chief of the Choctaw Nation. She jokingly suggested that the boy's name might be Peter Pitchlynn, and he accepted this: "the school broke out in laughter," wrote Hudson, "and of course I laughed too as I thought I had put something over on the teacher." More dramatic, but equally amusing for all but the victim, was the incident at Carlisle when Jeoffre, a Chiricahua Apache boy, made a spear from a piece of wood and charged the disciplinarian. "The man was so frightened he high-tailed it back to the school, Joeffre in full pursuit," wrote Asa Daklugie. When Joeffre explained to that it had all been a joke, Captain Pratt again demonstrated his tolerant sense of humor: he laughed, and refrained from punishing the boy. [17]

Stealing need not be romanticized as a form of cultural resistance, but it certainly could have cultural implications, as when Jim Whitewolf and other pupils at the Kiowa boarding school became involved in a carefully planned scheme. His main task was to steal meat from the butchering place, and then to pass it along to others who hid it until use. The episode reads like another example of the petty pilfering common at the schools, except for Whitewolf's attempt to explain the motivation: "I think the reason we stole food was that we wanted to cook it our own way, roasted in the ashes." Further, they gave some of the stolen food to a relative who worked at the school, and he took it back to Whitewolf's home—an attempt to involve the school within the tribal network of sharing. The enterprise appears to have been successful. "I never got caught at stealing food," concluded Whitewolf. "We were pretty careful about it." [18]

In order to return temporarily for cultural events in their tribes, pupils sometimes played truant. Once La Flesche fled the school to join his people on the annual buffalo hunt, only to be caught and returned by his uncle; there is no indication he intended to leave permanently. Boys at the Mescalero school made similar escapes, to hear the stories of the old men. "We planned to get back," wrote Chris significantly. Even when one of the Apache storytellers warned the narrator against returning before a storm broke, Chris endured the storm. "I had to get back," he wrote, "I was late for school and I got into trouble, for I was not supposed to go away like that." Whatever his motivation for returning, Chris, like La Flesche, knew that at that point he was engaged in an act of resistance rather than rejection. [19]

"I'm sorry to say that I played hookey sometimes," admitted Goodbird of his truancy to attend scalp dances. "The scalp was raised aloft on a pole, and the women danced about it, screaming and singing glad songs. Warriors painted their faces with charcoal, and danced, sang, yelled and boasted of their deeds. Everybody feasted and made merry." Hardly the environment for a future Christian minister, and indeed the young Hidatsa voluntarily returned to the school next day. But when the teacher scolded him, Goodbird enjoyed a sense of power over her. "She would tell me how naughty I was; but she never punished me, for she knew if she did, I would leave the school." [20] At moments like that it was difficult to tell just who was adjusting to whom.

Passive acceptance of punishment could also become an expression of cultural resistance. When Gray-beard thrashed the young Omaha who organized nightly escapes from the Presbyterian school to the village, the boy "gave no sign of pain . . . he stood unmoved, every muscle relaxed, even his hands were open, showing no emotion whatsoever." Finally the stick broke, and Gray-beard threw it to the floor. The boy "put on his coat, then, with head uplifted and unfaltering steps, went back to his desk, took his pen, and completed the unfinished word of the motto [he had been writing]." La Flesche may have romanticized "the stoic Indian." Yet he noted that although Brush also bravely withstood the beating, "we could see that he felt keenly the blows." That La Flesche admitted even this much weakness in the idolized Brush adds greatly to the impressiveness of the other boy's performance.[21]

Historians have noted that less-dramatic forms of passivity, such as refusing to participate actively in class or to achieve full scholarly potential, could also imply traditional conditioning, as young Indians resisted incorporation into the individualist ethic of the school. Articulate and ambitious narrators such as La Flesche, Eastman, Alford, and Winnie rarely exhibited this form of passive resistance; they epitomized the highly competitive ethic also typical of many tribal groups. Lame Deer, however, did refer to the outward passivity of many of his Lakota classmates and narrators such as Talayesva (Hopi) and Frank Mitchell (Navajo) conveyed little interest in the content of the curriculum. The jealousy provoked by Sekaquaptewa's scholarly success could also have been the expression of the Hopi conformist ethic (though the studious also inspire jealousy in white schoolrooms). Passive resistance combined with degrees of acceptance probably did exist at many of the schools attended by the narrators; but it is difficult to glean much about the extent or effect from the autobiographies. When taken to extremes, as we shall see in the next chapter, passivity and noncooperation could move beyond mere resistance and become powerful means of rejection of the school.[22]

III

Paul E. Willis has shown how, in the 1970s, a group of English working-class boys developed a counterculture bitterly antagonistic to the "official" culture and values of their school. Although always nominally in attendance at the school, these lads adopted specific "working class themes" in their counterculture: "resistance; subversion of authority; informal penetration of the weaknesses and fallibilities of the formal; and an independent ability to create diversion and enjoyment." Building on Willis's model, Celia Haig-Brown presents a similar phenomenon at the Kamloops Indian Residential School in Vancouver, Canada, during the first half of the twentieth century. She characterizes a counterculture or subculture as "groups of children who defined roles, projects, and ways of daily life for and with one another . . . without the sanction, and in some cases without the knowledge of those who officially held the power of administration" Haig-Brown does not see every act of resistance as the expression of a subculture. But such a patterned way of responding to the school did at times develop, and "these opposition movements live clearly in people's memories at times of strength."[23]

There is little in the autobiographies that corresponds to Willis's picture of a group of English youngsters waging "continual guerrilla warfare" against the school and book learning. Or to the picture Wax provides of the Pine Ridge Sioux reservation in South Dakota during the midtwentieth century when, especially with inexperienced teachers, "the peer group may become so powerful that the children literally take over the school."[24] Yet opposition movements and other unsanctioned group activities also lived in the memories of many of the Indian narrators. Unofficial subcultures certainly existed at some of the Indian schools, distinct from the official cultures with their football, socials, and other school-sanctioned activities.

Carefully planned group circumvention of the sexual rules, as at the Keams Canyon Boarding School, suggest the existence of such a subculture. So do the elaborate schemes for stealing and hiding food that Jim Whitewolf described at the Oklahoma school. When they continually spoke to each other in their own languages, pupils were obviously living in a subculture. Indeed, at schools comprising children of one tribe, much of the pupil subculture would be heavily influenced by that tribal culture. The subculture would not be a mere copy of the tribal patterns of children's activity, for children began to change the moment they entered and adjusted to the school.

Ironically, the English language too could become the expression of a student subculture. Lucille Winnie remembered the slang used by students at Haskell. Money was "kale"; a boy's girlfriend was "your aunt," and a girl's boyfriend was "your uncle"; delicious food was "good eats"; and a serious romance was a "bad case." Only from the opposite sex could you get "a pleasant"—a smile. Whether such slang was used elsewhere is irrelevant; once pupils at her school accepted it as their own slang, it had become a clear mark of a subculture.[25]

So was the ritual of battle, with its denigration of supposed cowardice. Often a go-between carried the taunts to and from sometimes reluctant combatants. Indeed, bullying and victimization of each other by groups of boys and girls could also be seen as characteristic of pupil subcultures. An anonymous Choctaw, for example, reported being brought before a secret student kangaroo court at Armstrong Academy, Oklahoma, during the early twentieth century. The tribunal met near a cemetery, and was made up of a "judge or the chairman, and members already in session." After questioning, the chairman asked the members of the tribunal for their decision on the fate of the accused. Before he gained admission into the group—into the subculture—he had to fight a number of boys, although fighting was against school rules. The student tribunal also demonstrated the way in which a subcultural element could simultaneously resist and support the school. Though convened out of sight and earshot of the teachers, the tribunal accused the Choctaw of breaking both its rules and, by speaking Choctaw, *the rules of the school.*[26]

La Flesche was especially alive to patterns of pupil behavior, and provided the clearest example of a student subculture developing independently of school-sanctioned activities. He recalled, for example, how more experienced mediators introduced newcomers to the school and to its pupil subculture. And he noted how the students began to use cake as currency. All the students at the school were from his own Omaha tribe, making it easier for him to see the syncretism, as tribal values mutated in the school situation. He noted how the hierarchy of Omaha society broke down, and students had to work out new arrangements, based on ability to fight and to attract friends.[27]

Yet elements of traditional social organization persisted. Although La Flesche conveyed a sense of general pupil community vis-à-vis the staff, more striking is the division of the student body—at least the boys—into gangs. Like tribal societies each of these new groupings, often age-graded, had its own roles, rules, and ritual. Gangs from different age levels possessed different privileges, as the leader of "the Big Seven" noted when he invited the boys of the Middle Five to sit with his gang:

> "There is not a 'gang' in the school that has not its secrets. . . . Ordinarily we do not interfere with each other's affairs; but now that you have the same privileges that we have had . . . we of the Seven think that your 'gang' should unite with ours in a secret that up to this time has been ours alone, and share in its pleasures. Are you willing to join in it?

The younger boys assented to escape each night from a high window, and return to the village for a prize, a bag of pemmican. Back at the dormitory they sat Indian-fashion on the floor, and the leader offered a piece of pemmican to Wakonda—with Gray-beard asleep downstairs! The whole affair was conducted in Omaha, and La Flesche leaves the impression that it was a form of initiation—the leader spoke "words which had been sacred to generations of boys who had preceded us." *Neither La Flesche nor the older leader made any specific connections with similar-*

aged Omaha boys at the village, however, suggesting that they had developed new kinds of groupings at the school, utilizing elements of their Omaha culture.[28]

According to Allen James (Pomo), there was also a gang-based subculture among the boys at Sherman Institute half a century later.[29] Obviously they felt the need for protection and mutual support, both against the school and against each other. Unfortunately, we know much less about such groupings among the girls.

Occasionally, subcultural activities included the plotting of flight from the school. But neither La Flesche nor the leader of the Big Seven even implied that the goal of the Omaha gangs or of other forms of resistance was to prevent learning or to plot permanent escape. The student subculture at the Omaha mission, then, and probably at many other schools, institutionalized both resistance and acceptance, and expressed fundamentally ambivalent pupil responses. Although always a threat to the total control sought by the school authorities, such subcultures could also work to their advantage by making the school more bearable to pupils.

Not every isolated act of mediation or every outburst of anger or malingering can be seen as a manifestation of the subculture. Especially in schools where large numbers of children from different tribes suddenly found themselves thrown together, many endured isolation and loneliness and even persecution until they attached themselves to friends or gangs; some never did so. Trapped behind a language barrier, Elsie Allen (Pomo) endured almost total isolation at Covelo Boarding School; by no stretch of the definition was she within a student subculture that terrible year.

Where they existed, then, pupil subcultures probably developed slowly and did not necessarily absorb all the students. Perhaps, as La Flesche's accounts implies, boys and girls sometimes developed quite different subcultures, or subcultures that partly overlapped and partly remained distinctive. Irene Stewart (Navajo), for example, suggested how an interest in fashion could cut across tribal differences among girls at the Haskell Institute in the 1920s.[30]

IV

Beyond merely "getting used to it," many claimed or implied that school had become a kind of home, and that they had grown apart from kin. In the case of Indians who had quarreled with family about going to school, such as Zitkala-Sa or Polingaysi Qoyawayma, this is understandable. The latter "almost dreaded the day when her four years at Sherman Institute would come to a close, and she would return to her home. She was certain she would not like it." She felt by then that she had outgrown village life: "She had burst like a butterfly from the confining chrysalis of her Hopi childhood."[31]

Other narrators had fewer reasons to dread the return: "The family tie is strong among Indians," wrote Ah-nen-la-de-ni. Yet there is little indication in his short autobiography that the Mohawk felt aggrieved by his nine-year separation from kin, many of whom had died in his absence. Irene Stewart, whose "attempt to live the traditional Navajo life was chopped up with the school life," was disarmingly explicit about her feelings at Fort Defiance. "By the time I entered fifth grade I had forgotten about my [dead] grandmother and other relatives," she wrote. "I was no longer always lonesome and homesick. And when I went home on summer vacations, I missed the fun I had at school." Although Kay Bennett enjoyed a warm relationship with her mother, the young Navajo remarked about how quickly the pupils got used to the school routine, "and forgot their families and family troubles at home." Fred Kabotie wrote to his Hopi family while away, and appeared disappointed that no one wrote back; he looked forward to going home. Yet upon return to the village of Shungapovi he felt foreign, and was glad to return to public school in Santa Fe, with its white student body. Fellow Hopi Helen Sekaquaptewa connived with the principal of the Keams Canyon Boarding School to circumvent the rules requiring a parent's permission before transferring to an off-reservation boarding school. "Time passed by, and I grew older, and it was better for me at school," she wrote. "I was weaned away from home."[32]

Despite his near-traumatic arrival at the Omaha mission school, Francis La Flesche soon learned the ways of the boys and the teachers, and began to understand his books. Even before he had joined a gang he "felt quite at home and independent," perhaps because Brush had already befriended him. Again and again James McCarthy noted how little he missed his Papago family once he adjusted to the various schools he attended. "I felt at home in Santa Fe School," wrote McCarthy; "I did not have homesick feelings because, I guess, I had my mind on work, play, school study, and everything else"—close to what the school authorities hoped would be the case. Later, upon leaving one school, he wrote that his class "was just like a family, and there were many tears— mine also." Long after he had left Carlisle and awaited a visit to the reservation of his old school principal, Jason Betzinez told how "we were as anxious to see General Pratt as if he were our own father."[33]

Such accounts may partly reflect nostalgia, but not always. Narrator claims for deep acceptance of the school are lent credibility, nevertheless, by "The Story of My Life" an essay written by Anna Bender, an Ojibway graduate of Hampton Institute in the early twentieth century, while she was still a student at Hampton, only a few years after the events and feelings described. Leaving home at the age of six for the Lincoln Institute in Philadelphia, she called this school the "first thing I can distinctly remember," and after seven years there felt "I had no reason for wanting to go home, except that other students went to theirs." Met at the station by her mother, sisters, and by two younger brothers she had never seen before, she immediately experienced reentry problems. She became "so lonesome that I did not know what to do except to cry to go back [to school]." Her father asked Anna if she recognized him, "which I didn't, and then he said I had changed a great deal from a loving child to a stranger and looked different." Bender's essay is that of *a young person* rather than an aged narrator. It demonstrates her deep transformation by the school, which had become for her, as for some other pupils, a second or even a first home.[34]

Part of the reason for such radical adjustment by many of the narrators was that—individually, in groups, and in broader subcultures—pupils developed many ways of resisting and thus of making school more bearable. The authorities would have been especially pleased to read that for pupils like La Flesche, McCarthy, Betzinez, and others, the school had become "a home"—that sacred word. Teachers and staff would have been less pleased to realize the mixed motivations behind such acceptance: Admittedly school offered real incentives, but it also became a more acceptable place because pupils could circumvent some of the rules and add the spice of defiance to their lives.

There were narrators, however, for whom school immediately or finally became unbearable. Neither institutional incentives nor pupil resistance and subcultural activities sustained them, and they rejected school.

Notes

1. On Zitkala-Sa's school experiences as both pupil and teacher, see *American Indian Stories*, 39–99. See also Foreword by Dexter Fisher, v–xx on her life. Also Johnson and Wilson, "Gertrude Simmons Bonnin," 28–29.
2. Ah-nen-la-de-ni, "An Indian Boy's Story," 1781–82; Rickard, *Fighting Tuscarora*, 8–9. Also Jim Whitewolf, *Life*, 86–87. On problems of discipline and resistance at white American schools, see, for example, Finkelstein, *Governing the Young*, 165–67, 170–71, 173–74, 214–17; Tyack and Hansot, *Learning Together*, 66, 177–79.
3. La Flesche, *Middle Five*, 97–98.
4. La Flesche, *Middle Five*, 74–75; Mitchell, *Navajo Blessingway Singer*, 66. Also, Lame Deer and Erdoes, *Seeker of Visions*, 34–36; McBeth, *Ethnic Identity*, 129–30.
5. Standing Bear, *My People the Sioux*, 144, 154; Creek, Narrative no. 4, Lowawaima, "Oral Histories," 248. Also Stinson, in Cash and Hoover, eds., *To Be an Indian*, 95.
6. Goodshot, "Oscar Good Shot," in Marquis, ed., *The Cheyennes*, 264–65; Ah-nen-la-de-ni, "An Indian Boy's Story," 1785. Also Talayesva, *Sun Chief*, 103–104, on playing sick. Haig-Brown also notes the absence of "any sense of regret," and sees various forms of resistance, including stealing, as "the actions of strong people against a system which degraded and dehumanized," *Resistance and Renewal*, 103 (Canada).
7. La Flesche, *Middle Five*, 66–68.
8. *Ibid.*, 49, 52–53; Lindsey, "Memories," 182. On evasions of similar restrictions in tribal societies, see, for example: Stands in Timber and Liberty, *Cheyenne Memories*, 292; Lame Deer and Erdoes, *Seeker of Visions*, 139–42; Fletcher and La Flesche, *Omaha Tribe*, vol. 1, 318–19; Mourning Dove, *Salishan*, 49–52, Chap. 2, note 18, above. Cf. Hyer, *One House*, 37, on the discomfort of pueblo boys and girls at being seated together at Santa Fe Indian School.
9. Shaw, *Pima Past*, 137. See also Trennert, *Phoenix Indian School*, 133–36: "students found numerous ways to avoid the system." A few young women became pregnant every year at the school; Jenkins, *Girl from Williamsburg*, 342; Wilbert H. Ahern, "'The Returned Indians': Hampton Institute and Its Indian Alumni, 1879–1893," *Journal of Ethnic Studies*, 10 (Winter 1983): 108. "Hampton proved to be a match-maker for many of its Indian students"; McBeth, *Ethnic Identity*, 131–132; Berkhofer, *Salvation and the Savage*, 41; Haig-Brown, *Resistance and Renewal*, 94–95 (Canada).
10. On Talayesva's sexual escapades as a student, see *Sun Chief*, 111–118, and 97–99 on the group violation of rules. Also, Woodruff, *Indian Oasis*, 139–41.
11. Mourning Dove, *Salishan*, 27; Zitkala-Sa, *American Indian Stories*, 59–61.
12. Sekaquaptewa, *Me and Mine*, 137; Lindsey, "Memories," 186.
13. Daklugie et al., *Indeh*, 150–51.
14. See also Daklugie et al., *Indeh*, 151 (in text); Standing Bear, *My People the Sioux*, 145; Coleman, "Credibility"; Pratt, *Battlefield and Classroom*.
15. Pratt, *Battlefield and Classroom*, 274–75; Report of Superintendent of Arapaho School, ARCIA (1895), *House Document* No. 5, vol. II, 54 Congress, 1 session, serial 3382, 249. Also, Jenkins, *Girl from Williamsburg*, 283–84.
16. Ah-nen-la-de-ni, "An Indian Boy's Story," 1783; Mitchell, *Navajo Blessingway Singer*, 66; Bennett, *Kaibah*, 226–27. Also McCarthy, *Papago Traveller*, 29–30, 40; La Flesche, *Middle Five*, 112. I recall surreptitiously speaking *English* at a camp where the Irish language was mandatory.
17. Peter Hudson, "Recollections of Peter Hudson," *Chronicles of Oklahoma* 10 (Dec. 1932): 507; Daklugie et al., *Indeh*, 151.
18. Jim Whitewolf, *Life*, 96. On theft, also: Mitchell, *Navajo Blessingway Singer*, 67; McCarthy, *Papago Traveller*, 41. Cf. note 6, above.
19. La Flesche, *Middle Five*, Chap. 10. For comments by missionaries on such flights to the buffalo hunt, see Coleman, "Credibility"; Chris, *Apache Odyssey*, 87–88. Also, Hyer,

One House, 62–63; pupils at Santa Fe "ran away often but fully intended to return to school."

20. Goodbird, *Goodbird the Indian*, 41.

21. La Flesche, *Middle Five*, 122. Also Jenkins, *Girl from Williamsburg*, 267–68.

22. McBeth, *Ethnic Identity*, 130–31; Adams, "From Bullets to Boarding Schools," 232; Wax, "Warrior Dropouts," 148; Michael C. Coleman, "The Responses of American Indian Children to Presbyterian Schooling in the Nineteenth Century: An Analysis Through Missionary Sources," *History of Education Quarterly* 27 (Winter 1987): 486–87; Lame Deer and Erdoes, *Seeker of Visions*, 33.

23. Paul E. Willis, *Learning to Labour: How Working Class Kids Get Working Class Jobs* (Aldershot, Hampshire: Gower, 1977), 84. These lads looked forward to leaving at the statutory minimum age of sixteen, 5; Haig-Brown, *Resistance and Renewal*, Chap. 4, quotations, 88, 104. Haig-Brown uses the terms "subculture" and "counterculture" interchangeably; I have confined myself to "subculture." The resistant pupil subculture is a major theme of a Canadian autobiography, Basil H. Johnson, *Indian School Days* (Norman: University of Oklahoma Press, 1988). Tyack and Hansot also use Willis in discussion of pupil countercultures within some white American schools in the late nineteenth and early twentieth centuries, *Learning Together*, 177–79.

24. Willis, *Learning to Labour*, 19; Wax, "Warrior Dropouts," 147.

25. Winnie, *Sah-gan-de-oh*, 52. Even in retrospect, Winnie makes no comment upon the incestuous implications of the terms "aunt" and "uncle." Also Hyer, *One House*, 36; La Flesche, *Middle Five*, xviii; and DeMallie on the "Indian English," a dialect that developed at multitribal boarding schools, Introduction to Nicholas Black Elk, *The Sixth Grandfather: Black Elk's Teachings Given to John G. Niehardt*, edited by Raymond S. DeMallie (Lincoln: University of Nebraska Press, 1984), 32.

26. Anonymous Choctaw, in *Nations Remembered: An Oral History of the Five Civilized Tribes, 1865–1907*, edited by Theda Perdue (Westport, Conn.: Greenwood Press, 1980), 131–32. Although autobiographers did not draw attention to the fact, student tribunals also became part of the officially sanctioned pupil culture at some schools; see, for example, United States Indian Service, Training School for Indian Youth Carlisle, ARCIA (1881), *House Executive Document* No. 1, part 5, vol. II, 47 Congress, 1 session, serial 2018, 246; Report of Hampton Normal and Agricultural Institute, Hampton, Va., ARCIA (1890), *House Executive Document* No 1, part 5, vol. II, 51 Congress, 2 session, serial 2841, 319–20. There was an Indian court martial, and a student-elected court called the Indian Council.

27. La Flesche, *Middle Five*, esp. Chaps. 1–4, on both unofficial and official mediation, and 71, on the use of gingerbread currency. Compared to the large boarding schools with their debating societies, clubs, and sports, there appears to have been little of an officially sanctioned, extracurricular student culture at the small Omaha mission school.

28. La Flesche, *Middle Five*, Chap. 13, quotation 113. Also, Lowawaima, ed., "Oral Histories," esp. 241–42; Haig-Brown, *Resistance and Renewal*, 96–98, on sometimes oppressive *male* gangs.

29. James, *Chief of the Pomos*, 40–42.

30. Stewart, *A Voice in Her Tribe*, 29–30. A Pima friend cut Stewart's hair so she would look like the "it" girl, Clara Bow.

31. Qoyawayma, *No Turning Back*, 64.

32. Ah-nen-la-de-ni, "An Indian Boy's Story," 1786–87; Stewart, *A Voice in Her Tribe*, 18–19; Bennett, *Kaibah*, 226; Kabotie, *Hopi Indian Artist*, 38–39; Sekaquaptewa, *Me and Mine*, 132–33. Also Winnie, *Sah-gan-de-oh*, 52–53.

33. La Flesche, *Middle Five*, 12; McCarthy, *Papago Traveller*, 42, 45, 55, 65; Betzinez, *I Fought with Geronimo*, 202. See also McBeth, *Ethnic Identity*, 144–45.

34. Annie Bender, "The Story of My Life," Annie Bender Student Record, Hampton University Archives. There is much overwriting on the MS, apparently in a teacher's hand, but I have quoted what seems to be the original text. See also Molin, "Training the Hand," 93–97.

CHAPTER 9

Rejection

"**K**ANSEAH WAS UNHAPPY AND not interested in school," wrote James Kaywaykla of one of the youngest Apache prisoners brought to Carlisle after the Geronimo campaign in 1886. "Captain Pratt let him return to his people after a few months." For a superintendent as determined as Pratt to surrender so soon to "savage" intransigence suggests that the boy's rejection of the school was complete. Kanseah was one of many pupils who could not or would not adjust to an alien method of education. Many narrators rejected school straight off by fleeing or trying to do so; many rejected it later, after having spent a number of difficult or productive years accepting some elements, resisting others. Sometimes a narrator could reject a particular school, yet accept another one, or reject school as an institution while continuing to value some of its learning.[1]

The line between resistance and rejection often blurred, therefore, and narrators crossed from one to another on many occasions. Yet this chapter will demonstrate that certain responses implied more than resistance-accommodation; they constituted rejection of the school or major elements of its program.

I

There is overwhelming agreement among the narrators, and between the narrators and contemporary white American sources, that Indian children sickened and died in large numbers at the schools. Irrespective of their mental attitudes, in other words, physically many of them rejected the new institution. Nowhere is this more poignantly conveyed than in the relieved comment by a missionary of the Presbyterian BFM in the 1850s: "Not one of our children died during the year." Eight decades later the Meriam Report castigated "the deplorable health conditions" at most of the Indian schools. And throughout the period covered by the present study, agents and teachers lamented the continual loss of children to sickness.[2]

It is impossible to know whether fewer Indian children would have died had they stayed at home. But it is likely that bringing together large numbers who had little resistance to many Euro-American diseases, especially in crowded boarding schools where pupils shared towels and musical instruments, significantly increased health hazards. White educators were deeply conscious of the problems, and attempted to alleviate them. In 1902, for example, the agent at Fort Apache, Arizona, reported the death of a number of children, which resulted in the bitter opposition of parents to further schooling. "I was compelled to resort to force, and every pupil was returned to the school by the police," wrote C. W. Crouse. But he also strove to improve the ventilation of the building in hopes of preventing further pupil death, the scourge of Indian schooling.[3]

Many schools were situated in areas remote from modern medical facilities, and few teachers availed themselves of Indian medical practices. But even at schools relatively close to "civilization," such as Hampton and Carlisle, young Indians died. "The death rate here has been very serious this year among pupils from Lower Brulé and Crow Creek Agencies, though not unusual or serious among the rest," conceded the annual report from Hampton Institute in 1885. The report also noted that "epidemic diseases" and serious illness struck some of its pupils. During his recruiting missions to the Pine Ridge reservation in the 1880s, Standing Bear faced the bitter complaints of older Sioux, some of whose children had died at Carlisle.[4]

Obviously not every pupil death implied attitudinal rejection of the school. Brush, the great friend of La Flesche, died convinced of the importance of the new learning.[5] Nevertheless, even if we can never be sure of the exact cause of illness, the sickness or death of pupils was a response, a form of physical (sometimes linked to psychological) rejection.

At Jim Whitewolf's school around 1893, a returned runaway infected a large number of boys with the measles. The Kiowa Apache himself was "sure sick" but recovered; his youngest brother was among the many dead pupils. The half-brother of Chris (Mescalero Apache) came back sick from Albuquerque school, and he too died. Irene Stewart (Navajo) believed that the double pneumonia she contracted at the Fort Defiance Boarding School almost killed her. And Elsie Allen too had a close escape. While taking care of a friend sick with tuberculosis at the Covelo Boarding School, the Pomo ate all the patient's leftovers. Allen credited her survival mostly to a curing ceremony earlier performed upon her by a Pomo "singing doctor."[6]

La Flesche, Chris (Mescalero), and others generally did not blame the schools for the sickness which struck them or kin or schoolmates. As we have seen, narrators often specifically noted the concern and dedication of teaching and medical staff during such crises. Sadly, but nevertheless with little rancor, Standing Bear once did imply that the schools were in part responsible for their pupils' health problems. An apparently healthy companion complained that he did not want to go to class; a few days later he was dead. Standing Bear volunteered an explanation which, if it cannot claim clinical validity, does suggest the strain of schooling for many young Indians. "That was one of the hard things about our education," wrote the Brulé Sioux, "we had to get used to so many things we had never known before that it worked on our nerves to such an extent that it told on our bodies." In a similarly critical but forgiving vein, Charles Eastman recalled how the confinement of the school led to the death of his younger cousin.[7]

Suicide was perhaps the most extreme expression of physical and psychological rejection, and the annual report of the Hampton Institute for 1885 almost accused one Indian of such a response. When asked by a nurse why he disregarded "all the laws of health" at the school, the pupil replied: "'Because the white man is afraid to die, but the Indian is not.'" There are few unambiguous accounts in the autobiographies, however, of Indian children taking their own lives to escape school. Referring to a period later than when he himself attended, the Oglala shaman Lame Deer claimed that "in these fine new buildings Indian children still commit suicide, because they are lonely among all that noise and activity. I know of a ten-year-old who hanged himself." But Lame Deer did not claim that any of his school companions in the early twentieth century took their own lives. Max Henley (Navajo) recounted how at certain times of year attempting to flee school could amount to near- or actual suicide. Some runaways suffered frostbitten ears and feet: "Others froze to death."[8]

Lending credence to such a claim of almost suicidal recklessness was the 1908 letter from E. J. Bost, superintendent of the Wittenberg Indian School, Wisconsin, to the commissioner of Indian Affairs. A Winnebago pupil had run away "no less than six times" in about three months, wrote Bost in despair:

> I have gone after him myself several times and have talked to him. We have been good to him, did not punish him at all for running away several times, not until *his people* [emphasis added] told me that I had better chain him or punish him some way, that they were afraid a storm would come up some time when he was on the road and *he would perish with the cold as two Menominee children had recently* [emphasis added]. I had the disciplinarian

keep him chained about a week one time and just as soon as he had a chance he ran away again.[9]

Tribal young were trained to seek physical hardship, so every case of a frozen runaway should not be seen as suicide. But considering the strains they faced at school, it is possible that some of the many children who died at, or in flight from, the schools during the decades under review committed suicide or acted so recklessly that death was likely. There is little concrete evidence in the autobiographies, however, to substantiate this speculation. Most of the irreconcilables physically survived their ordeals, and found other ways to express rejection.

II

A less dramatic method was that employed by the young Apache sent home by Captain Pratt: withdrawal of all cooperation and interest in learning. Luther Standing Bear remembered a similar case at Carlisle earlier in the same decade. When Standing Bear's father visited the school, the principal asked him to take an uncooperative boy back to the reservation: "he did not try to learn anything, nor seem inclined to want to," wrote Standing Bear. His father objected, feeling that the school had accepted responsibility for the difficult boy. But again the usually determined Pratt insisted that an individual Indian was beyond the help of the school. Standing Bear's father finally agreed, and the whole incident seemed to stimulate Standing Bear himself to greater effort: he became "more determined than ever to learn all the white people's ways, no matter how hard I had to study." The two boys thus manifested near-extremes in their responses to the school, from quiet rejection to intense dedication; yet some years later Standing Bear himself would reject Carlisle.[10]

White Americans also reported such expulsion of intransigent young Indians. In 1880—perhaps the year of the incident recalled by Standing Bear—Pratt himself noted somewhat ambiguously that fifteen pupils had been returned to their peoples "because of imperfect physical and mental condition." The agent for the Pimas and Maricopas was more specific when he remarked in 1882 how a pupil adamantly refused to have his hair cut: "he was one of our brightest and most moral boys, but I could not vary the rule, and he returned home." And in 1914 the assistant commissioner of Indian Affairs accepted the recommendation of the superintendent of the Wittenberg Indian Boarding School that an uncooperative Oneida pupil be expelled.[11]

As suggested in the previous chapter, passive noncooperation did not always imply *rejection* of the school. The student who stoically accepted a whipping at the Omaha mission continued his schooling. And some apparently passive Indians may have feared peer disapproval if they studied harder. But the passivity and noncooperation of pupils such as Kanseah the Apache or the boy described by Standing Bear were of a different nature, and expressed not merely resistance along with acceptance, but a determined rejection of the new institution.

Attempting to burn down the school was a radical form of rejection. Contemporary whites sometimes reported cases of arson by pupils. In 1899, for example, William A. Jones, commissioner of Indian Affairs, told of "the most disastrous fire of years" which occurred at the Mount Pleasant Boarding School in Michigan. "An Indian school girl was the incendiary," Jones claimed. "She confessed to having made ample preparations by placing oiled rags in one of the upper rooms and setting fire to them an hour before it was discovered." This girl was sent to a reformatory institution. Only rarely did a narrator relate possible instances of arson, but autobiography is hardly the best source for gleaning evidence of such criminal action. During the 1880s, when Narcissa Owen was teaching at the Cherokee Female Seminary in Tahlequah, Oklahoma, she visited an ex-schoolmate, now in an insane asylum. This man confided: "I burned up [a] schoolhouse to see the big fire." And Elsie Allen lamented the fact that the girls' dormitory at the Covelo Boarding School in California burned down in the early twentieth century, taking with it all her clothes. The fire, wrote the Pomo carefully, was "believed to have been started by some older girls who hated the school."[12]

III

"I opened the school October, 1, 1887, with an attendance of 52 pupils," reported superintendent James Gallagher of the Keams Canyon Boarding School for Hopis. "After being here about two weeks *there was a general stampede for the mesa*" [emphasis added]. Gallagher quickly quelled the rumor that he was about to kidnap the children and carry them off to Washington, and the school tentatively began again. Twenty years later Navajo policemen still had to catch Hopi children, and the problem of runaways plagued the authorities throughout the period under review. Significantly, early in the twentieth century government teachers sometimes employed the term "deserter" for runaways. This was partly in line with the military organization common at the schools. But adding the stigma of cowardice was no doubt intentional, especially around the time of World War I.[13]

Ensuring attendance in the new school systems on the home front was also a problem for educational reformers, as they struggled to inculcate democratic and Christian orthodoxies into Anglo children and into the more problematic children of non-English-speaking immigrants.[14] But chronic truancy or absenteeism do not appear to have been as big a problem in white schools as in Indian schools. By 1928 the Meriam Report expressed optimism about improvements in Indian attendance, yet noted that fewer eligible tribal children than whites were enrolled at school. The report also warned that the available statistics were "probably unduly optimistic in that they report enrollment only and say nothing of the serious irregularities of attendance"—runaways, no doubt—"among the full-bloods nearly everywhere."[15]

Teacher frustration can easily be understood: the imparting of English and difficult academic subjects required long-term, regular attendance from students. Truancy and all kinds of absenteeism thus sabotaged the whole educational effort. Further, the symbolic rejection of the Christian civilization implied by flight and nonattendance equally affronted school staff; thus the insistence upon compulsory education and the often harsh and humiliating punishments imposed on runaways.

The autobiographies abundantly corroborated contemporary reports of missionaries, agents, and others; many narrators recounted their own flights from school or those of fellow students. Perhaps the clearest cases of outright rejection occurred in the first terrible days, when shocked and lonely Indians sometimes succeeded in fleeing the schools, at least until hauled back. Fred Kabotie fled a Hopi day school after watching an enraged teacher try to thrash a boy. "Even when my sister said she was being punished for my absence, I couldn't make myself go back." The truant officer caught Kabotie, but he escaped again and for a period "ran wild." Such escapes could also involve the symbolic rejection of the new institution. On his first day at the Polocca day school, Albert Yava and fellow Hopis disliked the new school clothes "because they made us feel ridiculous." So when the teacher sent them outside for recess "we took off our [school] clothes and hid them under some bushes, then we ran naked back to the village up on the Mesa." But the Hopi truant officer finally caught them and "we had to put those clothes on again, and listen to the teacher . . ." Yava and Kabotie later *volunteered* to attend more advanced schools. Their flights from the day schools implied initial rejection, but their later actions indicate the changing responses of many narrators.[16]

"I ran away from school three times," declared Jim Whitewolf, the Kiowa Apache. Not all of these flights from boarding school could be characterized as rejection, however. Whitewolf *voluntarily* returned after the first escape, but other pupils who fled with him did not. For Whitewolf, in other words, this flight was a minor act of resistance; for the others it apparently became a final act of rejection. The second time he also fled with the encouragement of fellow pupils. Then Logan, Whitewolf's older mediator, came looking for the boys, as they were in danger of freezing to death. This time Whitewolf *was* engaged in an act of rejection: "I didn't want to go back," he wrote, "but I had to." The third time a group also escaped to the camp, only to be apprehended by the agency police; it is unclear whether the boys would later have returned of their own free will.[17]

Peers were obviously of crucial importance in this process of resistance or rejection, egging on or conspiring with each other to escape; "unofficial" pupil mediation did not always benefit the school. Sometimes, in extreme defiance of the sexual barriers at the school, couples fled. "Often a boy and a girl would have it planned," wrote Sekaquaptewa of the Phoenix school, "and go at the same time." Kay Bennett recalled the flight of four boys and girls—probably couples—from the Toadlena Boarding School on the Navajo reservation in New Mexico around 1930. More carefully supervised than boys, the girls were missed sooner. Upon recapture they faced public humiliation. "To have one's hair cut short was a drastic break in Navajo tradition," wrote Bennett, "but to have it all cut off, was a great disgrace." The other girls of the school "watched in shocked silence" as their companions were sheared, "thinking what if this should happen to them." But the punishment also had a counterproductive effect from the school's point of view. When word of the humiliation reached the families of the runaway girls, their parents came and removed them from the school. Whatever the motives for running away, the flight ended their schooling at Toadlena.[18]

On other occasions kin also helped effect the escape. The Navajo parents of Frank Mitchell were similarly aghast to see the way the boy's hair had been cut at the Fort Defiance Boarding School, and refused to let him return after a break. They so frightened him with stories of catching sicknesses from white people that he himself was happy to stay with his family. Three years later Mitchell's school clothes and shoes had worn out, however, so he "got to thinking about going back to school again." After a further period at Fort Defiance, he fled with a schoolmate to get a job on the railroad, and "never did go back to school again." When the white father of James and Sidney Huntington (Koyukuks) visited them at their Alaska boarding school, he asked with mock casualness if they wished to join him as trappers in the forest. "Sidney and I almost busted open with excitement," wrote James. "We said yes and danced around a little, for our dream had come true. So that was the end of my education." Yet James took pride in his school achievements. He had learned to read and write, and had gone through the third reader—"more than most kids do in this part of the world," he boasted. But after less than three full years of schooling he was now "ready to start the learning that was to keep me going for the rest of my life: how to use what the land has to give you." [19]

Some narrators who spent long periods at school claimed that they would have fled except for fear of punishment, kin disapproval, or other forms of retribution. G. W. Grayson (Creek) noted how other students fled his school; he might have done so himself had he not feared his father's threat of a beating. The Navajo father of Chester Yellowhair used a more subtle but no less effective approach. "Do not forget," he told the boy, "if you run away from school, I will have to go to jail." Irene Stewart heeded her Navajo father's warnings about dangerous animals who might eat runaways; she also feared the punishments meted out to offenders at the school, and remembered the frozen feet of one returned runaway. And Asa Daklugie claimed that the haunting memory of Geronimo, who had instructed him to learn the ways of the whites, and the equally haunting presence of his wife-to-be at Carlisle, kept him from permanently fleeing. [20]

When Annie Lowry (Paiute) fled a local day school in Nevada, her white father gave her "a good whipping with a willow birch," got her cleaned up, and returned her to the white family with whom she boarded. "Back in school I was faced with the fact that running away was useless," she recalled. Yet some years later, when the father insisted that she leave her mother and come with him to the East to attend a women's college, Lowry would not go. "After my father left," she wrote, "I never went to school again." Had her father not thwarted the first attempt to flee, her rejection of the school might have begun even earlier. [21]

One of the most intriguing of runaways was James McCarthy, the Papago. His warm, serene, almost whimsical autobiography conveys a strong sense of wanderlust. He was one of those for whom school became like a home, yet he fled a number of schools. And he described something of a subculture of runaways at Phoenix, as pupils plotted escape in their native language. "After listening to the boys talk I wanted to go home," he wrote. With an older boy as ringleader, McCarthy and a few other Pimas fled. Early in the trip two of the younger boys decided to return to the school, but McCarthy, the leader, and another boy continued. Three and a half days later, after an epic walk of about 115 miles, the twelve-year-old McCarthy introduced himself to his shocked mother, who at first did not recognize him.

If a mixture of loneliness, resentment of bullying Pimas, and the influence of older boys provoked his first flight, the second was the product of whimsy. After his "long walk" he attended other schools, and ended up in Santa Fe Indian School. He enjoyed the summer outings to Colorado, where he could make some money. Yet in 1914, during one of these outings and for no particular reason, he again fled. Out on a walk, he reached some railway tracks:

> I guess that I did not realize how far I walked that morning. After a while I came to a section house. A man came out and asked me if I wanted work. I asked him, "What kind of work?" He said, "To check the track joints." . . . I said "Yes," without thinking.

And he was off again, driving a three-wheeled track car. But ambivalence racked him, as he worried that his friends would worry about him, and he missed the Santa Fe school. He soon walked away from this job—he estimated at one point that he had walked 800 miles or more during his wanderings! He continually gravitated back to schools, so it is perhaps incorrect to categorize his actions as rejection of school as such. But his casualness toward attendance certainly expressed rejection of the rigid school ideals of order and regularity; he actually signed up for Phoenix school twice, under different names. Ambivalence characterized the schooldays of James McCarthy, punctuated as they were by his long walks away from the institution.[22]

IV

In a sense, any Indian who left school before he or she had graduated, even with permission of the school authorities, was rejecting the institution, or at least making an independent decision upon its continued relevance to life. The schooling of James McCarthy and many of his student companions ended suddenly in 1917, when they volunteered for the United States armed forces. Although the superintendent of Phoenix actually helped the undersized and underweight McCarthy gain admission into the National Guard, the Papago's patriotism or thirst for new adventure did signify final rejection of the school.[23]

Refugio Savala and Rosalio Moisés (both Yaquis) quit school to work, apparently without objections from school authorities. In retrospect Myrtle Begay (Navajo) was unsure why she quit in 1931. "I dropped out of Fort Apache before I had finished high school. I don't know why I never went back. I just stayed around home and worked for some families at Chinle." Her rejection of schooling for herself was final, but not bitter: later she worked for the principal of the Fort Defiance Indian School, and believed that "traditional education and Anglo education are the same in many ways." Despite the bullying and initial loneliness, Helen Sekaquaptewa greatly enjoyed her schooling at a number of institutions. When the three years she could spend at Phoenix Boarding School without parental consent were at an end, Superintendent Brown invited her to stay on. Although she still had not graduated, "something" told this dedicated student and entrepreneur to go home—she had not been back in thirteen years. She intended to continue at another institution, but soon married Emory Sekaquaptewa, her Phoenix sweetheart. So ended her schooling, but not her interest in American education, which she communicated to her own growing family.[24]

Fellow Hopi Don Talayesva did not tell exactly why he decided to finish at the Sherman Institute; decisions seem to have been made by himself and the authorities together. But a major factor in his decision to return to the old life was the vivid dream-vision he experienced when he fell sick after speaking badly of a "two-heart" witch. Before the vision, he appeared to be contentedly acculturating: "I was half-Christian and half-heathen [then]," he wrote in a striking passage, "and often wished that there were some magic that could change my skin into that of a white man." He stayed at Sherman for about a year and a half after the dream-vision, but back in his home village for the first time in many years, he reflected upon his life away:

> I thought about my school days and all that I had learned. I could talk like a gentleman, read, write and cipher. I could name all the states in the Union, with their capitals, repeat the names of all the books in the Bible, quote a hundred verses of scripture, sing more than two dozen Christian hymns and patriotic songs, debate, shout football yells, swing my partners in square dances, bake bread, sew well enough to make a pair of trousers, and tell "dirty" Dutchman stories by the hour.

Despite the note of irony, Talayesva was appreciative of what school had given him. "It was important that I had learned to get along with white men and earn money by helping them," he wrote, "and that he could face whites as an equal. Now he was through with school, partly because of age. But also because of his dream-vision: "My death experience had taught me that I had a Hopi Spirit Guide whom I must follow if I wished to live. I wanted to become a real Hopi again, to sing the good old Katcina songs, and to feel free to make love without fear of sin or rawhide." Of course Talayesva could never "become a real Hopi again," in the sense of being one untouched by Euro-American education and life. But after taking what he believed he needed, he too had decisively rejected the school before formal graduation, and finally returned to his people.[25]

Luther Standing Bear and Jason Betzinez separately came to similar conclusions at Carlisle, the former after only five years of school, the latter after a decade. Each decided for himself it was time to go, but neither wanted to flee. Standing Bear clearly stated his dilemma to Captain Pratt: "'I want to go home, but I want to go in the right way. Several of the boys have run away from you, but I do not want to do that.'" Betzinez had a similar meeting with the principal. Initially Pratt refused both requests, but when he realized the determination of the pupils—Betzinez was then thirty—he relented and allowed them go "in the right way." Their respect for Pratt emerges strongly in both accounts, as does their ambivalence and their appreciation for what the school had given them. "I knew that I would be sad at first to leave Carlisle and its happy memories," wrote Betzinez. But leave he did, and Standing Bear too, each at his own insistence.[26]

V

Personal motivations were obviously crucial in rejection of the school: loneliness, homesickness, fear of or disgust at the punishment of selves or comrades, resentment of the general difficulties of school life. "The hunger and hardship were the reasons why many pupils ran away," wrote Max Henly (Navajo), in a comment which applied to many beyond his own school. The desire for a paying job or the realization that school was no longer a useful vehicle for personal development also motivated dropouts. There were other personal factors, such as the embarrassment of larger pupils deposited into classes with smaller children.[27] Even the physical constitution of each boy or girl helped decide his or her response to disease. Romantic attachments also motivated Indians to violate rules or even flee the school, knowing full well the punishments they risked calling down upon themselves.

Kin influences were crucial in keeping reluctant young Indians at their desks or in encouraging discontent. But negative family attitudes did not always produce pupil rejection: in the case of the Hopis, Sekaquaptewa and Qoyawayma, and especially of the Yankton, Zitkala-Sa, bitter family opposition to schooling seemed to *intensify* the determination of the young girls to prove themselves as scholars. Kin attitudes, then, could have many different effects on pupil motivations and responses.

Cultural background was also deeply influential. Most of the runaways ran back to their homes or villages—back to kin and culture— rather than off to the big city or to white communities. The recklessness of some of the runaways can also be seen as a reflection of tribal cultures, which inculcated ethics of bravery and acceptance of physical suffering; flight on a freezing winter night could thus appear as yet another test for a young Indian boy or girl. Half a century ago, just after the end of the period covered by the present study, Clyde Kluckhohn and Dorothea Leighton noted a tendency in Navajos to withdraw from certain kinds of problems rather than risk confrontation. Withdrawal of cooperation within the classroom or withdrawal of physical presence by flight from a difficult situation were in part cultural responses by members of other tribes too. Asa Daklugie, for example, fled his own Apache people for a period as a young boy. And Don Talayesva told a fellow-Hopi that he would try out his new wife—"if she treats me unfairly, I may escape and go back to school."[28]

The staff and other whites similarly influenced both resistance and rejection. Narrator after narrator told of the harshness and even brutality of individual teachers—accounts made more convincing by the same narrators' descriptions of other teachers as kind and concerned. Indian disciplinarians and officers were often no easier to live with than white teachers.

Peers also influenced each other to acceptance, resistance, or rejection of the school. Many of the runaway episodes began with discussion among aggrieved pupils; often older boys or girls took the lead in such conspiracies. Peers had their effect in other ways too: their bullying and victimizing of each other, or their ostracism of deviants, also led to great individual suffering. Rosalie Wax has shown how, in midtwentieth century Lakota schools, it was often *fellow-pupils* who drove interested students from the school.[29] The evidence is less clear-cut here. But the victimization and bullying certainly led to greater individual misery and loneliness, and thus to less bearable school experiences.

The institutional regimen at the schools also powerfully impelled many Indians to rejection: the shearing of hair, the baths, the constant surveillance, the use of physical or humiliating punishments, the "obnoxious" military organization—to use Helen Sekaquaptewa's explanation for many flights from Phoenix school—all such arrangements became unbearable for some pupils. Even in the case of many who got used to the school regimen, or even came to like it, in the end the system became too much, especially for older pupils, and they asked to go home or fled.

The curriculum less obviously motivated pupils to reject the school. The demanding physical labor may, as Irene Stewart claimed, have provoked some boys and girls to flight. But many young Indians would have been engaged in physically demanding activities had they been among their own people. Despite the shocks sometimes produced by the new learning, no narrator complained that arithmetic or geography or the teachings of Christianity turned him or her into a runaway. The English language, however, was probably a major factor in producing acceptance or rejection. Those who learned English poorly, or not at all, were in a sense rejecting the school, even if they sat obediently in class for years.

These seven motivational influences overlapped and intertwined in complex ways for each individual who immediately or finally rejected the school. And the combinations changed over time, preventing a quantitative analysis of the responses: sometimes personal, sometimes kin or cultural or other motivations coming to the fore. At different periods, and sometimes at the same moment, Helen Sekaquaptewa, Irene Stewart, or Jim Whitewolf accepted some aspects of the school, resisted others, and rejected, or attempted to reject others. While at Sherman Institute in California, Don Talayesva yearned to be white, ignored the rules of sexual segregation, experienced his Hopi dream-vision, yet continued at the school for a year and a half longer, then left— rejected school—but appreciated much of what he had learned. He, like most of these narrators, could perhaps be classified as an acceptor/ resister, until he decided he no longer needed the school and then attempted to leave.

VI

Thus the reasons for the final break were many, but not all pupils nor all of these narrators left school willingly. Mountain Wolf Woman

(Winnebago) happily attended school for a period until her brother withdrew her. Similarly, Standing Bear reported how, when Spotted Tail visited Carlisle in 1880, the Brulé chief took his children and granddaughter home with him. After eighteen months "my dad took me off," recalled Sam Robertson (Sisseton Sioux), "and I never went back to school." Robertson's father apparently wanted the boy to work on the farm. The Navajo Family of Ernest Nelson had similar needs. Nelson "probably would have returned [to school], but my family told me to herd sheep." As War Between the States threatened in 1861, Arkansas College closed down—just as G. W. Grayson (Creek) had become accustomed to the place. "What made me leave school," declared an anonymous Navajo with some regret, "was sickness." And Francis La Flesche's formal schooling appears to have ended after about seven years, when the Presbyterian Omaha boarding school closed in 1869. Through personal effort and an increasingly close relationship with Alice C. Fletcher, he later became an ethnologist.[30]

And others, although they left voluntarily, did not reject the school either: they graduated. The criteria for successful completion of courses varied from school to school over these eight decades, but a small number of the narrators claimed to have graduated and received their diplomas. Thomas Alford graduated from Hampton in the early 1880s. Around the turn of the century Ah-nen-la-de-ni completed the nursing course in Manhattan, and afterwards took "a special course in massage treatment for paralysis." Lucille Winnie got her diploma from Haskell "with a high average" in 1916, and won a scholarship to the University of Kansas. But instead of continuing on to further schooling, she accepted a teaching job in the United States Indian Service. Anna Moore Shaw graduated from the Phoenix Union High School 1920. Two years later Irene Stewart took a diploma from the Fort Defiance Boarding School; she always regretted not having gone back to Haskell to finish high school, but she later received another diploma from the Albuquerque Indian School. Once Fred Kabotie overcame his early desire to flee school and "live wild," he progressed successfully through a number of institutions, graduating from Santa Fe Public High School in 1925. Academically, Charles Eastman was undoubtedly the star of the group. After graduation as a physician from Boston University in 1890, he took up his post as government physician at Pine Ridge Reservation—on the eve of the Ghost Dance disturbances and the Wounded Knee Massacre.[31]

Although a number would later live for periods in white society, most of these narrators initially returned to their own peoples after school. For some narrators the arrival home would be joyous, for others almost as great a shock as the first terrible days at school.

Notes

1. Kaywaykla, *In the Days of Victorio*, 200. Cf. Daklugie et al., *Indeh*, 145, 147.

2. BFM, AR (1851), 5; Institute for Government Research, *Indian Administration* (Meriam Report), 392–94. Also 314–39. Cf. Samuel H. Preston and Michael R. Haines, *Fatal Years: Child Mortality in Late Nineteenth-Century America* (Princeton, N.J.: Princeton University Press, 1991), 5: "Nearly two out of every ten children died before their fifth birthday."

3. Report of Agent for Fort Apache Agency, ARCIA (1902), *House Document*, No. 5, 57 Congress, 2 session, serial 4458, 149. Also, ARCIA (1868), *House Executive Document*, No. 1, 40 Congress, 3 session, serial 1366, 686; ARCIA (1900), *House Document*, No. 5, 56 Congress, 2 session, serial 4101, 33–34; Trennert, *Phoenix Indian School*, 76–77. And 101–09, 177–78, 191–92, on efforts made to improve health conditions.

4. Report of Hampton Institute, ARCIA (Washington, D.C.: Government Printing Office, 1885), 235, 244; Standing Bear, *My People the Sioux*, 162–66. Carlisle reports broadly corroborate his account of death at the school: for example, Report of Training School for Indian Youth (Carlisle), ARCIA (1881), *House Executive Document*, No. 1, part 5, vol. 2, 47 Congress, 1 session, serial 2018, 242. Also, Stinson, in Cash and Hoover, eds., *To Be an Indian*, 95.

5. La Flesche, *Middle Five*, Chap. 16. Cf. BFM AR (1864), 9, on deaths at school.

6. Jim Whitewolf, *Life*, 96–97; Chris, *Apache Odyssey*, 46–47. Also 88–90. Stewart, *Voice in Her Tribe*, 16; Allen, *Pomo Basketmaking*, 8–9.

7. Standing Bear, *My People the Sioux*, 159; Eastman, *Indian Boyhood*, 73.

8. Report of Hampton Institute, ARCIA (Washington, D.C.: Government Printing Office, 1885), 244; Lame Deer and Erdoes, *Seeker of Visions*, 35; Henly, in Johnson, ed., *Stories of Traditional Navajo Life*, 32.

9. E. J. Bost to CIA, March 18, 1908, CCF, File 821 for Wittenberg, RG 75, NA.

10. Standing Bear, *My People the Sioux*, 153.

11. Carlisle Report, ARCIA (1880), *House Executive Document*, No. 1, part 5, 46 Congress, 3 session, serial 1959, 301; E. J. Bost to CIA, Dec. 4, 1914, and Assistant CIA to E. J. Bost, Dec. 15, 1914, both in CCF, File 821 for Wittenberg, RG 75, NA.

12. ARCIA (1899), *House Document*, No. 5, 56 Congress, 1 session, serial 3915, 26; Owen, *Memoirs*, 53; Allen, *Pomo Basketmaking*, 11. Also, David W. Adams, "The Federal Indian Boarding School: A Study of Environment and Response," (Ed.D. dissertation, Indiana University, 1975), 232–35. I thank the author for sending me Chapters 5 and 6 of his study.

13. Report of School at Keams Canyon, Ariz., ARCIA (Washington, D.C.: Govern-

ment Printing Office, 1887), 248; Coleman, "Responses of American Indian Children," 484, 490–91; Use of "deserter," for example, supervisor in charge to Abel Greeley, Sept. 17, 1914, Records of Non-Reservation Schools, Records of the Carlisle Indian Industrial School, RG 75, NA; *The Carlisle Arrow* 12 (Nov. 19, 1915): 2; E. J. Bost to the superintendent of Indian Schools, May 18, 1916, File 821 for Wittenberg, CCF, RG 75, NA.

14. Kaestle, *Pillars of the Republic*, 107–10; Fass, *Outsiders In*, 30, 41; Tyack, "Ways of Seeing," esp. 363–64.

15. Fischbacher, "A Study of the Role of the Federal Government," 130; Institute for Government Research, *Indian Administration* (Meriam Report), 355–56. Also Szasz, *Education and the American Indian*, 2, 22–23, 124, 129, 146, 187.

16. Kabotie, *Hopi Indian Artist*, 12, 17; Yava, *Big Falling Snow*, 9–10. On rejection of one school, but acceptance of another, Rickard, *Fighting Tuscarora*, 9–11.

17. Jim Whitewolf, *Life*, 89–91. Also, Lame Deer and Erdoes, *Seeker of Visions*, 36.

18. Sekaquaptewa, *Me and Mine*, 137; Bennett, *Kaibah*, 227–28. Cf. Jenkins, *Girl from Williamsburg*, 283; at Fort Mohave school, Arizona, in the early twentieth century, some kindergarten students used a battering ram to break out fellow pupils committed to the school jail for running away, and all fled to hide out nearby. Also 280, 293–94.

19. Mitchell, *Navajo Blessingway Singer*, 67–69; James Huntington, *On the Edge of Nowhere*, as told to Lawrence Elliot (New York: Crown, 1966), 56–57.

20. Grayson, *Creek Warrior*, 42; Yellowhair, "I Was Born in the Dark Ages," 18; Stewart, *Voice in Her Tribe*, 18; Daklugie et al, *Indeh*, 151. Once he did flee temporarily.

21. Lowrie, *Karnee*, 61–64, 67–68.

22. McCarthy, *Papago Traveller*, 30–35, 53–61.

23. *Ibid.*, 68. See Russell Lawrence Barsh, "American Indians in the Great War," *Ethnohistory* 38 (Summer 1991): 279, on the large number of federal Indian school pupils who enlisted.

24. Savala, *Autobiography*, 45; Moisés, *Yaqui Life*, 43; Begay, in Johnson, ed., *Stories of Traditional Navajo Life*, 65–66. She later taught "Indian culture" at the Chinle Boarding School, 68–69; Sekaquaptewa, *Me and Mine*, 142–44, 153–66. And 217–20 on her children's educational achievements.

25. Talayesva, *Sun Chief*, 117, 119–134.

26. Standing Bear, *My People the Sioux*, 190; Betzinez, *I Fought with Geronimo*, 159.

27. Max Henly, in Johnson, ed., *Stories of Traditional Navajo Life*, 34. On bigger boys' discomfort in a class of smaller boys: Talayesva, *Sun Chief*, 96, 102; Qoyawayma, *No Turning Back*, 114–15; Robert Burtt, "descriptive catalogue," letter 180, 12–1, AIC.

28. Kluckhohn and Leighton, *The Navajos*, 306–308; Daklugie et al., *Indeh*, 92–94; Talayesva, *Sun Chief*, 220.

29. Wax, "Warrior Dropouts," 148–50.

30. Standing Bear, *My People the Sioux*, 157. See also, Training School for Youth, Carlisle Barracks, ARCIA (1880), *House Executive Document*, No. 1, part 5, 46 Congress, 3 session, serial 1959, 301; Robertson, in Cash and Hoover, eds., *To Be an Indian*, 93; Nelson, in Johnson, ed., *Stories of Traditional Navajo Life*, 269; Grayson, *Creek Warrior*, 55; Anonymous Navajo, in *Navajo Door*, 126; Mark, "Francis La Flesche," esp. 498–500; Black Elk requested that his son be sent home from Carlisle in 1917, possibly to avoid the war, De Mallie, Introduction to Black Elk, *Sixth Grandfather*, 24.

31. Alford, *Civilization*, 109. See also, Report of School at Hampton, Va., ARCIA (1903), *House Document*, No. 5, 58 Congress, 2 session, part 1, serial 4615, 437; Ah-nen-la-de-ni, "An Indian Boy's Story," 1787; Winnie, *Sah-gan-de-oh*, 57–58; Shaw, *A Pima Past*, 147; Stewart, *A Voice in Her Tribe*, 27, 34; Kabotie, *Hopi Indian Artist*, 25; Eastman, *Deep Woods*, esp. 70–75. Also, Angel de Cora, "Autobiography," 279–85; she graduated from Hampton; Hoke Denetsosie, in Johnson, ed., *Stories of Traditional Navajo Life*, 97.

CHAPTER 10

Return Home

"**M**Y HOMECOMING WAS A bitter disappointment to me," wrote Thomas Alford of his return to the Oklahoma Shawnees after graduation from Hampton Institute. Noticing the changes in his manner, dress, and speech, the people received him "coldly and with suspicion." There was "no happy gathering of family and friends, as I had so fondly dreamed there might be. Instead of being eager to learn the new ideas I had to teach them, they gave me to understand very plainly that they did not approve of me." Many narrators received a similar shock, intensified by their own belief that they possessed a superior kind of knowledge, and by their people's justifiable resentment of that very assumption. Alford's problems had only begun, and the remainder of his autobiography details his determination to be true to this self-image as a man mediating between American civilization and his own people.[1]

When Ah-nen-la-de-ni returned briefly to the Mohawk reservation in New York after a nine-year absence, his experience was quite different. Although many in his family were dead and the Mohawk felt like a stranger, he enjoyed renewing acquaintance with familiar places and objects, and with the friends who remained. He noted that "the people had progressed. The past and its traditions were losing their hold on them and white man's ways were gaining." His sense of cultural superiority was perhaps as great as Alford's, but his sense of mission was less, and he intended making his career in white society; therefore he alienated his people less.[2]

Narrators reacted in individual ways, then, but most faced demanding problems of readjustment. Indeed the so-called returned student generated considerable controversy, in the later nineteenth and early twentieth centuries, among reformers, missionaries, and government educators. Reports from schools such as Carlisle and Hampton claimed that only a small percentage of ex-students "backslid" into heathenism or otherwise failed to become credits to their alma mater.[3] But other whites frankly expressed concern about the many problems young Indians encountered upon return to their own peoples, and narrators later corroborated these reports.[4]

I

Alford was not alone in experiencing reentry shock. Although anxious to return to her homeland, Irene Stewart hardly knew her father when they met after a separation of four years, and the hoped-for joyful return was not to be. "When I had left the Navajo country years before, I felt heartbreak," she wrote, "now I was disappointed in it. I could not make up my mind to stay on the reservation. Hogan life—once a great pleasure to me, and in later years so satisfying—was not for me." As she indicates, this negative response did not last the rest of her life. But— just as teachers hoped would be the case—she felt that school had spoiled her for the older way: "having gotten used to living where there are hygienic facilities, it is very hard to live again in the old hogan life." The homecoming, intended to be final, turned into a mere break between schools. She was soon off to Albuquerque Indian School, and from thence to California, where for a period she became a Christian mission- ary to *white* Americans (mostly children). She returned to the reservation as a missionary worker, and after many jobs later became active in tribal political life.[5]

Helen Sekaquaptewa's return was just as problematic. "I didn't feel at ease in the home of my parents now," wrote the Hopi after thirteen years at school. The family told her to change into Hopi attire. Her mother relented somewhat, happy to have Helen home, but her older, more traditional sister continually clashed with the returnee, forcing Helen to move out of the house. She and Emory Sekaquaptewa began a life of their own, first on the reservation, then on the border of the Hopi– Navajo reservations. Helen developed her own syncretic blend of Hopi and American—including Mormon—values, and finally became recon- ciled with her always traditional father. But those first tension-filled months after return from Indian school obviously left a deep imprint upon her.[6]

For all his hopes of becoming "a real Hopi again," Don Talayesva too had changed deeply at school. While there, he began a relationship with a clan relative—incestuous by Hopi standards—and later incurred the wrath of some of his people by cooperating with white anthropologists. Yet his immediate return seems to have been relatively easy. Don and his brother reached Second Mesa, and their mother "nearly cried when we shook hands, but she did not kiss me, for that is not the Hopi way." Other relatives greeted them warmly, and the acting chief of Oraibi, an uncle, later invited them to eat with him. "We stayed around all day, talking about school and listening to stories of herding, farming, and fuel gathering"—a striking picture of the easy exchange of different cultural experiences. He then attempted to continue as before in Hopi society, marrying, participating in ceremonial life, and fearing witchcraft. Perhaps Talayesva's warmer reception partly related to the fact that his was a Friendly family, whereas that of Sekaquaptewa had been Hostile. Yet Hopis, like other Indians, responded as individuals to the problems and joys of return.[7]

II

The young Indian was at least partly responsible for whatever conflict occurred—although teachers too could claim a major role. Many "educated" Indians arrived home with a sense of cultural and indeed personal superiority, and this, as Alford admitted, produced strong resentment among the people. The narrators thus demonstrated that an explicit goal of the educational crusade, the cultural separation of child from family, had often been achieved, but at a high price in personal suffering for the returnee and kin.

Even while still at school, young Indians could exhibit this developing sense of superiority. Omaha students referred to unschooled Ponca boys as "little savages." And from a traditional perspective, Edward Goodbird's spirited espousal of the Copernican theory was a shocking example of a child presuming to teach his elders. Clinton Rickard's brother wrote letters home from Carlisle saying that, even though his brothers would become drunkards, "he would be steady and become a minister." Jim Whitewolf's sense of superiority was less strident, perhaps, but just as real. "They still had long braids," he wrote of Kiowa Apache boys he saw during his first summer holidays. "I combed my hair and kind of showed off to them. I used to tell the boys the names of things in English that I learned in school." Only in later life, when he himself faced an intolerant returnee and ethnocentric missionaries, did Whitewolf begin to realize how it felt to be on the receiving end of such affectations.[8]

Upon final return from Indian school, ex-students continued to demonstrate that they had learned their lessons only too well. "It is said that some Pimas who went to an Eastern school for two months came home thinking they had forgotten their own language," remarked George Webb sarcastically. "But they remembered the words for what went on a plate." Standing Bear enjoyed his homecoming, but was surprised to find that some of the older people hesitated to shake his hand. Only later did he discover the reason: "It seemed that some of the returned Carlisle students were ashamed of their old people and refused to shake hands with them; some even tried to make them believe they had forgotten the Sioux language."[9]

Once Qoyawayma recovered from reintroduction to the "poverty" of her Hopi home, she embarked upon a campaign of uplift, provoking a sad but significant response from her mother: "'What shall I do with my daughter, who is now my mother?'" The girl's father reacted in a practical way. When Qoyawayma berated the family for having no beds or table, he went out into the village and got boards enough to build a crude table. Qoyawayma rejected her mother's insistence that she marry in the Hopi way. It also annoyed her to see the older woman grinding corn on her knees, rather than by using a machine, and she rejected the explanation that this was both the traditional and most spiritually rewarding method. Qoyawayma outraged other Hopis by cooking as she had learned at school, wasting three full eggs for a cake! Looking back, she was highly critical of her own youthful enthusiasm and arrogance: "she was not then wise enough to see her lessons in home economics were wrong for her as a Hopi. . . . How could [her white teachers] know, or care to know, that even in good seasons the specter of starvation was always before the desert dwellers?"

Qoyawayma conveyed something of the anguished ambivalence she herself felt at the time, saddened by the hurt she caused her family, yet determined to be true to her school education. She would not let the other villagers claim that she was "just another foolish schoolgirl who couldn't stick with the white life, but had to come running back to her parents, back to the security of tribal ways." Soon Qoyawayma "became almost a stranger within her own home," and went to live with white missionaries. Later in her life she once again opened to elements of "the Hopi way," and as a teacher tried to combine traditional stories and values with the teaching of English. Ironically, some Hopi parents protested that they sent their children to school to learn white culture.[10]

Oscar Good Shot (Sioux) also critically remembered his insensitivity on returning from the Santee Normal Training School early in the twentieth century. When he logically criticized some of the old men's stories, one of them "just flared up and said: 'You young people who have been to the white man's school think you know everything, but you don't know anything.'"[11] Such a perhaps universal intergenerational conflict gained even greater intensity when, as often happened in these accounts, the young not only rejected specific wisdom of the old, but poured contempt upon their whole way of life.

In the long run, the old people did not completely lose the war. Many of the most contemptuous returnees grew to regret their earlier lack of sensitivity, and attempted to blend school education and traditional learning. But the sense of superiority could cling into adult life. In his autobiography G. W. Grayson referred unself-consciously to "wild or blanket Indians"—as distinct from "civilized" Creeks. And he told how, at gatherings of Indians he attended in later life, his light skin color and competence in Indian and American society "impressed the simple representatives of some of those tribes with the belief that I must be a person of very considerable importance and fully entitled to their confidence."[12]

III

If some of the tensions of homecoming could be attributed to the zeal of returning students, other problems were less of their making. Many returnees soon discovered that the knowledge, skills, and trades they had struggled to acquire at school were often irrelevant on the reservation. Ely S. Parker, a Seneca whose education at mission and other schools ultimately prepared him for the position of commissioner of Indian Affairs (1869–71), was acutely aware of this problem. Accepting that missionaries, government educators, and philanthropists had often provided "an excellent education" for young Indians, Parker nevertheless believed that much of the vocational training proved unsuitable to home conditions. When they returned to their people

> the young men found no wagons or carts to be made or mended, no horses or cattle to be shod, no houses, requiring skilled labor, to be built, no fashionable clothes to be made, no shoes to make or mend . . . the trade of dressmaking was alike unprofitable [to returning girls] . . . and hence all the time, money and patience expended upon these people has generally been a dead loss and has had the effect of retarding their general civilization.[13]

White American educators became increasingly concerned about this issue. The new "courses of study" developed by the BIA in the early twentieth century may have implied a lack of confidence in Indian mental capacity, but they also demonstrated a commitment to making the curriculum more relevant to life after school. Many returnees initially found little relevance. "With marriage I began a life of toil," wrote Don Talayesva, and discovered that education had spoiled me for making a living in the desert. I was not hardened to heavy work in the heat and dust and I did not know how to get rain, control winds, or even predict good and bad weather. I could not grow young plants in dry, wind-beaten, and worm-infested sand drifts; nor could I shepherd a flock of sheep through storm, drought, and disease. I might even lead my family into starvation and be known as the poorest man in Oraibi—able-bodied but unable to support a wife.

Although Talayesva elsewhere admitted that he gained much from his schooling, Sherman Institute hardly taught him skills to solve many of the problems facing a Hopi desert farmer. And, in a passage reminiscent of Commissioner Parker's, Luther Standing Bear recalled the frustration felt by Carlisle returnees who had no outlets for their school-learned trades. Those on his reservation formulated a plan that each should open "a little shop of his own," and wrote to the then commissioner of Indian Affairs for help. None was forthcoming, claimed Standing Bear.[14]

Zitkala-Sa did not return to live on the Yankton reservation, but her school-educated brother did, and lost his job as a reservation clerk to a white man. Since then he had "not been able to make use of the education the Eastern school had given him," remarked Zitkala-Sa's mother to her "inflamed" daughter. And in a melodramatic short story, the Yankton poured contempt upon a returnee "who hunted for the soft heart of Christ" at the school, became an ordained minister, but returned totally ill-equipped to take care of his starving father. Chris (Mescalero Apache) also found his school training of little use, as there was no suitable work on the reservation. Although he served as a reservation policeman for a time, he felt that even in his own day (the 1930s) the problem persisted. Young Apaches went away and learned trades, "and when they come back the trade jobs aren't given to them. The white man's got in the lead of them, and when they want jobs as mechanics or with the cattle they can't get them." Although George Webb did not discount the value of schooling, his later experience made the Pima wonder. "I had two years in business school," he wrote, "but only last year I let a white man on a business deal take me for two thousand dollars. And he had never even been to high school."[15]

When Anna Moore Shaw and Ross Shaw married—tribal *and* white ceremonies—and returned to the Pima reservation, they tried at first to do things the old way, living with Ross's parents in a traditional Pima home. "There was no plumbing, gas, or electricity," wrote Anna with scarcely concealed distaste. "How difficult this simple way of life seemed to Ross and me after our years of enjoying the white man's conveniences!" Although there appears to have been little of the intrafamily tension that plagued Sekaquaptewa and others, Anna noted that, despite hard work on the farm, Ross's parents were always poor, barely able to buy a few groceries. She and Ross realized "that laboring beside his parents in the field each day was not the way to help. The education they had strived so hard to give us had prepared us to bring in money from the white man's world; it would be wrong to waste all those years of schooling on a life of primitive farming." Even in retrospect Anna was unaware of the irony in her own words: making farmers of Indians had been an almost sacred goal of most missionary and government educators. But her message was clear. She and her husband believed that their schooling had prepared them for better things than could be found on the Pima reservation, and they headed for Phoenix (later in life she would return to her own version of Pima life).[16]

IV

Other returnees felt their education did help them in later life among their own people, or among whites. Sometimes the effect of schooling could be strikingly ironic. G. W. Grayson first learned *the Creek language* at mission school! (His parents spoke English at home.) And Ernest Nelson enjoyed telling his interviewer about the use to which he put his "civilized" education. "From the four years I attended school," he said,

> it seemed that I gained enough knowledge to be able to learn the singing of [Navajo] ceremonies. If I hadn't gone to school and learned to read I might not have been able to learn that much. Usually, I wrote the chants down on paper as they were sung by a medicine man. . . . I would use different kinds of colors of writing pens to help me remember the separate songs and prayers. That was how I learned. It was just like going to school. Thus, from lessons taught in reading and writing I learned the singing of ceremonies.[17]

No matter how bitter against school or white life, none of the narrators ever regreted learning the English language, and how to read and write.

Like Jason Betzinez, Anna Moore Shaw, and others, Howard Whitewolf (Comanche) felt that Christianity transformed his life. He also noted that English helped him gain his profession as an interpreter at the Comanche Mission of the Reformed Church in Oklahoma. Further, he believed strongly that schooling was a vital weapon to defend Indians against the depredations of white society. "The Indian young men and women who fail to get an education are like the warriors of the old days with their bows and arrows," he wrote. "The arrows would not reach as far as the white man's bullets." In the battles ahead, white men were "trained to do business. If the Indian does not take this training, like a soldier drilling with his rifle, he will be cheated and lose money and land." Reflecting a modern Indian patriotism, Whitewolf thus advocated acceptance of Christianity and other elements of white life, but insisted on Indian self-reliance. "We must not depend on white people too much, but must depend on ourselves also. If we do this we will make greater strides towards civilization." And in this struggle, schooling was crucial: "These are the people who will lead us,—men and women who are good Christians, who are educated, and who will fight for the Indians."[18]

Geronimo had made a similar argument when he insisted that Asa Daklugie and fellow-Apaches go to Carlisle. Many of them justified the faith of the Apache leader. Daklugie, James Kaywaykla, and others learned that they could hire lawyers to present Apache land claims. After a series of legal battles the Indian Claims Court in 1971 finally handed down a judgment against the United States Government of over $16 million. Similarly, Indians such as Charles Eastman validly believed that they used their schooling for the good of the people. Eastman's motives, like those of other narrators, were partly personal. But in serving as a doctor at Pine Ridge, in working on the land claims of the Santee Sioux, on the land allotment rolls of the Sioux, or as a lecturer, writer, and spokesman for "the Indian," he was also serving his people.[19]

For periods a number of narrators became teachers of fellow Indians—Lindsey (Creek), Standing Bear (Sioux), Alford (Shawnee), Winnie (Iroquois), Qoyawayma (Hopi)—an obvious use of school learning both for personal and ethnic "advance," and a continuation of the mediating role of broker. Chester Yellowhair, who claimed that until he was eight or nine years old he did not know there were other people on the earth besides his own Navajo family, learned the art of silversmithing at school in Santa Fe around 1930. Later he taught this craft to other Indian pupils at Albuquerque and Fort Wingate schools, and became the instructor of the general shop at the Sherman Institute. He also helped found the Navajo Arts and Crafts Guild. By painting Hopi ceremonials, Fred Kabotie gained respect and financial reward from white society, including a Guggenheim Foundation Fellowship in 1945–46; he too returned to his people to teach, and helped found the Hopi Cultural Center.[20]

Even some of the much-criticized vocational training would later prove relevant. Daklugie had no toleration for farming and even less for sheepherding, but he and other Apaches took to cattle raising, and the concepts they learned at Carlisle thus became useful, helping them get the most out of the poor land of the Mescalero reservation on which they finally settled. "Running cattle was more like the hunting we had done before captivity," he believed, indicating that the motivation for working with domesticated livestock was not quite what his teachers hoped it would be. Similarly, Jim Whitewolf noted that he "learned about farming in school, and to this day I have used that knowledge in planting my garden every spring."[21]

Others such as Jason Betzinez (Apache) and Carl Sweezy (Arapaho) also gained economic and personal satisfaction from their "industrial skills." The superintendent at Sherman Institute arranged a job for Ada Damon even before she finished school, and she began her life's work as a cook in government schools on the Navajo reservation. Jonas Keeble (Sisseton Sioux) believed that many vocational skills he learned at the Genoa Boarding School later proved valuable. But he achieved a special sense of fulfillment from one: "After I got home, I was interested in bricklaying, so we done [sic] a lot of stone work all through the reservation. I worked everywhere, nearly, in South Dakota." He, his son, and brothers, "did some wonderful work—all over, even in North Dakota and around Aberdeen."[22]

Like many of these narrators, Keeble went from job to job, and spent a period in the state militia. James McCarthy (Papago) and Clinton Rickard (Tuscarora) also served time in the military. Ross Shaw (Pima) also did a military stint and found employment off the reservation practicing tinning and plumbing as well, the trades he had learned at school; later he worked for the railroad. William Cadman also served in the armed forces during World War II—as one of the famous Navajo Marine Code Talkers, he utilized his Indian language "to send secret messages on the radio to the battle fronts in enemy [Japanese] territory." For him, both traditional and white learning had their later uses beyond the reservation.[23]

If few besides Kabotie, Eastman, La Flesche, and Zitkala-Sa achieved accolades in the white world, school education obviously helped them and some other narrators feel more at ease in modern civilization. Hampton Institute not only prepared Thomas Alford to teach Indian children and to work for his people; the school made him a gentleman, he believed. "I had learned those little details of toilet that were considered essential to the dress of 'a civilized man'," wrote the Shawnee. "I no longer felt awkward or self-conscious in the society of the opposite sex. I had learned those outward forms of manner that give one a comfortable feeling when in the company of well-bred people." Angel DeCora (Winnebago), who illustrated the cover of the first edition of La Flesche's *Middle Five*, emphasized the many white educational establishments she attended after graduation from Hampton, and the art-related jobs she performed in American society. Her short autobiography reads like an impressive curriculum vitae, leading finally to a teaching position at the Carlisle school. And to the hope that, through her efforts, Indian youth might begin to contribute "to American Art." In later life Luther Standing Bear also entered the dominant society, performing in Buffalo Bill's Wild West Show, and in films.[24]

With characteristic ambivalence Lucille Winnie admitted that Haskell was not all cranky officers, demerits, and matrons. "Whether we liked them or not," wrote the Iroquois, "they helped us to become better citizens and adjust to a better way of life when we left Haskell." She articulately recalled the usefulness of her training:

> The academic education we received at Haskell was not slanted to college entrance, but based on the needs of our people at the time. We learned what was to be essential to our future. No foreign languages were taught, but we got a good basic English foundation and were taught to speak and write English correctly. Vocational training . . . was offered to the boys, and the girls were trained in homemaking. During our junior year we could choose to specialize in home economics, business, or teaching. No matter what course we chose, our training was thorough; we were qualified to go out and make a living.[25]

To an energetic, talented, and acculturated young Indian like Winnie, her few years at Haskell provided an immensely useful basis for a satisfying and even exciting life, spent mostly in white society. After a stint as a teacher in the Indian service and a series of other jobs, she worked in the early air industry and for magnate Howard Hughes, met Amelia Earhart, and spent a period working and holidaying in Hawaii. Impelled by "her mission," she then helped Cheyennes organize a craft industry on their reservation.

Few of the narrators completed the equivalent of a contemporary high school education, however, and were far less aware than Winnie of the ways of white America when they began their schooling. Most received a school education which, as Hoke Denetsosie (Navajo) validly claimed, "only half prepared [Indians] to make a living in the dominant world around us."[26]

V

Thus, when we examine the immediate return of the narrators to their peoples or, in a few cases, to white society, the picture is one of diversity, and often of wrenching ambivalence as they faced the problems of readjustment to the family, the people, and the reservation. This chapter can only suggest the variety of jobs, the periods of inactivity, frustration, or satisfaction narrators experienced in the days after their return from school, and in later life. Many who initially expressed shock at reservation conditions would later reconcile themselves to some blended version of tribal and white life. Helen Sekaquaptewa spoke for more than herself and her husband, when she wrote: "Our lives were a combination of what we thought was the good of both cultures, the Hopi way and what we learned at school." [27]

A number of the narrators believed that young people in their own days (when they prepared their autobiographies) were often caught between cultures, without a firm grounding in either, that they were what anthropologists call "marginal" men and women, at peace in neither world. [28] From their own accounts, some of the narrators fall into this category. Although Zitkala-Sa later became a celebrated Indian reformer and author, her autobiography depicts a deeply anguished woman. For all Charles Eastman's success in the white world, and his claim to have been both an Indian and an American, he also confessed to difficulties in coming to terms with modern life. The *reality* of the so-called Christian civilization was "more confusing and contradictory" than "the simple, instinctive nature religion" of his childhood. As Raymond Wilson, Eastman's biographer, perceptively noted, "[i]t was never easy to be the most prominent Indian of one's day." [29]

Most of these narrators gravitated toward Malcolm McFee's model of the "150%" Indian. Such men and women were not necessarily at full peace with themselves and the world, but to some degree they achieved the ability to live in two cultures. Or perhaps—to use a formulation of L. G. Moses and Raymond Wilson—they lived not in two worlds, but in one "complex world of multiple loyalties." Some of the narrators, such as Helen Sekaquaptewa and many of the Navajos interviewed by Broderick H. Johnson, appeared to have achieved a kind of "relaxed" 150 percent-ness, despite the difficulties caused by schooling. The ambivalence of their responses to white education emerges strongly, but so does their sense of peace with the compromises made. Such Indians reinforce the claim of James A. Clifton that people caught between cultures do not necessarily become "psychologically diminished." Many of the narrators certainly became "more complicated psychologically," to use Clifton's expression; they mastered knowledge in both cultures, and as bicultural men and women indeed became "culturally enlarged."[30]

Not every member of his own Tewa–Hopi community would have agreed with him, but Albert Yava obviously worked out his own pragmatic compromise, one that involved a high degree of cultural enlargement, and one similar to that of many narrators:

> I have always thought that the only way we can save the old traditions is to recognize the new forces at work in our lives, accept that times have changed, and become part of the modern world. That way we can survive and preserve a part of our minds for the old values. If you don't survive you don't have anything.[31]

"The schools leave a scar," claimed Lame Deer, the Oglala (Sioux) medicine man. "We enter them confused and bewildered and we leave them the same way."[32] Almost all the narrators certainly entered the schools bewildered. Not all were equally bewildered by the return, however. For reasons that mixed pupil personality, school experience, family attitudes toward white culture, and historical and economic conditions among the people, some narrators found the return a happy occasion; some did not. Many who returned bewildered would later reaccommodate to home life. And although this chapter has touched on the highly varied adult experiences of the narrators, these later lives are another story, or indeed many other stories.

Notes

1. Alford, *Civilization*, 111. Like other narrators Alford missed friends, comforts, and the conveniences of school.

2. Ah-nen-la-de-ni, "An Indian Boy's Story," 1786–87.

3. See, for example, Report of School at Hampton, Va., ARCIA (1903), *House Document* No. 5, 58 Congress, 2 session, serial 4645, 437: it claimed that in twenty-five

years the school had taught 938 Indian boys and girls, of whom 673 were still living. "These returned students are doing work and exerting influences which, according to our best knowledge we classify them as follows: Excellent, 141; good, 333; fair, 149; poor, 42; bad, 8. According to this classification 474 returned students are entirely satisfactory, 50 have poor records, and 149 amount to but little either way. They are largely the sick and the deficient."

4. For example, Report of School at Fort Yuma, Ariz., ARCIA (1896), *House Document* No. 5, vol. II, 54 Congress, 2 session, serial 3489, 360; ARCIA (1904), *House Document* No. 5, 58 Congress, 3 session, serial 4798, 30; Board of Indian Commissioners, "Returned Student Survey," Bulletin 24 (1916–17), MS (copy) in Newberry Library, Chicago. Also, Trennert, *Phoenix Indian School*, 143–49; Ahern, "'The Returned Indians'," 113.

5. Stewart, *A Voice in Her Tribe*, 33–36.

6. Sekaquaptewa, *Me and Mine*, 144–46, 151–52, 153–66 (on marriage), 197–98, 224–44 (on syncretism), 247–49.

7. Talayesva, *Sun Chief*, 135–36. On troubles because of anthropologists, 307–11, 328–30, for example. Also, Sekaquaptewa, *Me and Mine*, 186–87. Qoyawayma, *No Turning Back*, 47–48, and note 10, below.

8. Rickard, *Fighting Tuscarora*, 12; Jim Whitewolf, *Life*, 95; Also Trennert, *Phoenix Indian School*, 145–46.

9. Webb, *A Pima remembers*, 49; Standing Bear, *My People the Sioux*, 191. Cf. Rogers, *Red World and White*, 3–8.

10. Qoyawayma, *No Turning Back*, 67–75, Chaps. 10–15. Cf. Kabotie, *Hopi Indian Artist*, 65–68.

11. Good Shot, "Oscar Good Shot," 269–70. Also Eve Ball, in Daklugie et al., *Indeh*, 282; Johnson *Indian School Days*, 186–88.

12. Grayson, *Creek Warrior*, 148, 152.

13. Parker, "General Parker's Autobiography," in "Writings of General Parker," 529–31.

14. Talayesva, *Sun Chief*, 224; Standing Bear, *Land of the Spotted Eagle*, 239–40.

15. Zitkala-Sa, *American Indian Stories*, 90–91, 109–125. Quotation, 112; Chris, *Apache Odyssey*, 68, 138, 189; Webb, *A Pima Remembers*, 125.

16. Shaw, *Pima Past*, 146–50, 199–234.

17. Grayson, *Creek Warrior*, 41–42. Grayson mentions the Creek language, "which we did speak at our home"—the context implies "did *not* speak"; Nelson, in Johnson, ed., *Stories of Traditional Navajo Life*, 241.

18. Howard Whitewolf, "A Short Story of My Life," 31.

19. Eve Ball, in Daklugie et al., *Indeh*, 290–291; Charles Eastman, *Deep Woods*, esp. Chaps. 6, 7; and 152–58, 180–85. Wilson, *Ohiyesa*, Chaps. 3–12, 94, 170, for example. A major theme of Rickard, *Fighting Tuscarora*, is the need for Indians to utilize elements of white culture while retaining their identity. Also Ahern, "'The Returned Indians'," esp. 112–18.

20. Lindsey, "Memories," 194–97; Standing Bear, *My People the Sioux*, esp. Chap. 19; Alford, *Civilization*, Chaps. 17–19; Winnie, *Sah-gan-de-oh*, Chap. 3; Qoyawayma, *No Turning Back*, Chaps. 9–15; Yellowhair, "I Was Born in the Dark Ages," 17–18; Kabotie, *Fred Kabotie*, 65–68, 106–14; Eastman, *Deep Woods*, Chaps. 6, 7.

21. Daklugie et al., *Indeh*, 84, 274; Whitewolf, *Life*, 96.

22. Betzinez, *I Fought with Geronimo*, esp. chaps. 17, 22, *passim*; Sweezy, *Arapaho Way*, esp. 40, 65; Damon, "'That's the Way We Were Raised'," 62; Keeble, in Cash and Hoover, eds., *To Be an Indian*, 60–61.

23. Keeble in Cash and Hoover, eds., *To Be an Indian*, 61; McCarthy, *Papago Traveller*, 68–98; Rickard, *Fighting Tuscarora*, Chap. 2; Shaw, *Pima Past*, 140–51; Cadman, in Johnson, ed., *Stories of Traditional Navajo Life*, 213.

24. Alford, *Civilization*, 108–109; DeCora, "Autobiography," 280–85; on her work

with La Flesche see Coleman, "Credibility." Standing Bear, *My People the Sioux*, 248–72, 284–86.

25. Winnie, *Sah-gan-de-oh*, 53, 58.

26. Denetsosie, in Johnson, ed., *Stories of Traditional Navajo Life*, 102; Robert A. Trennert, "Educating Indian Girls at Nonreservation Boarding Schools, 1878–1920," *Western Historical Quarterly* 13 (July 1982): 285–88, on the menial occupations, (many in the Indian Service itself) to which most such girls could look forward. Trennert believes that "trained women probably had more opportunities than their male counterparts"; Wilbert H. Ahern, "An Experiment Aborted: Returned Students in the Indian Service, 1881–1908," MS, 11, 21–23 (see statistical breakdown): "By 1899, Indian employment comprised 45.3 percent of Indian School Staff." By 1905, however, this figure had dropped to 25 percent. I thank the author for sending me an early draft of this article.

27. Sekaquaptewa, *Me and Mine*, 186.

28. Daklugie et al., *Indeh*, 59. Also, Kaywaykla, *In the Days of Victorio*, 203–204; Alford, *Civilization*, 198. On marginality, James A. Clifton, "Alternate Identities," in Clifton, ed., *Being and Becoming Indian*, 29.

29. Eastman, *Deep Woods*, 194; Wilson, *Ohiyesa*, 192, also esp. 188–93.

30. McFee, "150% Man"; L. G. Moses and Raymond Wilson, eds., *Indian Lives: Essays on Nineteenth- and Twentieth-Century Native American Leaders* (Albuquerque: University of New Mexico Press, 1985), 3; Clifton, "Alternative Identities," in Clifton, ed., *Being and Becoming Indian*, 29–30. Clifton also draws on McFee.

31. Yava, *Big Falling Snow*, 133.

32. Lame Deer and Erdoes, *Seeker of Visions*, 35.

CHAPTER 11

Conclusions

TWO MAJOR CONCLUSIONS ARISE out of this analysis of the responses of American Indian children to missionary and government schooling from the 1850s to the 1920s. The first is that they responded to an alien educational institution with a high degree of ambivalence. The second conclusion is that the narrators' accounts of their school experiences are highly consistent both with each other and with contemporary white American sources; the autobiographical accounts thus provide a credible understanding of the narrators'—and of many of the Indian pupils'—responses to schooling during the decades under review.

I

Most of the Indian narrators certainly fit Christopher Boehm's understanding of ambivalence as a dynamic state, which permits many and changing kinds of conflicting feelings about an issue, sometimes leading to decisions that involve compromise. To paraphrase him, people can blend their ambivalent tendencies on an issue into many combinations, according to their socialization and cultural perceptions, and depending upon the situation.[1]

For some narrators, negative factors predominated early in the school experience, to be partly balanced later by positive factors; for others the reverse was the case, as they gradually became less and less willing to persist with schooling. What should have emerged powerfully from the present study was the *individuality* of the Indian narrators as pupils responding to the school (not to speak of their individuality as reminiscing adults). To claim ambivalence as a major theme of the study, then, is not to lump all these narrators into one monolithic category; nor is it to claim that each pupil developed merely dualistic, either/or responses toward the school. Obviously each narrator responded with his or her own complex and shifting attitudes. The present study analysed this ambivalence in terms of adjustment, resistance, and rejection, showing how closely intertwined and overlapping such analytically discrete categories were in the everyday student life of the narrators.

Motivations for such responses involved changing and complex interactions within and between seven motivational clusters. A shocked and unhappy student like Lucille Winnie resented much of the *institutional* regimen of the Haskell Institute, yet learned to accept the school because of *kin* influences, *personal* ambition, and interest in the *curriculum*. Don Talayesva, on the other hand, was driven mostly by personal motivation, stimulated by envy of school-going *peers* and by *cultural* factors—especially the desire to avoid the rigors of Hopi life. School *staff*, of course, massively influenced all the narrators. And such motivations shifted as students grew older, made more friends, experienced personal crises, or became intellectually stimulated by some of the curriculum—a number of the more gifted narrators powerfully communicated the joy of learning. Again, the seven-factor categorization should be seen as an analytical device, meant to convey the diversity, complexity, and shifting nature of motivation.

II

Certain patterns did not emerge to the expected extent in the accounts of schooling. *Change* is obviously a theme in almost every autobiography; not just change across a long life, but changing responses across a few years of schooling. It is also possible to discern the expanding nature of the education offered, at least for those students who went beyond the basic curriculum of the small local day schools, and moved on to the ambitious programs of the big off-reservation schools. But the narrators give little indication that they were markedly influenced by the changing educational controversies stirring in the decades around the turn of the century. Indian autobiographies demonstrate that a heavy manual labor element had been a feature of school life from the beginning of the period under review. And there is little evidence in these autobiographies of a discernible increase in racism—indeed of biological racism at all.

Nor did the narrators communicate much significant difference in character between Presbyterian or Roman Catholic and supposedly secular government schools. The mission schools of course emphasized the beliefs of their denominations, but they also taught a heavily secular and "civilized" curriculum. And government schools generally tried to inculcate "republican" and Christian ethics. Many of these narrators moved around from school to school, and a few went to public or other white schools, leaving little significant comment on the differences.[2]

Indian men wrote about two thirds of the hundred school accounts, leaving a substantial proportion by women. But there was no clear sexual patterns in the responses to school. We can easily discern that girls generally received training in the domestic arts, and the boys in farming and trades. The stricter supervision of girls sometimes emerges. But Indian boys and girls shared much in the schools: all experienced the shock of entry, the loneliness, the harsh regimen, and significantly the ethnocentric academic and religious curriculum. Further, even if the content of the work was different, *both* sexes were required to perform manual labor. Haig-Brown claims that, at the Kamloops Residential School in British Columbia, the resistance of girls was "more subtle" than that of boys. These accounts, however, contain cases of girls attacking teachers, setting fire to the school, and harshly treating each other. Thus the broad patterns of response were characteristic of both sexes at the schools.[3]

III

Other subthemes emerge. Kin were obviously crucial to motivation and response. Family sometimes split on the issue of schooling, but their admonitions to learn the white ways echoed in the minds of many Indian pupils long after they had been physically separated from home. On other occasions kin encouraged resistance or rejection of the school. But the influence upon responses could be unexpected, as when pupils intensified their commitment to schooling in the face of kin opposition.

No typical Hopi or Navajo or Sioux response to the school emerged; yet the powerful and often ironic influence of tribal cultures upon motivation and response were striking. Their own cultures continually drew individual narrators out of the schools—to hunts, to dances, to story-telling sessions—and continued to influence them while there. Yet tribal culture could also work to the advantage of the school. Respect for adults, for incremental learning, for the increasing status that went with increasing knowledge and expertise, acceptance of hard physical labor— such tribal patterns were clearly compatible with school goals.

As was the "inclusive" cultural ethos of the tribes. Although some pupils rejected and fled the schools, tribal children were generally more tolerant than their culturally exclusive teachers and willingly accepted useful values, knowledge, and skills of an alien culture. In later life many narrators continued this inclusive approach, and developed their syncretic blends of tribal and white cultural traditions.

The demanding mediatory roles accepted by the narrators, or forced upon them, indicates the importance of *children* as contacts between American and Indian cultures. Some of the narrators brought disruption into their families and communities, some brought peaceful change; all brought some degree of contact with a different world. During these decades, tens of thousands of other Indian children attended schools, fled, reattended, returned to and attempted to influence their peoples, visited white society, were "shown off" to presidents and at expositions. They often had far different experiences of white life than tribal adults. Therefore we need to know much more about these young but major participants in cross-cultural interaction.

Obviously the school exploited such children. But symbiosis, mutual exploitation, characterized the whole school situation. Indian adults who realized the need to adapt to the white world developed an instrumental approach to the school, enrolling their children for personal, familial, and ethnic advantages. Such Indians therefore became dependent upon the expanding, white-controlled educational system. Yet secular and Christian educators also came to need Indians: to maintain the support of the American public, they had to keep their schools filled with happy or at least obedient children. Thus the constant battle against runaways and the constant effort to convince Indian parents of the need for schooling. Even Indian children participated in the symbiosis. Once they had adjusted to the school, many of them developed their personal and highly pragmatic motivations for cooperation.

Therefore this study reinforces a major contention of the new social history and of the new Indian history: non-Western peoples are not merely passive victims; they too have influenced events.[4] But although it is important to emphasize the resilience of Indian children and adults, and their pragmatic, even manipulative approach to Western education, one must not minimize the development of increasingly uneven power relationships. During these decades, white settlers inundated tribal lands, and the economic, political, and military power of the United States increased massively. On the one hand, a major contribution of the new historical approaches has been to bring groups previously slighted by scholars back into the picture as active participants, but on the other there has been a concomitant tendency to overcompensate, to romanticize Indian resilience and manipulation of the dominant civilization. It is well to remember the pointed question that David Brion Davis asked in the late 1970s in relation to the new approaches to African-American experiences: who was adjusting to which, and why? Which group, in other words, had greater capacity to force its will upon the other?[5]

Even if they never succeeded in remaking Indian children to their own formula, white educators obviously possessed far greater access to power, ultimately to the use of police and the military. Teachers too made adjustments, as when missionaries learned Indian languages, but such concessions to "savagery" were unusual. It does not diminish the impressive resilience and adaptive abilities of Indian children to claim that, generally, they were adjusting to the school, rather than the other way around.

IV

Much work remains to be done by historians to ascertain the responses to school and mediating roles of other Indian children in other periods and places.[6] A potentially rich field for comparative analysis might be between pupils of the missionary and government schools, on the one hand, and those Indians who in the same period began to attend the American public schools, on the other. Further areas for fruitful comparison would be of Indian and Anglo children in common or other schools, and especially of Indian and immigrant children from various ethnic backgrounds. In their responses to the school, perhaps immigrant children occupied, and today occupy, a middle ground between white American children and Indian children.[7]

A number of Canadian Indian autobiographies, along with studies by historians such as J. R. Miller, J. Donald Wilson, Celia Haig-Brown, and others, indicate that the broad patterns of Indian pupil responses at Canadian schools were very similar to those presented in the present study. But Haig-Brown, for example, demonstrates a more clearly negative response at one Canadian school, and Miller shows a greater degree of Indian family influence over certain schools than the narrators in the United States remembered. Canadian Indian school experiences cry out for systematic comparisons with counterparts in the United States.[8]

This is only to hint at the need for further studies of non-Western children and schooling. The present writer has compared the motivations of seven of these Indian narrators with the motivations of eight African missionary school pupils. Despite different time frames (1860s–

1920s for the Indians, and 1950s–1960s for the Africans), and despite enormous historical, cultural, economic, and demographic differences, the Africans showed remarkably similar responses and motivations to those of Indians at missionary and government schools. There were differences, of course. But this comparative study suggests the possibility of many broadly similar patterns of response to Western schooling among non-Western peoples.[9]

The period under review is thus a rich one, not only for further studies of Indian children and schooling, but for a multitude of comparative approaches focusing upon the role of children in cross-cultural interactions.

V

My second major conclusion is that the accounts of schooling are historically credible.[10]

The *consistency* of the autobiographical accounts is expecially impressive. Narrator after narrator recalled the military regimentation, the half-and-half curriculum, the rules against speaking an Indian language, the exploitation of pupils as mediators and officers, the fact that, although some found subjects in the academic curriculum difficult to learn, none objected to the totally non-Indian content of the new knowledge. Almost to a man and woman, the narrators reinforced each other's recollections. This strongly suggests that, when they cast their minds back, the narrators recovered the *child's response*, accepting the school as a place that taught only the knowledge of the white tribe.

Some of the consistency could have arisen through a process of "conversations with others," to use David Thelen's expression. Thus narrators might have remolded their school memories, through discussions with other ex-students or by reading each others' views in school publications.[11] But it is unlikely that over one hundred narrators from widely different parts of the United States, providing their accounts decades apart, could have produced such consistent accounts if they had not undergone similar experiences.

Paradoxically, the *diversity* in the autobiographical accounts also reinforces their credibility. Although the narrators agreed on what happened, their attitudes and responses toward much of the school experience different widely. In these accounts pupils castigated, reacted indifferently to, or praised teachers; loathed, accepted, or enjoyed the regimentation and labor demands of the school; thrilled to, merely endured, or resented learning the new language and academic curriculum. *And this diverse picture of pupil responses generally emerges regardless of the adult attitude of the narrator.* Those with highly positive and those with more negative memories of the school leave essentially similar accounts of the diversity of pupil responses decades earlier.

Further, there is powerful mutual corroboration between the narrators' accounts and contemporary reports by American government officials, teachers, missionaries, and others. These white sources agree with most of what the narrators remember of the major patterns and events; they also reinforce the claims of the narrators that Indian children responded in a variety of ways. White Americans too attested to the diverse adjustments, resentments, resistance, health problems, rejections, joys, and miseries of school life for young Indians.

The school obviously was such a radically new experience that it imprinted itself deeply upon the minds of the narrators—they recalled the arrival with special vividness. Further, most of them began life in oral cultures, where accurate recall and the faultless performance of ritual and other duties were seen as vital to survival. This is not to claim that memory is infallible in such cultures, merely that the deeply ingrained need to remember accurately did not dissolve the moment the narrators entered the school gates.[12]

This study, therefore, has sought to contribute both to the history of Indian education and to those fields of scholarship that focus upon human memory, especially to the field of autobiography studies. Memory may often deceive, but it can also provide startlingly vivid and accurate recall of past events. The present work is intended to strike a discordant note among those many recent studies which emphasize the limitations of human memory. Indian autobiographical accounts of schooling certainly justify Robert R. Sayre's claim, made a decade and a half ago, that self-telling can offer the scholar a broad and direct contact with American experience.[13]

Notes

1. Boehm, "Ambivalence and Compromise," 930.
2. Kabotie conveyed a sense of greater freedom and openness to Indian culture at the Santa Fe Indian School, *Hopi Indian Artist*, 17–33.
3. See Lowawaima, "Oral Histories," 247, on the more varied activities of boys at Chilocco; Haig-Brown, *Resistance and Renewal*, 50. Also Hyer, *Open House*, 20–21. Cf. Coe; there was no "revealing difference" between men and women in their approach to the writing of childhood autobiographies, *Where the Grass Was Taller*, 275–76.
4. For a powerful statement of the major trends and achievements of the "new Indian history," see R. David Edmunds, "Coming of Age: Some Thoughts Upon American Indian History," *Indiana Magazine of History*, 85 (Dec. 1989): 312–21, esp. 316. Also, Shepard Krech III, "The State of Ethnohistory," *Annual Review of Anthropology* 20 (1991): 345–75. Scholars of Indian autobiography, discussed in Chapter 1, have also contributed toward "Indian centered" understandings of American experience—as, of course, have anthropologists.
5. David Brion Davis, review of Herbert G. Gutman, *The Black Family in Slavery and Freedom, 1750–1925*, in *American Historical Review* 82 (June 1977): 744–45. Excellent recent studies which, in my view, come close to such overcompensation: Haig-Brown, *Resistance and Renewal*; Albert L. Hurtado, *Indian Survival on the California Frontier* (New Haven, Conn.: Yale University Press, 1988).
6. See Richard C. Trexler, "From the Mouths of Babes: Christianization by Children in 16th Century New Spain," *Religious Organization and Religious Experience*, edited by J. Davis (London: Academy Press, 1982), 115–35. I thank Nancy Farriss for alerting me to this important article.
7. See Fass, *Outside In*, 24–25, 30, for example.
8. Haig-Brown, *Resistance and Renewal*; Miller, "Owen Glendower, Hotspur, and Canadian Indian Policy," esp. 396–405; all the essays in Barman et al., eds., *Indian Education in Canada*, Vol. 1.
9. Coleman, "Western Education, American Indian, and African Children." The Indians: Francis La Flesche, Charles Eastman, Luther Standing Bear, Zitkala-Sa, Edward Goodbird, Don Talayesva, Helen Sekaquaptewa. The Africans: in Edward H. Berman, ed., *African Reactions to Missionary Education* (New York: Teachers College Press, Columbia University, 1975); Colin Turnbull, *The Lonely African* (New York: Simon & Schuster, 1962), 148–58. Other autobiographies by Africans generally reinforce the conclusions of my essay, esp. Don Mattera, *Sophiatown: Coming of Age in South Africa* (Boston: Beacon Press, 1987), Chap. 3 and *passim*., Ezekiel Mphalele, *Down Second Avenue* (London: Faber & Faber, 1959), esp. Chaps. 1, 7, 13, 17, 19; Kwame Nkrumah, *Ghana: the Autobiography of Kwame Nkrumah* (New York: International Publishers, 1957), Chaps. 1–3, *passim.*; Peter Abrahams, *Tell Freedom* (London: Faber & Faber, 1954, 1981), esp. 138–61, 190–202, and 214–46.
10. Assertions in the next five paragraphs are more fully discussed in Coleman, "Credibility."
11. Thelen, *Memory and American History*, ix.
12. For example, Daklugie et al., *Indeh*, 14. On accurate ritual performance, Fletcher and La Flesche, *Omaha Tribe*, 596, for example. On some strengths and limitations of oral cultures: Axtell, *Invasion Within*, 14–15; Walter J. Ong, *Orality and Literacy: the Technologizing of the World* (London: Methuen, 1982). Cf. Marie Battiste, "Micmac Literacy and Cognitive Assimilation," in Barman et al., eds., *Indian Education in Canada*, Vol. 1, 23–44.
13. I play somewhat freely with Sayre's words in "The Proper Study," 241: "Autobiographies, in all their bewildering number and variety, offer the student in American Studies a broader and more direct contact with American experience than any other kind of writing."

Appendix

Tribal backgrounds of Indian autobiographical narrators who related school experiences, c. 1850–1930.

Below are listed the tribal backgrounds of narrators who described or showed a discernible influence of schooling (as stated in the text, many were of mixed tribal or tribal-white ancestry). Dakotas, Nakotas, and Lakotas are listed as *Sioux*. Mohawks, Senecas, Onondagas, Tuscaroras are listed as *Iroquois*. Lucille Winnie is also listed as Iroquois: her father was of three-quarters Seneca, and one-quarter Dutch ancestry; her mother was of three quarters Seneca–Cayuga, and one quarter French ancestry. Narrators who recalled attending school from the mid-1930s are not included. As a few narrators produced more than one autobiography, there is discrepancy between the number of narrators and number of autobiographies.

NARRATORS		AUTOBIOGRAPHIES
Apache	4	4 books
Arapaho	1	1 book
Cherokee	3	1 book; 2 shorter accounts
Cheyenne	4	3 books; 1 shorter account
Choctaw	2	2 shorter accounts
Comanche	2	1 book; 1 shorter account
Creek	4	1 book; 5 shorter accounts
Eskimo		
(St. Lawrence Island, Alaska)	1	1 book
Hidatsa	1	1 book
Hopi	5	5 books
Iroquois	6	2 books; 4 shorter accounts
Kiowa Apache	1	1 book
Koyukuk	2	1 book; 1 shorter account
Navajo	19	4 books; 15 shorter accounts
Ojibway (Chippewa)	3	1 book; 2 shorter accounts
Omaha	2	1 book; 1 shorter account
Paiute	2	2 books
Papago	1	1 book
Pima	2	2 books

Pomo	3	1 book; 2 shorter accounts
Ponca	1	1 shorter account
Potawatomi	2	2 shorter accounts
Salish	1	1 book
Sauk and Fox	1	1 shorter account
Shawnee	1	1 book
Sioux	17	7 books; 13 shorter accounts
Winnebago	8	2 books; 7 shorter accounts
Yaqui	2	2 books
Zuni	1	1 shorter account
	102	108

A Note on the Citation of Authors

I T IS NOT ALWAYS CLEAR from the title page of an autobiography whether the narrator, editor, or other collaborator should appear in the citation as the "author." In conventional notes and bibliographies, the editor/collaborator usually appears as "author." Because I focus on the *narrator*, however, I regard him or her as author and enter the work under that name in the notes and bibliography of the present work.

Bibliography

This is a select bibliography, which lists all materials cited in the notes, along with other immediately relevant sources. Many of the works listed below contain extensive bibliographies. For details concerning "author," see page 202.

A. Primary Sources

1. AMERICAN INDIAN AUTOBIOGRAPHIES

Individual autobiographies and collections of autobiographies. Those in which narrators show little or no influence of schooling are marked thus: (*). Those by Canadian Indians are marked thus: (Canada).

Ah-nen-la-de-ni (Daniel La France). "An Indian Boy's Story." *The Independent* 55 (July 30, 1903): 1780–87.

Alford, Thomas Wildcat. *Civilation, and the Story of the Absentee Shawnees.* As Told to Florence Drake. Norman: University of Oklahoma Press, 1936.

Allen, Elsie. *Pomo Basketmaking: A Supreme Art for the Weaver.* Edited by Vinson Brown. 7–16. Healdsburg, Cal.: Naturegraph, 1972.

Anonymous. "The Narrative of a Southern Cheyenne Woman." Edited by Truman Michelson. *Smithsonian Miscellaneous Collections* 87, No. 5 (1932): 1–13.

Anonymous Choctaw. In *Nations Remembered: An Oral History of the Five Civilized Tribes, 1865–1907.* Edited by Theda Perdue. 130–32. Westport, Conn.: Greenwood Press, 1980.

Anonymous Navajo. In *The Navajo Door: An Introduction to Navajo Life.* Edited by Alexander H. Leighton and Dorothea C. Leighton. 119–32. Cambridge, Mass.: Harvard University Press, 1944.

Apes, William. *A Son of the Forest. The Experience of William Apes, a Native of the Forest* . . . New York: Privately printed, 1829.

Bennett, Kay. *Kaibah: Recollections of a Navajo Girlhood.* Los Angeles: Westernlore Press, 1964.

Betzinez, Jason. *I Fought with Geronimo.* With William Sturtevant Nye. 1959; rpt., Lincoln: University of Nebraska Press, 1987.

Black Eagle. See William Whitman, below.

Black Elk, Nicholas. *Black Elk Speaks: Being the Life Story of a Holy Man of the Oglala Sioux.* Edited by John G. Neihardt. 1932; rpt., Lincoln: University of Nebraska Press, 1961, 1979 (*).

————. *The Sixth Grandfather: Black Elk's Teachings Given to John G. Niehardt.* Edited by Raymond J. DeMallie. Lincoln: University of Nebraska Press, 1984 (*).

Black Hawk. *Black Hawk: An Autobiography.* Edited by Donald Jackson. Urbana: University of Illinois Press, 1964 (*).

Cash, Joseph H., and Herbert T. Hoover, eds. *To Be an Indian: An Oral History.* New York: Holt, Rinehart & Winston, 1971.

Chris (pseudonym). *Apache Odyssey: A Journey Between Two Worlds.* Edited by Morris E. Opler. New York: Holt, Rinehart & Winston, 1969.

Colson, Elizabeth, ed. *Autobiographies of Three Pomo Women.* 1956. Rpt. Berkeley: Archaeological Research Facility, Department of Anthropology, University of California, 1974.

Crashing Thunder (pseudonym for Sam Blowsnake). *Crashing Thunder: The Autobiography of an American Indian.* Edited by Paul Radin. 1926; rpt., Lincoln: University of Nebraska Press, 1983.

Crow Dog, Mary, and Richard Erdoes, *Lakota Woman.* New York: Harper-Collins, 1990.

Daklugie, Asa, et al. *Indeh: An Apache Odyssey.* Edited by Eve Ball. Norman: University of Oklahoma Press, 1988.

Damon, Ada "'That's the Way We Were Raised': An Oral Interview with Ada Damon." Edited by Yvonne Ashley, *Frontiers* 2 (1977): 59–62.

DeCora, Angel, "Angel DeCora—an Autobiography," *The Red Man* 3 (1910): 279–85.

Deloria, Vine V., Sr. "The Standing Rock Reservation: A Personal Reminiscence," *South Dakota Review* 9 (Summer 1971): 167–95.

Doxon, Charles. "Address by Mr. Charles Doxon," *The Red Man* 5 (May 1913): 423–26.

Eastman, Charles A. (Ohiyesa). *From the Deep Woods to Civilization: Chapters in the Autobiography of an Indian.* 1916; rpt., Lincoln: University of Nebraska Press, 1977.

————. *Indian Boyhood.* 1902; rpt., New York: Dover, 1971.

————. *The Soul of an Indian: An Interpretation.* 1911; rpt., Lincoln: University of Nebraska Press, 1980.

FASISO47A (pseudonym). "Autobiographical Statement by FASISO47A. In *Zuni Daily Life.* Edited by John M. Roberts, 100–07. 1956; rpt., New Haven: Human Relations Area Files Press, 1965.

Geronimo. *Geronimo: His Own Story.* Edited by S. M. Barrett. 1906; rpt., New York: Ballentine, 1970 (*).

Gladstone, James. "Indian School Days." *Alberta History* 15 (1967): 18–24. (Canada).

Good Shot, Oscar. "Oscar Good Shot, The Narrative of a Sioux Visitor." In *The Cheyennes of Montana.* By Thomas Marquis, 264–77. Algonac, Mich.: Reference Publications, 1978.

Goodbird, Edward. *Goodbird the Indian: His Story.* Edited by Gilbert L. Wilson. 1914; rpt., St. Paul: Minnesota Historical Society Press, 1985.

Grayson, G. W. *A Creek Warrior for the Confederacy: The Autogiography of Chief G. W. Grayson.* Edited by W. David Baird. Norman: University of Oklahoma Press, 1988.

Griffis, Joseph K. *Tahan: Out of Savagery, into Civilization.* New York: Doran, 1915.

Gros-Louis, Max. *Max Gros-Louis: First Among the Hurons.* With Marcel Bellier. Translated by Sheila Fischman. Montreal: Harvest House, 1973 (Canada).

Harris, George William. "Autobiography." In *Growing Older.* By George Ancona. New York: Dutton, 1978.

Hensley, Albert. "Autobiography, 1908." In *American Indian Autobiography.* By H. David Brumble III, 132–33. Berkeley: University of California Press, 1988.

———. To Miss M. V. Gaither, Feb. 22, 1916. In *American Indian Autobiography.* By H. David Brumble III, 134–35. Berkeley: University of California Press, 1988.

Herman, Jake. "Pine Ridge." In *The American Indian Reader: Literature.* Edited by Jeanette Henry. 130–34. San Francisco: The Indian Historian Press, 1973.

Highwalking, Belle. *Belle Highwalking: The Narrative of a Northern Cheyenne Woman.* Edited by Katherine M. Weist. Billings: Montana Council for Indian Education, 1979.

Hopkins, Sarah Winnemucca. *Life Among the Piutes: Their Wrongs and Claims.* Edited by Mrs. Horace Mann. 1883; rpt., Bishop, Cal.: Sierra Media, 1969.

Hudson, Peter. "Recollections of Peter Hudson." *Chronicles of Oklahoma* 10 (Dec. 1932): 501–19.

Huntington, James. *On the Edge of Nowhere.* As told to Lawrence Elliot. New York: Crown, 1966.

Inkanish, Mary Little Bear. *Dance Around the Sun: The Life of Mary Little Bear Inkanish: Cheyenne.* Edited by Alice Marriott and Carol K. Rachlin. New York: Crowell, 1977.

Jacobs, Peter. *Journal of the Reverend Peter Jacobs, Indian Wesleyan Missionary. . . . With a Brief Account of His life.* New York: Privately printed, 1857.

James Allen. *Chief of the Pomos: Life Story of Allen James.* Edited by Ann M. Connor (Santa Rosa, Cal.: Privately printed, 1972).

Johnson, Basil. *Indian School Days.* Norman: University of Oklahoma Press, 1988 (Canada).

Johnson, Broderick H., ed. *Stories of Traditional Navajo Life and Culture, by Twenty-Two Navajo Men and Women.* Tsaile, Navajo Nation, Ariz.: Navajo Community College Press, 1977.

Jones, David E., *Sanapia: Comanche Medicine Woman.* Prospect Heights, Ill.: Waveland Press, 1972.

Kabotie, Fred. *Fred Kabotie: Hopi Indian Artist. An Autobiography Told with Bill Belknap.* Flagstaff: Museum of Northern Arizona/Northland Press, 1977.

Kakianak, Nathan (pseudonym). *Eskimo Boyhood: An Autobiography in Psychosocial Perspective.* Edited by Charles C. Hughes. Lexington: University Press of Kentucky, 1974.

Kaywaykla, James. *In the Days of Victorio: Recollections of a Warm Springs Apache.* †ited by Eve Ball. Tucson: University of Arizona Press, 1970.

King, Kenneth Coe. "The Autobiography of Kenneth Coe King." Vol. 1. *The Carlisle Arrow* 11 (June 4, 1915): 3–4.

La Flesche, Francis. *The Middle Five: Indian Schoolboys of the Omaha Tribe.* 1900; rpt., Madison: University of Wisconsin Press, 1963.

Lame Deer/John Fire, and Richard Erdoes, *Lame Deer, Seeker of Visions: The Life of Sioux Medicine Man.* New York: Simon & Schuster, 1972.

Le Clair, Peter. "Peter Le Clair—Northern Ponca: An Autobiographical Sketch with an introduction and comments by James H. Howard." *American Indian Tradition* 8 (1961): 17–20.

Left Handed. *Son of Old Man Hat: A Navajo Autobiography.* Edited by Walter Dyk. 1938; rpt., Lincoln: University of Nebraska Press, 1966 (*).

Levering, Levi. "Does it Pay to Christianize the Indian?" *American Indian Missions.* New York: Presbyterian Board of Homes Missions, 1913. 6–7.

Lindsey, Lilah Denton. "Memories of the Indian Territory Mission Field." *Chronicles of Oklahoma* 36 (1958): 181–98.

Lowawaima, K. Tsianina, "Oral Histories from Chilocco Indian Agricultural School, 1920–1940." *American Indian Quarterly* 11 (Summer 1987): 241–54.

Lowry, Annie. *Karnee: A Paiute Narrative.* Edited by Lalla Scott. Greenwich, Conn.: Fawcett, 1966.

McCarthy, James. *A Papago Traveller: The Memories of James McCarthy.* Edited by John G. Westover. Tucson: Sun Tracks and University of Arizona Press, 1985.

McDaniel, Mary. In *The Death of the Great Spirit: An Elegy for the American Indian.* Edited by Earl Shorris, 156–61. New York: New American Library, 1971.

Manitowabi, Edna. "An Ojibwa Girl in the City." *This Magazine Is About Schools* 4 (Fall 1970): 8–24 (Canada).

Maxidiwiac. *Waheenee: An Indian Girl's Story, Told by Herself to Gilbert L. Wilson, Ph.D.* 1927; rpt., Lincoln: University of Nebraska Press, 1981.

Mitchell, Emerson Blackhorse, and T. D. Allen. *Miracle Hill: The Story of a Navajo Boy.* Norman: University of Oklahoma Press, 1967.

Mitchell, Frank. *Navajo Blessingway Singer: The Autobiography of Frank Mitchell, 1881–1967.* Edited by Charlotte J. Frisbie and David P. McAllester. Tucson: University of Arizona Press, 1978.

Moisés, Rosalio, Jane Holden Kelley, and William Curry Holden. *A Yaqui Life: the Personal Chronicle of a Yaqui Indian.* 1971; rpt., Lincoln: University of Nebraska Press, 1977.

Momaday, N. Scott. *The Names: A Memoir.* Tucson: Sun Tracks/University of Arizona Press, 1976.

———. *The Way to Rainy Mountain.* 1969; rpt., Albuquerque: University of New Mexico Press, 1976.

Mountain Wolf Woman. *Mountain Wolf Woman: Sister of Crashing Thunder. The Autobiography of a Winnebago Indian.* Edited by Nancy Oestreich Lurie. Ann Arbor: University of Michigan Press, 1961.

Mourning Dove (Christine Quintasket). *Mourning Dove: A Salishan Autobiography.* Edited by Jay Miller. Lincoln: University of Nebraska Press, 1990.

One Bull, Oscar. "The Narrative of Oscar One Bull." Edited by H. Inez Hilger. *Mid-America* 28 New Series 17 (July 1946): 147–72 (*).

Owen, Narcissa. *Memoirs of Narcissa Owen, 1831–1907.* Rpt., Siloam Springs, Ark.: Siloam Springs Museum, 1980.

Parker, Ely S. "Writings of General Parker." *Publications of the Buffalo Historical Society* 8 (1905): 520–36.

Pelletier, Wilfred. "Childhood in an Indian Village." *This Magazine Is About Schools* 3 (Spring 1969): 6–22 (Canada).

Pokagon, Simon. "Indian Superstitions and Legends." In *Native American Folklore in Nineteenth-Century Periodicals.* Edited by William M. Clements. 237–52. Athens, Oh.: Swallow Press/Ohio University Press, 1986.

Poor Man, Mercy. "Christian Life Fellowship Church." In *Sioux Indian Religion.* Edited By Raymond J. DeMallie and Douglas R. Parks. 149–55. Norman: University of Oklahoma Press, 1987.

Pretty-shield. *Pretty Shield: Medicine Woman of the Crows.* Edited by Frank B. Linderman. 1932; rpt., Lincoln: University of Nebraska Press, 1974 (*).

Qoyawayma, Polingaysi (Elizabeth Q. White). *No Turning Back: A True Account of a Hopi Indian Girl's Struggle to Bridge the Gap Between the World of Her People and the World of the White Man.* As told to Vada F. Carlson. Albuquerque: University of New Mexico Press, 1964.

Rain-in-the-Face. "Rain-in-the-Face: The Story of a Sioux Warrior." Edited by Charles A. Eastman. *Outlook* 84 (Oct. 27, 1906): 507–12 (*).

Rickard, Clinton. *Fighting Tuscarora: The Autobiography of Chief Clinton Rickard.* Edited by Barbara Graymont. Syracuse, N.Y.: Syracuse University Press, 1973.

Rogers, John. *Red World and White: Memories of a Chippewa Boyhood.* 1957; rpt., Norman: University of Oklahoma Press, 1974.

Sanapia (pseudonym). See Jones, David E., above.

Savala, Refugio. *Autobiography of a Yaqui Poet.* Edited by Kathleen M. Sands. Tucson: University of Arizona Press, 1980.

Sekaquaptewa, Helen. *Me and Mine: The Life Story of Helen Sekaquaptewa.* As told to Louise Udall. Tucson: University of Arizona Press, 1969.

Shadlow, Ann. "Autobiography." In *Growing Older.* By George Ancona. New York: Dutton, 1978.

Shaw, Anna Moore. *A Pima Past.* Tucson: University of Arizona Press, 1974.

Sewid, James. *Guests Never Leave Hungry: The Autobiography of James Sewid, a Kwakiutl Indian.* Edited by James P. Spradley. 1969; rpt., Kingston: McGill-Queen's University Press, 1972 (Canada).

Silko, Leslie Marmon. *Storyteller.* New York: Arcade, 1981.

Standing Bear, Luther. *Land of the Spotted Eagle.* 1933; rpt., Lincoln: University of Nebraska Press, 1978.

———. *My Indian Boyhood.* 1931; rpt., Lincoln: University of Nebraska Press, 1988.

———. *My People the Sioux.* Edited by E. A. Brininstool. 1928; rpt., Lincoln: University of Nebraska Press, 1975.

Stands in Timber, John, and Margot Liberty. *Cheyenne Memories.* 1967; rpt., Lincoln: University of Nebraska Press, 1972.

Stewart, Irene. *A Voice in Her Tribe: A Navajo Woman's Own Story.* Edited by Dorris Ostrander Dawdy and Mary Shepardson. Anthropological Paper No. 17. Socorro, N.M.: Ballena Press, 1980.

Swann, Brian, and Arnold Krupat, eds. *I Tell You Now: Autobiographical Essays by Native American Writers.* Lincoln: University of Nebraska Press, 1987.

Sweezy, Carl. *The Arapaho Way: A Memoir of an Indian Boyhood.* Edited by Althea Bass. New York: Clarkson N. Potter, 1966.

Swims Under, Mike. "A Sun Dance Child of the Blackfeet." In *Children of the Sun: Stories by and about Indian Kids.* Edited by Adolf and Beverly Hungry Wolf. 175–79. New York: William Morrow, 1987 (Canada).

Talayesva, Don. *Sun Chief: The Autobiography of a Hopi Indian.* Edited by Leo W. Simmons. New Haven, Conn.: Yale University Press, 1942.

Theriault, Madeline (Ka kita wa pa no kwe). *Moose to Moccasins.* N.p.: n.d. (Canada).

Two Leggings. *Two Leggings: The Making of a Crow Warrior.* Edited by Peter Nabokov. Lincoln: University of Nebraska Press, 1967 (*).

Webb, George. *A Pima Remembers.* Tucson: University of Arizona Press, 1959.

Whitewolf, Howard. "A Short Story of My Life." *The American Indian Magazine* 5 (Jan–Mar. 1917): 29–31.

Whitewolf, Jim (pseudonym). *Jim Whitewolf: The Life of a Kiowa Apache Indian.* Edited by Charles S. Brant. New York: Dover, 1969.

Whitman, William. "Xube, A Ponca Autobiography." *American Journal of Folklore* 52 (April–June 1939): 180–93 (*).

Winnemucca. See Hopkins, Sarah Winnemucca.

Winnie, Lucille (Jerry). *Sah-gan-de-oh: The Chief's Daughter.* New York: Vantage Press, 1969.

Yava, Albert, *Big Falling Snow: A Tewa–Hopi Indian's Life and Times and the History and Traditions of His People.* Edited by Harold Courlander. Albuquerque: University of New Mexico Press, 1978.

Yellow Wolf. *Yellow Wolf: His Own Story.* Edited by Lucullus Virgil McWhorter. 1940; rpt., Caldwell, Ida.: Caxton, 1986.

Yellowhair, Chester. "I was Born in the Dark Ages." *Desert Magazine* 23 (Nov. 1960): 17–18.

Zitkala-Sa (Gertrude Bonnin). *American Indian Stories.* 1921; rpt., Lincoln: University of Nebraska Press, 1985.

2. OTHER PUBLISHED PRIMARY SOURCES

Abrahams, Peter. *Tell Freedom.* 1954; rpt., London: Faber & Faber, 1981.

American Board of Commissioners for Foreign Missions. *First Ten Annual*

Reports of the American Board of Commissioners for Foreign Missions. 1810–20. Boston: American Board of Commissioners for Foreign Missions, 1834.

———. *Annual Report of the American Board of Commissioners for Foreign Missions.* Boston: American Board of Commissioners for Foreign Missions, 1821–40.

———. *Memorial Volume of the First Fifty Years of the American Board of Commissioners for Foreign Missions.* Boston: American Board of Commissioners for Foreign Missions, 1861.

Basso, Keith H., ed. *Western Apache Raiding and Warfare. From the Notes of Grenville Goodwin.* Tucson: University of Arizona Press, 1971.

Berman, Edward H., ed. *African Reactions to Missionary Education.* New York: Teachers College Press, Columbia University, 1975.

Board of Foreign Missions of the Presbyterian Church in the United States of America. *Annual Report of the Board of Foreign Missions . . .* New York: Board of Foreign Missions, 1838–93.

Bronson, Ruth Muskrat. *Indians Are People, Too.* New York: Friendship Press, 1944.

The Carlisle Arrow 5 (June 11, 1909); 11 (June 4, Nov. 20, Dec. 18, 1915); 12 (Nov. 19, 1915).

Clark, William Leslie, and Walker D. Wyman. *Charles Round Low Cloud: Voice of the Winnebago.* River Falls: University of Wisconsin/River Falls Press, 1973.

Cremony, John C. *Life Among the Apaches* 1868; rpt., Lincoln: University of Nebraska Press, 1983.

Eastman, Elaine Goodale. *Pratt: The Red Man's Moses.* Norman: University of Oklahoma Press, 1935.

———. *Sister to the Sioux: The Memoirs of Elaine Goodale Eastman, 1885–91.* Edited by Kay Graber. Lincoln: University of Nebraska Press, 1978.

Fowler, Lois J., and David H. Fowler, eds., *Revelations of Self: American Women in Autobiography.* Albany: State University of New York Press, 1991.

Golden, Gertrude. *Red Moon Called Me: Memoirs of a Schoolteacher in the Government Indian Service.* San Antonio, Tex.: Naylor, 1954.

Institute for Government Research. *The Problem of Indian Administration* (The Meriam Report). Baltimore: Johns Hopkins Press, 1928.

Jenkins, Minnie Braithwaite. *Girl from Williamsburg.* Richmond: The Dietz Press, 1951.

McBeth, Sue L. "Diary of a Missionary to the Choctaws, 1860–61." Edited by Anna Lewis. *Chronicles of Oklahoma* 17 (Dec. 1939): 428–47.

McCallum, James Dow, ed. *The Letters of Eleazar Wheelock's Indians.* Hanover, N.H.: 1932.

Mattera, Don. *Sophiatown: Coming of Age in South Africa.* Boston: Beacon Press, 1987.

Mirza, Sarah, and Margaret Strobel, eds. and trans. *Three Swahili Women: Life Histories from Mombasa, Kenya.* Bloomington: Indiana University Press, 1989.

Mphahlele, Ezekiel. *Down Second Avenue.* 1959; rpt., London: Faber & Faber, 1971.

The Native American 4 (April 11, 1903); 7 (June 16, 1906).

Nkrumah, Kwame. *Ghana: The Autobiography of Kwame Nkrumah*. New York: International Publishers, 1957.

Pratt, Richard Henry. *Battlefield and Classroom: Four Decades with the American Indian, 1867–1904*. Edited by Robert M. Utley. 1964. rpt., Lincoln: University of Nebraska Press, 1987.

Prucha, Francis Paul, ed. *Americanizing the American Indians: Writings by the "Friends of the Indians," 1880–1900*. Cambridge, Mass.: Harvard University Press, 1973.

The Red Man 1–5 (1909–13).

Riggs, Stephen R. *Mary and I: Forty Years with the Sioux*. 1880; rpt., Williamstown, Mass.: Corner House, 1971.

United States Commissioner for Indian Affairs. Annual Report of the Commissioner for Indian Affairs. 1851–1941. (Available, along with appended materials, in different publications, or sometimes as a separate publication; in notes I cite the specific publication.)

Washburn, Wilcomb E., ed. *The American Indian and the United States: A Documentary History*. Vol. 1. New York: Random House, 1973.

Woodruff, Janette. *Indian Oasis*. As told to Cecil Dryden. Caldwell, Ida.: The Caxton Press, 1939.

3. PRIMARY SOURCES: ARCHIVAL

Hampton University Archives, Hampton, Virginia
　　Annie Bender student file.
National Archives, Washington, D.C.
　　Records of the Bureau of Indian Affairs. Record Group 75.
　　Central Classified Files, 1907–1939.
　　　　File 821 for Fort Shaw and Wittenberg.
　　Letters Received, 1824–1881 (M234).
　　　　Schools, 1824–1873.
　　Records of the Education Division.
　　　　Examination Papers, 1915 (Haskell Institute).
　　Records of Nonreservation Schools.
　　　　Records of Carlisle Indian Industrial School.
　　　　　　School Records.
　　Reports of Inspection of the Field Jurisdictions
　　　　of the Office of Indian Affairs, 1873–1900
　　　　　　(M1070).
　　Superintendents' annual Narrative and Statistical
　　　　Reports from Field Jurisdictions of the
　　　　Bureau of Indian Affairs, 1907–1938.
National Anthropological Archives, Smithsonian Institution, Washington, D.C.
　　Alice C. Fletcher and Francis La Flesche Papers.

Newberry Library, Chicago.
   Board of Indian Commissioners. Returned Student Survey. Bulletin No.
   24. 1916–17 (copy).
   John Howard Payne Papers, Vol. 8.
Presbyterian Historical Society, Philadelphia.
   American Indian Correspondence.

B. Secondary Sources

Books, articles, theses, reports.

Abbott, Philip. *States of Perfect Freedom: Autobiography and American Political Thought.* Amherst: University of Massachusetts Press, 1987.

Adams, David Wallace. "The Federal Indian Boarding School: A Study of Environment and Response." Ed.D. dissertation. Indiana University, 1975. Chaps. 5, 6.

———. "From Bullets to Boarding Schools: The Educational Assault on the American Indian Identity." In *The American Indian Experience. A Profile: 1524 to the Present.* Edited by Philip Weeks. 218–39. Arlington Heights, Ill.: Forum Press, 1988.

———. "Fundamental Considerations: The Deep Meaning of Native American Schooling, 1880–1900." *Harvard Educational Review* 58 (Feb. 1988): 1–28.

———. "Schooling the Hopi: Federal Indian Policy Writ Small, 1887–1917." *Pacific Historical Review* 48 (August 1979): 335–56.

Adams, Timothy Dow. *Telling Lies in Modern American Autobiography.* Chapel Hill: University of North Carolina Press, 1990.

Ahern, Wilbert, H. "An Experiment Aborted: Returned Students in the Indian Service." MS.

———. "Indian Education and Bureaucracy: The School at Morris, 1887–1909." *Minnesota History* (Fall 1984): 82–98.

———. "'The Returned Indians': Hampton Institute and Its Indian Alumni, 1879–1893." *Journal of Ethnic Studies* 10 (Winter 1983): 101–24.

Alexander, Ruth Ann. "Elaine Goodale Eastman and the Failure of the Feminist Protestant Ethic." *Great Plains Quarterly* 8 (Spring 1988): 89–101.

Allen, Paula Gunn. "The Mythopoeic Vision in Native American Literature: The Problem of Myth." *American Indian Culture and Research Journal* 1 (1974): 3–13.

Ames, R. E., and C. Ames, eds. *Research on Motivation in Education.* Vol. 1. *Student Motivation.* Orlando, Fla.: Academic Press, 1984.

Anderson, Gary Clayton. *Kinsmen of Another Kind: Dakota–White Relations in the*

Upper Mississippi Valley, 1650–1862. Lincoln: University of Nebraska Press, 1984.

Axtell, James. *The European and the Indian: Essays in the Ethnohistory of Colonial North America.* New York: Oxford University Press, 1981.

———. *The Invasion Within: The Contest of Cultures in Colonial North America.* New York: Oxford University Press, 1985.

Barman, Jean, Yvonne Hebert, and Don McCaskill, eds. *Indian Education in Canada.* Vol. 1: *The Legacy.* Vancouver, B.C.: University of British Columbia Press, 1986.

Barsh, Russel Lawrence. "American Indians in the Great War." *Ethnohistory* 38 (Summer 1991): 276–303.

Bataille, Gretchen M., and Kathleen Mullen Sands. *American Indian Women: Telling Their Lives.* Lincoln: University of Nebraska Press, 1984.

Bauman, Zygmunt. *Modernity and Ambivalence.* Cambridge, Mass.: Polity, 1991.

Beaver, R. Pierce, ed. *American Missions in Bicentennial Perspective.* South Pasadena, Cal.: William Carey Library, 1977.

Bender, Norman J. *"New Hope for the Indians": The Grant Peace Policy and the Navajos in the 1870s.* Albuquerque: University of New Mexico Press, 1989.

———, ed. *Missionaries, Outlaws, and Indians: Taylor F. Ealy at Lincoln and Zuni, 1878–1881.* Albuquerque: University of New Mexico Press, 1984.

Berg, S. Carol. "Memories of an Indian Boarding School: White Earth Minnesota, 1909–1945." *Midwest Review* 11 (Spring 1989): 27–36.

Berkhofer, Robert F., Jr. *Salvation and the Savage: An Analysis of Protestant Missions and American Indian Response, 1787–1862.* 1965; rpt. New York: Atheneum, 1972.

Bingham, Edwin R. "American Wests Through Autobiography and Memoir." *Pacific Historical Review* 56 (Feb. 1987): 1–24.

Bloodworth, William. "Varieties of American Indian Autobiography." *Melus* 5 (Fall 1978): 67–81.

Boehm, Christopher. "Ambivalence and Compromise in Human Nature." *American Anthropologist* 91 (Dec. 1989): 921–39.

Bolles, Edmund Blair. *Remembering and Forgetting: An Inquiry into the Nature of Memory.* New York: Walker, 1988.

Bolt, Christine. *American Indian Policy and American Reform: Case Studies of the Campaign to Assimilate the American Indians.* London: Allen & Unwin, 1987.

Bonvillain, Nancy. "Gender Relations in Native North America." *American Indian Culture and Research Journal* 13 (1989): 1–28.

Borland, Hal. *When Legends Die.* Harmondsworth, Middlesex: Penguin, 1965.

Bowden, Henry Warner. *American Indians and Christian Missions: Studies in Cultural Conflict.* Chicago: University of Chicago Press, 1981.

Brady, Margaret K. *"Some Kind of Power": Navajo Children's Skinwalker Narratives.* Salt Lake City: University of Utah Press, 1984.

Brenner, Elise M. "To Pray or to be Prey: That Is the Question. Strategies for Cultural Autonomy of Massachusetts Praying Town Indians." *Ethnohistory* 27 (Spring 1980): 135–52.

Brumble, H. David, III. *American Indian Autobiography*. Berkeley: University of California Press, 1988.

———. *An Annotated Bibliography of American Indian and Eskimo Autobiographies*. Lincoln: University of Nebraska Press, 1981.

Bruss, Elizabth W. *Autobiographical Acts: The Changing Situation of a Literary Genre*. Baltimore,: Johns Hopkins University Press, 1976.

Bryde, John F. *The Indian Student: A Study of Scholastic Failure and Personality Conflict*. Vermillion: Dakota Press, University of South Dakota, 1970.

Burgess, Charles. "The Goddess, the School Book, and Compulsion." *Harvard Educational Review* 46 (May 1976): 199–216.

Canfield, Gae Whitney. *Sarah Winnemucca of the Northern Paiutes*. Norman: University of Oklahoma Press, 1983.

Carrithers, Michael, et al., eds. *The Category of the Person: Anthropology, Philosophy, History*. Cambridge, Eng.: Cambridge University Press, 1985.

Cazden, Courtney B., and Vera P. John. "Learning in American Indian Children." In *Anthropological Perspectives on Education*. Edited by Murray L. Wax, Stanley Diamond, and Fred O. Gearing. 252–72. New York: Basic Books, 1971.

Clifton, James A., ed. *Being and Becoming Indian: Biographical Studies of North American Frontiers*. Chicago: Dorsey, 1989.

Coe, Richard N. *When the Grass Was Taller: Autobiography and the Experience of Childhood*. New Haven, Conn.: Yale University Press, 1984.

Cogley, Richard W. "John Eliot in Recent Scholarship [Review Essay]." *American Indian Culture and Research Journal* 14 (1990): 77–92.

Coleman, Michael C. *Presbyterian Missionary Attitudes Toward American Indians, 1837–1893*. Jackson: University Press of Mississippi, 1985.

———. "American Indian School Pupils as Cultural Brokers: Cherokee Girls at Brainerd Mission, 1828–29." In *The Cultural Broker: Link Between American Indian and White Worlds, 1690s–1990s*. Edited by Margaret Connell Szasz. Norman: University of Oklahoma Press. Forthcoming.

———. "The Credibility of American Indian Autobiographical Accounts of Schooling." Paper delivered to Annual Meeting of Organization of American Historians, Chicago, April 3, 1992.

———. "The Mission Education of Francis La Flesche: An American Indian Response to the Presbyterian Boarding School in the 1860s." *American Studies in Scandinavia* 18 (1986): 67–82.

———. "Motivations of Indian Children at Missionary and U.S. Government Schools, 1860–1918: A Study Through Published Reminiscences." *Montana: The Magazine of Western History* 40 (Winter 1990): 30–45.

———. "Not Race, but Grace: Presbyterian Missionaries and American Indians, 1837–1893." *Journal of American History* 67 (June 1980): 41–60.

———. "The Responses of American Indian Children to Presbyterian Schooling in the Nineteenth Century: An Analysis Through Missionary Sources." *History of Education Quarterly* 27 (Winter 1987): 473–97.

———. "Western Education, American Indian and African Children: A Comparative Study of Pupil Motivation Through Published Reminiscences, 1860s–1960s." *Canadian and International Education/Education Canadienne et Internationale* 18 (1989): 36–53.

Cox, James M. *Recovering Literature's Lost Ground: Essays in American Autobiography*. Baton Rouge: Louisiana State University Press, 1989.

Crum, Steven J. "Henry Roe Cloud, a Winnebago Indian Reformer: His Quest for American Indian Higher Education." *Kansas History* 11 (Autumn 1988): 171–84.

Cuban, Larry. *How Teachers Taught: Constancy and Change in American Classrooms, 1890–1990*. New York: Longman, 1984.

Davis, David Brion. Review of Herbert G. Gutman, *The Black Family in Slavery and Freedom*. In *American Historical Review* 82 (June 1977): 744–45.

DeMallie, Raymond J., and Douglas R. Parks, eds. *Sioux Indian Religion: Tradition and Innovation*. Norman: University of Oklahoma Press, 1987.

Doriani, Beth Maclay, "Black Womanhood in Nineteenth-Century America: Subversion and Self-Construction in Two Women's Autobiographies." *American Quarterly* 43 (June 1991): 199–222.

Eakin, Paul John, ed. *American Autobiography: Retrospect and Prospect*. Madison: University of Wisconsin Press, 1991.

Edmunds, R. David. "Coming of Age: Some Thoughts upon American Indian History." *Indiana Magazine of History* 85 (Dec. 1989): 312–21.

Eggan, Dorothy. "Instruction and Affect in Hopi Cultural Continuity." In *Education and Culture: Anthropological Approaches*. Edited by George D. Spindler, 321–50. New York: Holt, Rinehart & Winston, 1964. Reprinted from *The Southwestern Journal of Anthropology* 12 (1956): 347–70.

Fass, Paula. *Outside In: Minorities and the Transformation of American Education*. New York: Oxford University Press, 1989.

Feher-Elston, Catherine. *Children of Sacred Ground: America's Last Indian War*. Flagstaff, Ariz.: Northland Publishing, 1988.

Fienup-Riordan, Ann. *The Real People and the Children of Thunder: The Yup'ik Eskimo Encounter with Moravian Missionaries John and Edith Kilbuck*. Norman: University of Oklahoma Press, 1991.

Finkelstein, Barbara. *Governing the Young: Teacher Behavior in Popular Primary Schools in Nineteenth-Century United States*. New York: The Falmer Press, 1989.

Fischbacher, Theodore. "A Study of the Role of the Federal Government in the Education of the American Indian." Unpublished Ph.D. dissertation. Arizona State University, 1967.

Fleishman, Avrom. *Figures of Autobiography: The Language of Self-Writing in Victorian and Modern England*. Berkeley: University of California Press, 1983.

Fletcher, Alice C., and Francis La Flesche. *The Omaha Tribe*. Vols. 1 and 2. The Twenty-Seventh Annual Report of the Bureau of American Ethnology to the Secretary of the Smithsonian Institution, 1905–1906. 1911; rpt., Lincoln: University of Nebraska Press, 1972.

Fox-Genovese, Elizabeth. "Between Individualism and Fragmentation: American Culture and the New Literary Studies of Race and Gender." *American Quarterly* 42 (March 1990): 7–34.

Fried, Risto. "Remembering—Forgetting and Clinging—Going in Search." *Ryhmätyö* 19 (1990): 5–12.

Fuchs, Estelle, and Robert J. Havighurst. *To Live on This Earth: American Indian Education.* Albuquerque: University of New Mexico Press, 1972; 1983 edition, introduction by Margaret Connell Szasz.

Geertz, Armin W. "A Container of Ashes: Hopi Prophecy in History." *European Review of Native American Studies* 3 (1989): 1–6.

———. "Hopi Prophecies Revisited: A Critique of Rudolf Kaiser." *Anthropos* 86 (1991): 199–204.

Gilman, Carolyn, and Mary Jane Schneider. *The Way to Independence: Memories of a Hidatsa Indian Family, 1840–1920.* St. Paul: Minnesota Historical Society, 1987.

Glenn, Elizabeth. "Education of the Miami and Potawotomi of the Fort Wayne Indian Agency, 1820–1840." Paper Presented at the Annual Meeting of the American Society for Ethnohistory, College of William and Mary, Williamsburg, Va., November 1988.

Goleman, Daniel. *Vital Lies, Simple Truths: The Psychology of Self-Deception.* New York: Simon & Schuster, 1985.

Grant, John Webster. *Moon of Wintertime: Missionaries and the Indians of Canada in Encounter Since 1534.* Toronto: University of Toronto Press, 1984.

Green, Norma Kidd. *Iron Eye's Family: The Children of Joseph La Flesche.* Lincoln, Neb.: Johnsen, 1969.

Guenther, Richard L. "The Santee Normal Training School." *Nebraska History* 51 (Fall 1970): 359–78.

Hagan, William T. "Full Blood, Mixed Blood, Generic, and Ersatz: The Problem of Indian Identity." *Arizona and the West* 27 (1985): 309–26.

Hagedorn, Nancy L. "'A Friend to Go Between Them': The Interpreter as Cultural Broker During Anglo–Iroquois Councils, 1740–70." *Ethnohistory* 35 (Winter 1988): 60–80.

Haig-Brown, Celia. *Resistance and Renewal: Surviving the Indian Residential School.* Vancouver, B.C.: Tillacum Library, 1988.

Hareven, Tamara. "The History of the Family and the Complexity of Social Change." *American Historical Review* 96 (Feb. 1991): 95–124.

Hassrick, Royal B. *The Sioux: Life and Customs of a Warrior Society.* Norman: University of Oklahoma Press, 1964.

Havighurst, Robert J., and Bernice L. Neugarten. *American Indian Children and White Children: a Sociopsychological Investigation.* Chicago: University of Chicago Press, 1955.

Hegeman, Susan, "Native American 'Texts' and the Problem of Authenticity. *American Quarterly* 41 (June 1989): 265–83.

Heller, Thomas C., et al., eds. *Reconstructing Individualism: Autonomy, Individuality and the Self in Western Thought.* (Stanford, Cal.: Stanford University Press, 1986).

Henriksson, Markku. *The Indian on Capitol Hill: Indian Legislation and the United States Congress, 1862–1907.* Helsinki: Finnish Historical Society, 1988.

Hewes, Dorothy, "The First Good Years of Indian Education: 1894 to 1898." *American Indian Culture and Research Journal* 5 (1981): 63–82.

Hoebel, E. Adamson. *The Cheyennes: Indians of the Great Plains.* New York: Holt, Rinehart & Winston, 1960.

Holler, Clyde. "Lakota Religion and Tragedy: The Theology of *Black Elk Speaks.*" *Journal of the American Academy of Religion* 52 (1984): 19–45.

Holly, Carol T. "*Black Elk Speaks* and the Making of Indian Autobiography." *Genre* 12 (Spring 1979): 117–36.

Holte, James Craig. *The Ethnic I: A Sourcebook for Ethnic-American Autobiography.* Westport: Greenwood Press, 1988.

Hoxie, Frederick E. *A Final Promise: The Campaign to Assimilate the Indians, 1880–1920.* Lincoln: University of Nebraska Press, 1984.

———, ed. *Indians in American History: An Introduction.* Arlington Heights, Ill.: Harlan Davidson, 1988.

Hurtado, Albert H. *Indian Survival on the California Frontier.* New Haven, Conn.: Yale University Press, 1988.

Hyer, Sally. *One House, One Voice, One Heart: Native American Education at the Santa Fe Indian School.* Santa Fe: Museum of New Mexico Press, 1990.

Jahner, Elaine. "Cognitive Style in Oral Literature." *Language and Style* 16 (Winter 1983): 32–51.

James, Harry C. *Pages from Hopi History.* Tucson: University of Arizona Press, 1974.

James, Thomas. "Rhetoric and Resistance: Social Science and the Community Schools for the Navajos in the 1930s." *History of Education Quarterly* 28 (Winter 1988): 599–626.

Jellison, Katherine. "'Sunshine and Rain in Iowa': Using Women's Autobiography as a Historical Source." *Annals of Iowa* 49 (Winter 1989): 591–99.

Johnson, David L., and Raymond Wilson. "Gertrude Simmons Bonnin, 1876–1938: 'Americanize the First American.'" *American Indian Quarterly* 12 (Winter 1988): 27–40.

Kaestle, Carl F. *Pillars of the Republic: Common Schools and American Society, 1780–1860.* New York: Hill & Wang, 1983.

———. "Ideology and American Educational History." *History of Education Quarterly* 22 (Summer 1982): 123–37.

Katz, Michael B. *Reconstructing American Education.* Cambridge, Mass.: Harvard University Press, 1987.

Keller, Robert H., Jr. *American Protestantism and United States Indian Policy, 1869–82.* Lincoln: University of Nebraska Press, 1983.

Ketcham, Ralph. *Individualism and Public Life: A Modern Dilemma.* New York: Blackwell, 1987.

King, Wilma, "Multicultural Education at Hampton Institute—the Shawnees: A Case Study, 1900–1923." *Journal of Negro Education* 57 (1988): 524–35.

Kluckhohn, Clyde, and Dorothea Leighton. *The Navajo*. Rev. ed. Garden City, N.Y.: Doubleday, 1962.

Krech, Shepard, III. "The State of Ethnohistory." *Annual Review of Anthropology* 20 (1991): 345–75.

Krupat, Arnold. *For Those Who Come After: A Study of Native American Autobiography*. Berkeley: University of California Press, 1985.

———. *The Voice in the Margin: Native American Literature and the Canon*. Berkeley: University of California Press, 1989.

Krutz, Gordon V. "The Native's Point of View as an Important Factor in Understanding the Dynamics of the Oraibi Split." *Ethnohistory* 20 (Winter 1973): 78–89.

Kugel, Rebecca. "Religion Mixed with Politics: the 1836 Conversion of Mang'osid of Fond Du Lac." *Ethnohistory* 37 (Spring 1990): 126–57.

Kuper, Adam, and Jessica Kuper. *The Social Science Encyclopedia*. London: Routledge & Kegan Paul, 1985.

Langness, L. L., and Geyla Frank. *Lives: An Anthropological Approach to Biography*. Novato, Cal.: Chandler & Sharp, 1981.

Lawson, William. *The Western Scar: The Theme of the Been-to in West African Fiction*. Athens, O.: Ohio University Press, 1982.

Leibowitz, Herbert. *Fabricating Lives: Explorations in American Autobiography*. New York: Knopf, 1989.

Leighton, Dorothea, and John Adair. *People of the Middle Place: A Study of the Zuni Indians*. New Haven, Conn.: Human Relations Area Files, 1966.

Liberty, Margot. "Francis La Flesche: The Osage Odyssey. Omaha, 1857–1932." In *American Indian Intellectuals*. Edited by Margot Liberty. 45–59. St. Paul: West Publishing, 1978.

Lionnet, Françoise. *Autobiographical Voices: Race, Gender, Self-Portraiture*. Ithaca, N.Y.: Cornell University Press, 1989.

Littlefield, Daniel F., and J. W. Parins, eds. *A Bibliography of Native American Writers, 1772–1924*. Metuchen, N.J.: The Scarecrow Press, 1981; Supplement, 1985.

Loftin, John D. *Religion in Hopi Life in the Twentieth Century*. Bloomington: Indiana University Press, 1991.

Lowenthal, David. *The Past Is a Foreign Country*. Cambridge, Eng.: Cambridge University Press, 1985.

McBeth, J. Sally. *Ethnic Identity and the Boarding School Experience of West-Central Oklahoma American Indians*. Lanham, Md.: University Press of America, 1983.

McCoy, Ronald. "Fred Kabotie: Hopi Artist, 1900–1986." *American Indian Art Magazine*. 15 (Autumn 1990): 40–49.

McDonnell, Janet A. *The Dispossession of the American Indian, 1887–1934*. Bloomington: Indiana University Press, 1991.

McFee, Malcolm. "The 150% Man, a Product of Blackfeet Acculturation." *American Anthropologist* 70 (Dec. 1968): 1096–1103.

McLoughlin, William G. *Cherokees and Missionaries, 1789-1839.* New Haven, Conn.: Yale University Press, 1984.

———. *Cherokee Renascence in the New Republic.* Princeton, N.J.: Princeton University Press, 1986.

McNabb, Steven L. "The Uses of 'Inaccurate' Data: A Methodological Critique and Applications of Alaska Native Data." *American Anthropologist* 92 (March 1990): 116-29.

Makofsky, Abraham. "Experience of Native Americans at a Black College: Indian Students at Hampton Institute, 1878-1923." *Journal of Ethnic Studies* 17 (1989): 31-46.

Mandel, John Barrett. "The Autobiographer's Art." *The Journal of Aesthetics and Art Criticism* 27 (Fall 1968): 215-26.

Mark, Joan. *A Stranger in Her Native Land: Alice Fletcher and the American Indians.* Lincoln: University of Nebraska Press, 1988.

———. "Francis La Flesche: The American Indian as Anthropologist." *Isis* 73 (1982): 497-510.

Marashio, Paul. "'Enlighten My Mind . . .': Examining the Learning Process Through Native Americans' Ways." *Journal of American Indian Education* 21 (May 1982): 2-10.

Meyer, Roy W. *The Village Indians of the Upper Missouri: The Mandan, Hidatsas, and Arikaras.* Lincoln: University of Nebraska Press, 1977.

Miller, David Reed. "Charles Alexander Eastman, the "Winner": From Deep Woods to Civilization. Santee Sioux, 1858-1939." In *American Indian Intellectuals.* Edited by Margot Liberty. 61-73. St. Paul: West Publishing, 1978.

Miller, J. R. "Owen Glendower, Hotspur, and Canadian Indian Policy." *Ethnohistory* 37 (1990): 386-415.

Milner, Clyde A., II. *With Good Intentions: Quaker Work Among the Pawnees, Otos, and Omahas in the 1870s.* Lincoln University of Nebraska Press, 1982.

———. "The Shared Memory of Montana's Pioneers." *Montana: the Magazine of Western History* 37 (Winter 1987): 3-13.

——— and Floyd A. O'Neill, eds. *Churchmen and the Western Indians, 1820-1920.* Norman: University of Oklahoma Press, 1985.

Misch, J. O. "Lilah D. Lindsey." *Chronicles of Oklahoma* 33 (Summer 1955): 193-201.

Molin, Paulette Fairbanks. "Training the Hand, the Head, and the Heart: Indian Education at Hampton Institute." *Minnesota History* 51 (Fall 1988): 82-98.

Morrison, Kenneth M. "Baptism and Alliance: The Symbolic Mediations of Religious Syncretism." *Ethnohistory* 37 (Fall 1990): 416-37.

Moses, L. G., and Raymond Wilson, eds. *Indian Lives: Essays on Nineteenth- and Twentieth-Century Native American Leaders.* Albuquerque: University of New Mexico Press, 1985.

Murray, David. *Forked Tongues: Speech, Writing, and Representation in North American Indian Texts.* London: Pinter Publishers, 1991.

Mählmann, Peter. "Sport as a Weapon of Colonialism in Kenya: A Review of the Literature." *Transafrican Journal of History* 17 (1988): 152–71.

Nichols, Roger L. "The United States, Canada, and the Indians: 1865–1876." *Social Science Journal* 26 (1989): 249–63.

Nock, David A. *A Victorian Missionary and Canadian Indian Policy: Cultural Synthesis vs. Cultural Replacement.* Waterloo, Ont.: Wilfrid Laurier University Press, 1988.

O'Brien, Lynne Woods. *Plains Indian Autobiographies.* Boise, Ida.: Boise State College Western Writers Series, 1973.

Olney, James, ed. *Autobiography: Essays Theoretical and Critical.* Princeton, N.J.: Princeton University Press, 1980.

———. "The Autobiography of America." *American Literary History* 3 (Spring 1991): 376–95.

Olson, James S., and Raymond Wilson. *Native Americans in the Twentieth Century.* Urbana: University of Illinois Press, 1984.

Ong, Walter J. *Orality and Literacy: The Technologizing of the World.* (London: Methuen, 1982).

Padilla, Genaro M. "The Recovery of Chicano Nineteenth-Century Autobiography." *American Quarterly* 40 (Sept. 1988): 286–306.

Pettitt, George A. *Primitive Education in Native North America.* Berkeley: University of California Press, 1946.

Philips, Susan Urmston. *The Invisible Culture: Communication in Classroom and Community on the Warm Springs Indian Reservation.* New York: Longman, 1983.

Preston, Samuel H., and Michael R. Haines. *Fatal Years: Child Mortality in Late Nineteenth-Century America.* Princeton, N.J.: Princeton University Press, 1991.

Prucha, Francis Paul. *American Indian Policy in Crisis: Christian Reformers and the Indian, 1865–1900.* Norman: University of Oklahoma Press, 1976.

———. *The Churches and the Indian Schools, 1888–1912.* Lincoln: University of Nebraska Press, 1979.

———. *The Great Father: The United States Government and the American Indians.* Vols. 1 and 2. Lincoln: University of Nebraska Press, 1984.

Ramsey, Jarold. *Reading the Fire: Essays in the Traditional Indian Literatures of the Far West.* Lincoln: University of Nebraska Press, 1983.

Rayman, Ronald. "Joseph Lancaster's Monitorial System of Instruction and American Indian Education, 1815–1838." *History of Education Quarterly* (Winter 1981): 395–409.

Reyhner, Jon, and Jeanne Eder. *A History of Indian Education.* Billings: Eastern Montana College: 1989.

Rhodes, Robert W. "Holistic Teaching/Learning for Native American Students." *Journal of American Indian Education* 27 (Jan. 1988): 21–29.

Rock, Roger O. *The Native American in American Literature.* Westport, Conn.: Greenwood Press, 1985.

Ronda, James. "'We Are Well as We Are': An Indian Critique of Seventeenth Century Christian Missions." *William and Mary Quarterly*, 3d series. 34 (Jan. 1977): 66–82.

———. "Generations of Faith: The Christian Indians of Martha's Vineyard." *William and Mary Quarterly* 38 (July 1981): 369–94.

Rubin, David C., ed. *Autobiographical Memory*. Cambridge, Eng.: Cambridge University Press, 1986.

Ruoff, A. LaVonne Brown. "American Indian Literatures." *American Studies International* 24 (Oct. 1986): 2–52.

———. "American Indian Oral Literatures." *American Quarterly* 33 (Bibliography Issue, 1981): 327–38.

Salisbury, Neal. *Manitou and Providence: Indians, Europeans, and the Making of New England, 1500–1643*. New York: Oxford University Press, 1982.

———. "Red Puritans: The 'Praying Indians' of Massachusetts Bay and John Eliot." *William and Mary Quarterly*, 3d Series. 31 (Jan. 1974): 27–54.

Sanborn, Geoff. "Unfencing the Range: History, Identity, Property, and Apocalypse in *Lame Deer Seeker of Visions*." *American Indian Culture and Research Journal* 14 (1990): 39-57.

Sands, Kathleen Mullen. "Telling 'A Good One': Creating a Papago Autobiography." *Melus* 10 (1983): 55–65.

Sayre, Robert F. "The Proper Study: Autobiographies in American Studies." *American Quarterly* 29 (Bibliography Issue, 1977): 241–62.

Shea, Daniel B., Jr. *Spiritual Autobiography in Early America*. Princeton, N.J.: Princeton University Press, 1968.

Sheehan, Bernard. *Seeds of Extinction: Jeffersonian Philanthropy and the American Indian*. Chapel Hill: University of North Carolina Press, 1973.

Schöler, Bo. "Images and Counter-Images: Ohiyesa, Standing Bear and American Literature." *American Indian Culture and Research Journal* 5 (1981): 37–62.

Simmons, William S. "Cultural Bias in New England Puritans' Perception of Indians." *William and Mary Quarterly* 38 (Jan. 1981): 56–72.

Smith, Donald B. "The Life of George Copway or Kah-ge-ga-gah-bowh (1818–1869)—and a Review of His Writings." *Journal of Canadian Studies/Revue d'Études Canadiennes* 23 (Fall 1988): 5–37.

Smith, William F., Jr. "American Indian Autobiographies." *American Indian Quarterly* 2 (Autumn 1975): 237–45.

Smits, David D. "The 'Squaw Drudge': A Prime Index of Savagism." *Ethnohistory* 29 (1982): 281–306.

Spengemann, William C., and L. R. Lundquist. "Autobiography and the American Myth." In *The American Culture: Approaches to the Study of the United States*. Edited by Hennig Cohen. 92–110. Boston: Houghton Mifflin, 1968.

Steinmetz, Paul B. *Pipe, Bible, and Peyote Among the Oglala Lakota: A Study in Religious Identity*. Knoxville: University of Tennessee Press, 1990.

Szasz, Margaret Connell. *Education and the American Indian: The Road to Self-Determination Since 1928*. Albuquerque: University of New Mexico Press, 1974, 1977.

————. *Indian Education in the American Colonies, 1607–1783.* Albuquerque: University of New Mexico Press, 1988.

————. "Listening to the Native Voice: American Indian Schooling in the Twentieth Century." *Montana: the Magazine of Western History* 30 (Summer 1989): 42–53.

Tanis, Norman Earl. "Education in John Eliot's Indian Utopias, 1646–1675." *History of Education Quarterly* 10 (Fall 1970): 308–23.

Taylor, Rodney L. "The Centered Self: Religious Autobiography in the Neo-Confucian Tradition." *History of Religions* 17 (1978): 266–83.

Tedlock, Dennis. *The Spoken Word and the Work of Interpretation.* Philadelphia: University of Pennsylvania Press, 1983.

Theisz, R. D. "The Critical Collaboration: Introductions as a Gateway to the Study of Native American Bi-Autobiography." *American Indian Culture and Research Journal* 5 (1981): 65–80.

Thelen, David, ed. *Memory and American History.* Bloomington: Indiana University Press, 1989. Book version of issue of *Journal of American History* 75 (March 1989).

Thompson, Laura. *Culture in Crisis: A Study of the Hopi Indians.* New York: Harper & Brothers, 1950.

Trennert, Robert A., Jr. *The Phoenix Indian School: Forced Assimilation in Arizona, 1891–1935.* Norman: University of Oklahoma Press, 1988.

————. "Corporal Punishment and the Politics of Indian Reform." *History of Education Quarterly* 29 (Winter 1989): 595–617.

————. "Educating Indian Girls at Nonreservation Boarding Schools, 1878–1920." *Western Historical Quarterly* 13 (1982): 271–90.

————. "From Carlisle to Phoenix: The Rise and Fall of the Indian Outing System, 1878–1930." *Pacific Historical Review* 52 (August 1983): 267–91.

————. "Victorian Morality and the Supervision of Indian Women Working in Phoenix, 1906–1930." *Journal of Social History* 22 (1988): 113–28.

Trexler, Richard C. "From the Mouths of Babes: Christianization by Children in 16th Century New Spain." In *Religious Organization and Religious Experience.* Edited by J. Davis. 115–35. London: Academy Press, 1982.

Tyack, David. "Ways of Seeing: An Essay on the History of Compulsory Schooling." *Harvard Educational Review* 46 (August 1976): 355–89.

———— and Elisabeth Hanshot. *Learning Together: A History of Coeducation in American Schools.* New Haven, Conn.: Yale University Press, 1990.

———— and Michael Berkowitz. "The Man Nobody Liked: Toward a Social History of the Truant Officer, 1840–1940." *American Quarterly* 29 (Spring 1977): 31–54.

———— and Thomas James. "Education for a Republic: Federal Influence on Public Schooling in the Nation's First Century." *This Constitution*, No. 9 (Winter 1985): 17–24.

Van Lonkhuyzen, Harold W. "A Reappraisal of the Praying Indians: Acculturation, Conversion, and Identity at Natick, Massachusetts, 1646–1730." *New England Quarterly* 63 (Sept. 1990): 396–428.

Vecsey, Christopher. *Imagine Ourselves Richly: Mythic Narratives of North American Indians*. New York: Crossroads, 1988.

Vinovskis, Maris A. "Family and Schooling in Colonial and Nineteenth-Century America." *Journal of Family History* 12 (1987): 19–37.

Waters, Frank. *Pumpkin Seed Point: Being Within the Hopi*. 1969; rpt., Athens, O.: Ohio University Press, 1981.

Wax, Rosalie. "The Warrior Dropouts." In *Native Americans Today: Sociological Perspectives*. Edited by Howard M. Bahr, Bruce A. Chadwick, and Robert C. Day. 146–55. New York: Harper & Row, 1972. Reprinted from *Trans-action*, May 1967.

Weintraub, Karl Joachim. *The Value of the Individual: Self and Circumstance in Autobiography*. Chicago: University of Chicago Press, 1978.

——. "Autobiography and Historical Consciousness." *Critical Inquiry* 1 (1975): 821–48.

Westerhoff, John H., III. *McGuffey and His Readers: Piety, Morality, and Education in Nineteenth-Century America*. Nashville: Abingdon, 1978.

White, Richard. *The Roots of Dependency: Subsistence, Environment, and Social Change Among the Choctaws, Pawnees, and Navajos*. Lincoln: University of Nebraska Press, 1983.

Whiteley, Peter M. *Deliberate Acts: Changing Hopi Culture Through the Oraibi Split*. Tucson: University of Arizona Press, 1988.

Wiget, Andrew. *Native American Literature*. Boston: Twayne, 1985.

——, ed. *Critical Essays on Native American Literature*. Boston: Hall, 1985.

Willis, Paul E. *Learning to Labour: How Working Class Kids Get Working Class Jobs*. Aldershot, Hampshire: Gower, 1977.

Wilson, Raymond. *Obiyesa: Charles Eastman, Santee Sioux*. Urbana: University of Illinois Press, 1983.

Wright, Bobby. "'For the Children of the Infidels'?: American Indian Education in the Colonial Colleges." *American Indian Culture and Research Journal* 12 (1988): 1–14.

Wong, Hertha D. "Pre-Literate Native American Autobiography: Forms of Personal Narrative." *Melus* 14 (Spring 1987): 17–32.

Index

Absenteeism, 45, 61–63, 166–70
Adams, David Wallace, 42
Adaptability of Indians, 29–30, 63–68, 193–97. *See also* Responses; Motivation
African pupils, 196–97, 125 n25
Ah-nen-la-de-ni (Daniel La France) (Mohawk), 27, 83–84, 88, 106, 113–14; graduates, 175; racism, and, 140; resents exploitation, 136–37; returns home, 178
Albuquerque Indian School, 15, 90, 92, 98, 120, 132, 163, 175, 179, 185
Alford, Thomas Wildcat (Shawnee), 15, 23, 24, 68, 86, 88, 94–95, 109–10, 121, 132, 142, 146, 148, 151–52, 154, 158; begins school, 65–66; conversion, 117–19; education helps, 186–87; graduates, 175; love of learning, 109; loyalty to alma mater, 138–39; as recruiter, 136; as teacher, 185; trip to East, 75–76
Allen, Elsie (Pomo), 67, 106, 157, 163, 166
Ambivalence, 85, 91, 118, 122, 129, 150, 181, 188, 192–93; subculture expresses, 157; defined, 85, 182. *See also* Responses
American Board of Commissioners for Foreign Missions (ABCFM), 40
American Indian Autobiography, 9
American Indian Defense Association, 50
American Indians: as citizens/wards, 46; identity, question of, 13. *See also* tribal names; individual narrators
An Annotated Bibliography of American Indian and Eskimo Autobiography, 9
Antagonism, inter-tribal, at school, 140–41
Apaches, 19, 26–28, 74, 82, 140; Mescalero, 31, 35 n35, 65, 120; Warm Springs, 18, 61. *See also* Geronimo; individual narrators
Apes, William (Pequod), 6
Apostle of the Indians. *See* Eliot, John
Arkansas College, 65, 175
Asbury Manual Labor School, Alabama, 85, 108
Arapaho School, 151

Armstrong Academy, Oklahoma, 155–56
Armstrong, Gen. Samuel C., 87–88, 136
Atkins, J. D. C., 105
Autobiography, 42; audience, 8–9; captivity narrative and, 5; as confession, 4; construction of past, 8; credibility, 8; defined, 3–4; ethnic groups and, 5; Euro-American genre, 3–5; history of, 5; women and, 5
—American Indian: adult life, focus upon, 32 n4; audience, 8–9; "Carlise made me" narrative, 157; categories of modern, 5–8, 9–10; collaboration and, 5–8, 9–10, 197; credibility, 4, 7–8, 11, 32 n4, 192, 197–98; defined, 3–5, 12 n4; dialogical, 6–7, 12 n5; ethnicity of narrator, 9; gender and, 194; history of, 5; hostility of Indians to, 12 n3; monological, 6–7, 12 n5; narrative plots, 6–8; narrator, citation form, 202; preliterate traditions, 4–5, 7; sample for present study, 9–10; self-written, 6–9
Axtell, James, 37

Baptists, 37
Bataille, Gretchen M., 6
Begay, Myrtle (Navajo), 171
Bender, Anna (Ojibway), 159
Bennett, Kay (Kaibah) (Navajo), 23, 37, 82, 91, 95, 113, 129, 132, 152, 158, 168; begins school, 71
Berkhofer, Robert F., Jr., x
Betzinez, Jason (Apache), 19, 61, 82, 99, 113, 122, 134–35, 158–59, 173, 185–86; begins school, 61; and Christianity, 82, 117, 121; leaves, 171
Black Eagle (Ponca), 28
Black Hawk (Sauk and Fox), 6
Blatchford, Paul (Navajo), 89
Board of Foreign Missions of the Presbyterian Church in the United States of America, 39, 41, 193
—Omaha Boarding School, 58 n43, 64, 81, 84, 86, 87, 90, 93–95, 98, 108–10,

59; Indian people and, 63–68, 194–96; languages (tribal), prohibited, 106, 151–52; loyalty to team, 91–92; on- and off-reservation school controversy, 42–46; negative incentives, 87, 88–90, 97; positive incentives, 91–96; publications of, 91; racism and, 46–50, 98–100, 193; regimentation, 44, 86–88, 132; sexual surveillance, 94–95, 148–49, 168; tribal education, compared to, 53–54; trips to, 72–76; "socials," 94–95, 148–49; symbol, boarding school as, 104 n62. *See also* Brokers, cultural; Curriculum; Education—Indian: goals; names of individual schools; Responses; Staff; United States Government: Indian Education
—Public: and Indians, 10, 45–46, 48–49, 99–100, 194, 196; and white children, 38, 61, 101 n5, 146–51 *passim*, 167, 196
Second Great Awakening, 39
Sekaquaptewa, Emory (Hopi), 171, 179, 143 n16
Sekaquaptewa, Helen (Hopi), 8–9, 15–16, 21, 87–88, 90, 94, 109, 129, 141, 158; academic success, 129, 154, 171; begins school, 62–63; blends two cultures, 188–89; leaves school, 171; religious views, 116–17, 179; responsibility and, 114–15; returns home, 179
Shaw, Anna Moore (Pima), 8, 19, 27, 67, 91–92, 96, 109, 118, 121, 131–32; graduates, 175; racial views, 100; resistance, 149; returns home, 183–84
Shaw, Ross (Pima), 149, 183–84, 186
Sherman Institute, Riverside, California, 89, 93, 113, 116, 157–58, 171, 174, 182, 185
Shiprock Indian Boarding School, Arizona, 95
Shungapovi Day School, Arizona, 168, 174
Sign language, 140
Silko, Leslie Marmon (Laguna), 7
Sioux Indians, 140. *See also* Dakota; Lakota; Nakota; individual narrators
Societies (within tribes), 20–21, 23, 25–26, 156–57
Spencer, A. B., 95–96
Spotted Tail (Lakota), 15, 175
Staff (white American), 79, 96–100, 106–07, 109, 115, 117–18, 119, 124 n19, 146–47, 164, 169, 180; open to new knowledge, 110, 124 n13, 137
—Indian teachers, 86, 96, 106. *See also* Education—Indians: goals; Motivation; names of individual staff; responses
Standing Bear, Luther (Lakota), 9, 16–17, 21–23, 43, 73–75, 83–84, 93–94, 96, 106, 110–11, 113–15, 135–37, 139, 141, 163–64, 175; begins school, 69–70; Christianity and, 116; leaves, 165, 172; motivations change, 139; outing, 95, 113; as recruiter, 114–15, 135; resists, 147; returns home, 180–81, 183; as teacher, 109, 185; works in white society, 187
Stands in Timber (Cheyenne), 24, 27
Stealing, 152–53, 160 n6
Stewart, Irene (Navajo), 17, 72, 80–81, 91–92, 108, 112–13, 121, 152, 157–58, 163, 169, 174; ambivalence, 85; begins school, 68, 80–81; graduates, 175; returns home, 179
Stinson, Mildred (Lakota), 30, 91, 130
Stockbridge Indian School, Oklahoma, 152
Stone, Albert E., 4, 8
Sub-cultures. *See* Pupils, Indian
Sweezy, Carl (Arapaho), 186
Symbiosis. *See* Exploitation
Syncretism, 117–21, 151–57 *passim*, 179–82, 188–89, 194
Szasz, Margaret Connell, 16, 29, 37, 127

Talayesva, Don (Hopi), 6, 22, 24–26, 62, 72, 80, 89, 91, 106, 111, 114–16, 130, 133, 140–42, 154, 173, 193; begins school, 69; leaves, 171–72; motivation changes, 174; resistance, 149; returns home, 179–80, 182–83
Teachers. *See* Staff
Tewa-Hopi Indians, 3, 10, 20, 72–73, 189. *See also* Yava, Albert
Toadlena Indian Boarding School, New Mexico, 132, 152, 168
Tohono O'Odham. *See* Papago Indians
Trennert, Robert A., Jr., 44, 50
Tribal patriotism, modern, 68, 185
Two Leggings (Crow), 24, 26–27
Tsosie, Archie (Navajo), 71–72
Tuba City Boarding School, 133
Tucson Indian Mission School, 131
Tuscarora Indian Reservation, New York, 97, 128, 147

University of Pennsylvania, 44
"Uplift," 36–38, 105, 181. *See also* Education of Indians: goals

Printed in the United States
128161LV00003B/71/A